D1049736

Agony and Epitaph

Also by Albert Hofstadter

LOCKE AND SCEPTICISM
TRUTH AND ART
PHILOSOPHIES OF ART AND BEAUTY *(co-editor)*

ALBERT HOFSTADTER

Agony and Epitaph

Man, his art, and his poetry

George Braziller • *New York*

Copyright © 1970 by Albert Hofstadter
All rights reserved.
Published simultaneously in Canada by Doubleday Canada, Limited

For information, address the publisher:
George Braziller, Inc.
One Park Avenue, New York, N.Y. 10016

Standard Book Number: 0-8076-0544-1
Library of Congress Catalog Card Number: 75-104963
First Printing
Designed by Jennie Bush
Printed in the United States of America

Acknowledgment is gratefully made to the following authors, editors, translators, agents, and publishers who have granted permission to use selections from copyrighted publications.

Maria Bradford, for quotations from Curtis B. Bradford's article, "Yeats's Byzantium Poems: A Study of Their Development," which appeared in *Yeats, a Collection of Critical Essays,* edited by John Unterecker, Englewood Cliffs, N.J., Prentice-Hall, 1963.

Robert Duncan, for permission to quote from his poem "The Dance," which originally appeared in *Measure,* now reprinted by Kraus Reprint Corporation.

Harcourt, Brace & World, Inc., for the extensive excerpts from *Four Quartets* by T. S. Eliot, copyright, 1943, by T. S. Eliot.

Harper & Row, Publishers, for the quotation from my translation of "The Origin of the Work of Art," by Martin Heidegger, originally published in *Philosophies of Art and Beauty,* edited by Albert Hofstadter and Richard Kuhns, Modern Library Giant G90, New York, Random House, 1964.

Alfred A. Knopf, Inc., for quotations from several poems by Wallace Stevens, all of which appear in *The Collected Poems of Wallace Stevens,* copyrights extending from 1923 through 1954 by Wallace Stevens, First Collected Edition, 1954.

The Macmillan Company, for quotations from poems by W. B. Yeats, all of which appear in *The Collected Poems of W. B. Yeats,* Definitive Edition, New York, 1956, with copyrights of different years by Bertha Georgie Yeats and by The Macmillan Company.

Man and World, for permission to reprint in revised form my article, "From Beauty to Aesthetic Validity," which appeared in Volume

II, 1968, and now forms part of "The Voice of the Dead Wife" in the present book.

New Directions Publishing Corporation, for the quotations from "Spring and All" by William Carlos Williams, in *Collected Earlier Poems,* copyright 1938 by William Carlos Williams (paperback *Selected Poems,* New York, 1963), and from *Paterson,* copyright 1958 by William Carlos Williams.

Oxford University Press, for quotations from *Hegel's Philosophy of Right,* translated by T. M. Knox, 1952; Paul Tillich, *Theology of Culture,* edited by Robert C. Kimball, 1959; and *Aristotle's Metaphysica,* translated by Sir W. D. Ross, 2nd edition, 1928.

Philosophy East & West, for permission to reprint two of my articles: "On the Consciousness and Language of Art," Volume 19, Number 1, January, 1969 (substantially identical with "The Kin-Consciousness of Art" in the present book); and "The Poem is Not a Symbol," Volume 19, Number 3, July, 1969.

Prentice-Hall, Inc., for quotations from the article by Curtis B. Bradford, "Yeat's Byzantium Poems: A Study of their Development," in *Yeats, a Collection of Critical Essays,* edited by John Unterecker, Englewood Cliffs, N.J., 1963.

Princeton University Press, for quotations from *The Collected Works of Paul Valéry,* edited by Jackson Mathews, Bollingen Series XLV, Volume 7, *The Art of Poetry,* translated by Denise Folliot (Copyright © 1958 by Bollingen Foundation, Inc.)

G. P. Putnam's Sons, for the quotation from John Dewey, *Art as Experience,* Capricorn Book, Cap. 1, 1958.

Review of Existential Psychology and Psychiatry, for permission to reprint my article, "The Vocation of Consciousness," which appeared in Volume IV, 1, 1969, ©, *The Review of Existential Psychology and Psychiatry.*

University of California Press, for quotations from Conrad Fiedler, *On Judging Works of Visual Art,* translated by H. Schaefer-Simmern and F. Mood, Berkeley and Los Angeles, 1949; reprinted by permission of The Regents of the University of California.

Verlag Gerd Hatje, for the quotation from W. Kandinsky, *Essays über Kunst und Künstler,* edited by Max Bill, Stuttgart, 1955.

Yale University Press, for the quotation from Martin Heidegger, *An Introduction to Metaphysics,* translated by Ralph Manheim, a Doubleday Anchor Book, Doubleday and Company, Inc., Garden City, 1961; acknowledgments are hereby extended also to Doubleday and Company, Inc.

Michael Yeats, for quotations from unpublished drafts of poems by W. B. Yeats appearing in the above-cited article by Curtis B. Bradford.

*For
Manya and Marc,
first of kin
and
always*

Preface

This is a book of essays; it is one as a book and many as its essays. Aside from the *Foreword,* which was actually written last and represents a certain conspectus of the whole, it consists of eight separate essays in philosophical reflection which move back and forth between man and his being on the one side and the arts on the other. The two subjects are connected because in art man articulates his being in the form of an image that is given to intuition. Consequently one of the best ways to approach an understanding of human being—and through that, of being more generally—is through philosophical reflection on the arts. Conversely, a fundamental understanding of art as a human reality and a reality in the world can be reached only through a comprehension of it as the articulation of man's being.

Each of the eight essays is offered as complete in itself. At the same time they are all bound together by an essential tie and form a natural sequence. The tie depends on the fact that they encompass a common center, a single idea which receives special application in each of them. This idea is briefly denominated in the title of the final essay: "Being: The Act of Belonging."

The first essay makes the point in general that the being of philosophy itself lies in its being the thought that belongs to its age and to which its age belongs. And that the philosophy which belongs to our own age is precisely the philosophy which understands that being is the act of belonging.

The essay on "The Vocation of Consciousness" tries to show how consciousness comes upon the scene by first distinguishing and separating the nonego from the ego, the world from the self, objects from the subject, so as later—not in time, but in the order of being—to be able, in the form of own-consciousness, to reach the unity of belonging of ego and nonego, self and world, subject and object. Through consciousness man is able to attain to the being of which his own-consciousness is the psychological organ. By this means he is able to determine what is his own and what is not his own and therefore is able to be a man, existing in the context of the act of belonging.

With "The Touch of Art" a first approach is made to the application of this idea about being to the arts. The phenomenon of "touch" in the graphic arts may be generalized in a somewhat metaphorical manner to the whole act of artistic creation, and then it becomes possible to see how by its touch art transforms the alien character of the world into ownness, granted to us in a vision that bears witness to our belonging.

"The Voice of the Dead Wife"—Henri Rousseau said he painted best when he heard the voice clearly within himself—speaks about the art that belongs to our age, namely, the art that seems purposely to depart from beauty in its search for its own integrity. That integrity is seen as the peculiar rightness that modern artists—in the visual arts, literature, music, and elsewhere—so frequently put in the place of beauty. This rightness, described as an aesthetic validity, is intelligible as the form of the ownness or belonging that constitutes man's being and that comes to show in its individual configurations in the works of individual artists. It is not something calculable but determinable by feeling and by feeling only, since feeling is the means by which man's being determines what belongs and what does not belong. The voice of the dead wife is the voice of the man's spirit itself.

In "The Kin-Consciousness of Art" an attempt is made to show how human consciousness—i.e., the consciousness of own and not own, the consciousness of the act of belonging—articulates itself in the language of art. For this purpose poetry is used to stand for all of art, and the structure of the articulation is described in terms of a particular poem, Matthew Arnold's "Dover Beach."

The following essays, in which the poem (again taken as representative of all art) is examined in regard to the symbolic process, deal with a paradoxical quality of art: it becomes symbolic precisely by overcoming the symbolic gap between that which does the standing for and that which is stood for.

On the one hand, however much of representation, expression, and symbolism may occur in the art work, the being of the work itself remains the key feature. This being is described in the first of the two essays as "the agony of the being there together which is enough." That description explains itself in the text. It is a way of speaking of the aesthetic validity and the kin-consciousness that belong to essential poetry and essential art. Yeats's two Byzantium poems form the subject matter of the analysis that leads to this conclusion. "Agony" comes from the agony of the trance of the fire-dance in "Byzantium"; the "being there together (which) is enough" comes from

Wallace Stevens' "Final Soliloquy of the Interior Paramour."

On the other hand, the very being of the poem makes it into a symbol of man's being and of being generally, if we take the word "symbol" in Tillich's intense sense: the genuine symbol is one that does not merely point to something beyond itself, like a sign, but does so by participating in the power and the being of the symbolized. The poem which *is not* a symbol, in the sense of an entity that merely stands for and points to something other than itself, like a hieroglyph, *is* a symbol in the sense in which a symbol brings us into connection with a transcendent reality by participating in the power and the being of that reality. This point is developed in an examination of T. S. Eliot's *Four Quartets,* a work that teaches us much about the nature of the poetic nonsymbol-symbol both by its speaking and its being. In it we learn by precept and performance how, by the belonging together of its words, the poem is able to join the times with time and the timeless with time, thus symbolizing true being by its own true being, forming the connecting link between finite and infinite.

The path of contemplation leading from philosophy, through human consciousness, the arts in general, and poems and poetic language in particular, returns in the end to its beginning and completes the circle of its idea. That idea, which first appeared as a philosophical one belonging to our age, having reappeared as defining the vocation of consciousness, the function of art, and the being and symbolic force of poetry, has attained sufficient determinateness to be able to stand direct statement on its own account. So the final essay attempts to give this statement, first by means of a straightforward analytical examination of the uses of the verb *be,* which results in an understanding of it as meaning "to be related to other as to own; to be related to by other as to its own"; and secondly, by means of a factual examination of being, especially human being, in some of the varied forms the being-relationship exhibits, from the ownership of property, the appropriation of one's body, the self-possession of one's own mind, etc., to the mutual ownness of love, which is indeed the source, the heart, and the lifeblood of all being.

Some of the essays have been delivered as lectures or have appeared in print.

"What Philosophy Is and Does" was given as an inaugural lecture in the Third Annual Series of Professors' Inaugural Lectures at the University of California at Santa Cruz on January 22, 1969.

"The Vocation of Consciousness" appears in, IX, I, 1969, *The Review of Existential Psychology and Psychiatry.*

"The Voice of the Dead Wife" is a revised version of the article "From Beauty to Aesthetic Validity," published in *Man and World,* Volume 2, 1968, pp. 165–190.

"The Kin-Consciousness of Art" was read, under the title "On the Consciousness and Language of Art," on October 26, 1968, at the Seventh Annual Meeting of the Society for Phenomenology and Existential Philosophy held at Yale University. It appears in *New Essays in Phenomenology,* edited with an introduction by James M. Edie, Quadrangle Books (Chicago, 1969) and also in *Philosophy East & West,* Volume 19, Number 1 (January 1969), pp. 3–15, in both instances under the title as read at the meeting.

"The Poem Is Not a Symbol" was read at an East-West conference in aesthetics on "The Nature and Function of

Symbolism in Eastern and Western Art" at the East-West Center, University of Hawaii, Honolulu, on December 16, 1968. It appears in *Philosophy East & West,* Volume 19, Number 3 (July, 1969), pp. 221–233.

The Foreword and Essays III, VII, and VIII appear for the first time in this book.

For an appointment to the Humanities Institute for 1969–1970 designed to help me to complete the present work, I owe thanks to President Charles J. Hitch and Chancellor Dean E. McHenry of the University of California.

I owe a considerable debt of gratitude to the Center for Advanced Study in the Behavioral Sciences, Stanford, California. Although this book was not written during my term there as a Fellow in 1966–1967, it is the direct outgrowth of the year's reflections. But that is the least of it. The Center is a uniquely fruitful institution: gathering its band of scholars each year to assemble in perfect freedom, it grants to each the rarest opportunity to gather his own self anew. For me, as for many others through the years, this chance at self-gathering turned out to be decisive, and for it I remain ever thankful to the Center, to Ralph Tyler, who was then its director, Preston Cutler, and the whole devoted staff. Among the Fellows whose counsel profited me were Albert Cook and Ian Watt, and very special thanks go to my dear friend Leo Lowenthal, who listened patiently—though, indeed, over the shared bottle—to thousands of words that have now blessedly joined the ranks of the shades.

For the inspiration of his courageous painting and the many years of our common experiences of art I am grateful to another dear friend, Samuel Huber. As ever, the encouragement and faith of my son Marc have been an inestimable resource. And to my wife Manya I owe most of all—a lifetime's participatory education in the meaning of belonging.

ALBERT HOFSTADTER

Santa Cruz
September, 1969

Contents

The poem lashes more fiercely than the wind,
As the mind, to find what will suffice, destroys
Romantic tenements of rose and ice.

WALLACE STEVENS

The Measure of Man

Protagoras is credited with the statement: Man is the measure of things.

His principle is obviously untrue. It could be true only if man were the infinite being, God. For then he would not be subject to being measured by something other than himself and could be the principle of measure of all things. But since man is finite his being is limited. He has a boundary beyond which he vanishes. A little too little salt in his blood and his body disintegrates; a little too little love in his soul and his mind disintegrates. Man is measured, not by himself as measure, but by a principle that lies at the ground of his being.

The measure of something is the quantity that belongs to that being's essential quality, to what it is. The measure of a flea is the quantity that belongs to being a flea. It is not that of an elephant. The living body's observance of its measure—its cybernetic keeping within the limits of its existence—has been called by W. B. Cannon the body's wisdom.[1] Every being has its own wisdom. Human being entails a human wisdom. Philosophy, whose name designates the love of wisdom, searches for the wisdom that belongs to man's being as a man, a wisdom that man is able to have because he is man and that he must have in order truly to be man. It spells out the measure of man.

What does philosophy tell us about man's measure?

It does not give it to us in a formula. Man's measure is not a quantity that can be calculated. Only man's being itself can tell what its measure is, by the fiery test of the living encounter of the human self with reality. The encounter is the individual's own. No one can perform it for him. He is in the world along with other individuals as a dancer is in the arena along with other dancers. He has to find the rhythm that belongs to him as one among the others. So every man must be his own philosopher, thinking the fundamental thought of his life for himself. No one can think it for him.

Philosophy tells us where to look to find the quality, the being, of which man's measure is the quantity. Being is the act of belonging—of belonging to and being belonged to, of owning and being owned. When we understand this, we understand that human measure is to be sought in the quantity of our belonging—in the magnitude, direction, and degree of our being with the other as with our own. The measure of man is the quantity of love exercised as his individual being. It is the incalculable quantity of the ownness, the kinship, with which he is called upon to relate himself to all that is inside and outside his world.

The quantity is finite. The human spirit is the spirit of its body, rooted in time and space, hunger and sexual lust, complexities of mire and blood. Yet it partakes of the infinite as well, if the infinite is that which is not limited by something other than itself. For when the other becomes kin and own, in a relation of reciprocal belonging, then it no longer limits but complements, completes, and liberates. It is through kinship with what is other than myself that I am able, in my being, to point toward that other and participate with it in our belonging to one another. My being then assumes a meaning that transcends the limitations of my existence in space and time and the body, while yet I remain in space, time, and the body. In this world and this body, in this place and this time, I participate in that which transcends world, body, place, and time.

Such a split or tension belongs essentially to man's being. He has the foot of a goat and a heart that yearns to heaven. His being is "satyrical." His measure is the measure of the movement by which, in the world of body and time, he is able to overcome his separation from things by stretching his kinship with them to the limit. This movement is the dance by which, moving in his body, he becomes bodiless; moving in time, he stands timeless; moving as one, he participates in all. Wisdom is the knowledge of the stretching of kinship to our limit, participating in the rhythm of the dance of life according to the measure of our capacity. That is the one genuine knowledge that belongs to us as human beings.

> We know nothing and can know nothing
> but
> the dance, to dance to a measure
> contrapuntally,
> Satyrically, the tragic foot.[2]

The poet knows about these things because his poem is itself always such a dance. Out of words in time he weaves a timeless fabric; in the rhythm of the words he dances a timeless dance; therefore he can say in simple truth

> our words are
> our articulations,   our measures.[3]

Because the poem is such a dance—an articulation of human being according to its own measure as a poem— it is no mere symbol of something apart from itself. It is what it means. And yet, as speech that articulates our kinship with things, it reaches out and participates in them and in the nature of kinship itself; and so it turns out to be the best symbol of transcendence that can be formed.

By his poetic understanding the poet knows about things that are not poems but that also suffice—the rose, for instance, which as a symbol once

> carried the weight of love
> but love is at an end—of roses.
> It is at the edge of the
> petal that love waits.[4]

The rose's end is the edge, the end that is the beginning of the geometry of roses, which is the measurement of roses, at which

> a line starts
> that being of steel
> infinitely fine, infinitely
> rigid, penetrates
> the Milky Way.[5]

Unbruised, the fragile flower penetrates space. It is the power of the love at its edge that carries it from one extremity to the other of the world's diameter. The rose can join the earth with the heaven above because it assembles at its edge—the limit of its being at which it reaches its measure—the love that is the secret of the kinship of other with other.

Man is not the measure of the rose. The rose, as symbol, shows in an image the measure of man. So the poem, too, shows the measure of man, and more intimately than the rose, for it is of man's own making.

Philosophy here lets man's being speak, in the poem, the painting, the dance, and, listening, learns to hear the words which are its own articulation, its own measure.

I

What Philosophy Is and Does

Philosophy does not let things alone. It is constantly raising questions about them. It is not willing even to let itself alone. It wants to know what it itself is and does, and why. It wants to examine the rationality of its own procedure. It is never satisfied with the mere fact that something is so. It wants always an explanation of the fact, insofar as an explanation is possible; and where an explanation is not possible it wants to know why.

Philosophy is the unremitting restlessness of thought. It penetrates every sphere searching for ultimate comprehension. Nothing is sacred to it, not even the sacred itself. Is there not also a philosophy of the sacred, called by the name of the philosophy of religion? So, too, of everything else there is a philosophy, though it may not always get a special name for itself. For instance, philosophy has something to think about automobiles, but its questioning in this region has not yet been christened "philosophy of the automobile." That is because the automobile is but one among many of the phenomena of our technological culture. There is indeed a philosophy of culture, and within it a philosophical comprehension of the means and instrument, handicraft and industry, work, automation, the technical, and the technological. That is where philosophy of the automobile belongs.

Wherever thought is at work seeking to understand, there we feel the working of the philosophical spirit. When a child begins to ask questions about things, he behaves in essentially the same way as the thinker grown gray in the philosophical quest. His questioning is, in the end, the same as the thinker's, for he is always asking "Why?" Why does the sun shine? Why does it rain? Why don't the flowers last more than a day? Where did grandma go and why can't she come back again? Why can't we fly like the birds and why can't the birds talk like us? If God made the world why isn't everyone happy?

We ask other questions—what, when, where, who, by what means, in what manner—ultimately in order to be able to ask why and get an answer. We ask about the facts, about what things are and what they are like, but philosophy remains unsatisfied by facts alone. It looks for their grounds. And if it reaches the point at which no further ground seems to be available—the point at which it appears forced to admit that the thing is so, that there is no reason for it, it is simply the case and that is the end of it—then philosophy, that is, thought, may submit, but only with a heavy heart. For its heart is set upon the light of truth, the radiance of insight, and it falls only unwillingly into the darkness of incomprehension.

But if philosophy is thought in search of ultimate understanding, what does it do? What is the practice that ultimate thinking engages in? If philosophy looks eventually toward the timeless and eternal, it nevertheless exists in time and has a historical role to play. What is that role?

Can it be, perhaps, that the practical work of philosophy is directed toward the future? Does philosophy begin something, usher in and initiate some career, hopefully with good omens? Is the function of philosophy, in a word, inauguration?

When we look at the history of thought we discover as a fact that philosophy does indeed inaugurate. All the important sciences that we have today originated in philosophy and became separated from it only as they passed through their infancy nurtured by philosophical minds. In Western thought such men as Thales and Pythagoras were initiators of mathematical thinking; the Sophists brought grammar and rhetoric into being; the Wise Men were the great legislators, founders of law and jurisprudence, an achievement that was later matched by the great contribution of the Stoic philosophers to thought about law and the state; Aristotle was the first great encyclopedist, whose writings bring into coherent order the findings of biology and chemistry, physics and astronomy, psychology, logic, ethical and political theory, poetics and rhetoric.

I mention only these few instances to remind us of the familiar process of the budding of the particular disciplines from the central stem of thought itself, that is, philosophy. It was not long ago that physics was still called natural philosophy and its instruments philosophical instruments. The great scientists of early modern times— Galileo, Kepler, Descartes, Leibniz, Newton—were philosophers. In our own day we have seen mathematical logic begin with the philosophers, grow more and more technicalized, and enter into the passage from philosophy to mathematics and communication theory.

Within the particular sciences themselves the function of inaugurating tends to be philosophical in quality, just because it is thinking that is doing the initiating. The great originators of new scientific ideas have not been mere technicians but men of a philosophical cast of mind, men for whom to think is to imagine and to imagine to think. Einstein's achievements came out of a search for new beginnings. His was a thinking that could puzzle about what it means for two events to be described as simultaneous, raising questions about the seemingly simplest sort of fact, much as a child does about what seems so simple to us. The same thing holds true of other great scientists, like Darwin and Freud. Their ideas had within themselves the power of inaugurating new epochs of human thought, because their thinking went to the principles of their subject, sharing in the restive search of philosophy for the grounds of things.

But philosophical thinking is originative not only in the sphere of thought. It has also had a great part in the initiation of the historical stages of man's existence. One naturally thinks here of Karl Marx's notion of the function of thought as being not just to reflect the world but to change it. Marx himself is undoubtedly the outstanding example of a philosophical mind that influenced and continues to influence world history by the direction of its ideas. The fundamental Marxist theses of natural and historical dialectics and materialism have been the philosophical equivalent of a scripture to the socialist movement of the past hundred years. Marxist philosophy worked to inaugurate a new life for millions of people on our planet, and a large part of earth's life bears the shape of its impress. So, too, philosophical thinking played its role in the initiation of earlier revolutions, particularly the two great revolutions of the eighteenth century, the American and the French.

It is in keeping with the philosophical temper so closely akin to the spirit of recent American life—namely, pragmatism—that philosophy should be seen in its function of contributing to the shaping of history. For pragmatism, the very meaning and nature of an idea lie in its ability to lead conduct toward a foreseen end. Ideas are, in John Dewey's expression, plans of action, instruments for guiding a problematic situation toward a resolution of its inherent conflicts. This holds particularly for philosophical ideas. Much of classical philosophy has been concerned to give an eternal sanction to cultural values and beliefs by relating them to notions of an absolute truth and reality. But the true function of philosophy, Dewey thought, lies in its use for dealing with the current problems of cultural and social transformation. Its basic task lies in confronting traditional beliefs and values with the facts and problems of present existence. It acts as a critic of the large-scale ideas that determine the direction of human thought and action. It is best imagined as what Dewey called an organon of criticism, a logic, as it were, not merely of ordinary rational thinking or the more technical procedures of scientific thought and methodology, but eventually of the whole activity of the human mind and spirit—of poetry, painting, and music, of political and moral imagination, of religious worship, in short, of the movement of the human mind in every form of life.

That indeed is the way in which it has functioned in actual history. The life of all thought, Dewey believed, is to join the new and the old, to adjust deep-sunk customs and unconscious dispositions that are brought to attention by some conflict with novel directions of behavior.

Every act of living perception, purposeful planning, or serious contemplation occurs within such a process of the growth of experience. Even the activities of fantasy, dream, and the poetic imagination find their source and role in the process. Philosophy is only this culture-transforming role writ large. Philosophies arise in the course of man's efforts to come to terms with the deepest and broadest transformations of his life. Socrates confronting the traditional beliefs of Athenian culture with new, trenchant critical concepts and methods, contrasting inherited institutions and beliefs with ideal standards, on the one hand, and a realistic perception of current shortcomings, on the other hand, is a type of all genuine philosophers. His was a dangerous occupation, fighting at the forefront of history by trying to let intelligence guide history's changes; and Socrates here too is the ideal type of the genuine philosopher, sealing his mission with the nobility of his death.

There can be no serious question of the important role philosophical thinking has played in historical change, all over the world. One need think only of the shaping influence of the powerful philosophical thoughts contained in Buddhism, Taoism, and Confucianism in determining the whole character of Indian, Chinese, and Japanese culture, or again of the role of philosophy in the determination of medieval Christian culture by way of the efforts of the Church Fathers to institutionalize and give systematic order to basic Christian ideas and ideals. Dewey's claim that philosophies define the larger patterns of continuity that are woven in joining a stubborn past with an insistent future is only a literal description of the actual facts.

Nevertheless, Martin Heidegger also is right in pointing out that philosophy itself does not and cannot supply the energies or create the opportunities and methods that produce historical change. Among recent philosophers it has been Heidegger who has most vividly conceived of the function of philosophy as that of the inauguration of stages in man's historical existence. But it does not operate directly as a controlling power. Its work is indirect. It begins with the few, the creative thinkers, who institute profound changes of ideas. Their ideas spread in a devious way, not by plan or design, but following the paths opened up in current thought and life. In the end, these ideas permeate the whole consciousness of a people and a period, giving to it its peculiar cast and orientation.

We have only to look at the root concepts and principles of our own language and culture to find illustrations: being and nothing; finite and infinite; matter and form; force and manifestation; substance, causality, and reciprocity; mechanism and teleology; the true, the good, and the beautiful; the unconscious, consciousness, and self-consciousness; theoretical, practical, and critical reason; freedom and responsibility. It is due to the labors of the great philosophers of our civilization that these words and ideas and the principles that embody them have been so articulated as to become essential shaping forces of our minds. We are what we are precisely because of the ways in which the ideas of being and nothing, finite and infinite, and all the rest have given form to our speech and thought. Reality is comprehensible to us only in terms of them. The very meaningfulness of things for us depends on how such concepts and principles have taken root and grown into living thoughts in our minds. Your moral stance depends essentially on your moral comprehension as one of its prime factors; but your moral comprehension is determined by how you think the concepts and principles of rights and obligations, freedom and responsibility, means and ends, inclination and duty, objectivity and personality. You need not think these things out explicitly, as they might be written in a philosophical treatise; but you must have them immanently at work within your mind if you are to be at all a civilized person. But if they are there, it is because they have come to you from the work of the philosophical intellect over the ages, seeking, analyzing, sifting, synthesizing, searching always for the utmost comprehension that the human mind can attain.

Our age differs from other ages in part, and in essential part, because we think differently from them. Our thoughts bear the profound impress of experiences of rapid change, instantaneous communication, the chattering of the media over all the earth, worldwide clashes, violence within the personality and the culture, the dehumanizing of nature and the denaturalizing of man, the nihilistic questioning and crumbling of standards and values and visions once dominant. While science and technology register daily advances that would in earlier ages be thought of as miracles—we still on occasion use that word, though it is becoming empty with passing time—we find ourselves beset by paradoxical problems. The world that sees men land on the moon sees at the same time the existence of massive misery along with the greatest possibility of plenty, the growing polarization of men on the basis of race and nationality in a period when they are more and more crowded together in their single living space, and the suddenly increasing meaninglessness of moral and religious codes that have existed for millennia.

Science is often idolized. People look to the scientist as they did earlier to the shaman, the miracle worker, the hero. Today he is giving them space to travel in and new hearts for old; tomorrow what will he bring? Some philosophers have so forgotten their mission and have been so smitten by the successes of the natural sciences that they have thrown off everything that philosophy is and does except logic and the analysis of concepts and words. They are the positivists and the analytic philosophers, the ones who are most widespread on the campuses of American and British universities at the present time. Carnap, Wittgenstein, and their disciples display great conceptual and technical facility in dealing with matters relating to language and methodology in the sciences or in ordinary language, but absolute vacuity as far as problems of the meaningfulness of life and the destiny of culture are concerned. We see in them, too, something that philosophy may do—namely, confronted by the terrors of existence and the danger of falling into an abyss of meaninglessness, philosophy can also retire, turn its back and flee, for it too can experience a failure of nerve.

Other philosophers have not hesitated to face the existent world and the realities of its life. The existentialists, especially, educated in the tradition of Pascal, Kierkegaard, and Nietzsche, have tried to articulate man's sense of the threat of nothingness in our time. Heidegger, Jaspers, Sartre, Buber, Marcel, and Tillich have looked into the face of nonbeing; they have tried to say what it is and what we are who are challenged by it.

It is sometimes alleged that existentialism simply preaches the absurdity of existence; but that allegation comes from a shallow view of existential thought or from a limited reading of its representatives. Existentialism's central thought, more central than any thought about nonbeing or nothingness or absurdity, has been the immeasurable quality, dignity, and destiny of the individual person. Existentialism has realized more intensely than any recent philosophical movement the burden of anxiety and responsibility that freedom imposes on the human individual and the challenge thrown down to him by that very fact in a world of organization, automation, mass existence, mass violence, and terror. Refusing to allow man to be reduced to animality by science and psychology, refusing to allow him to be reduced to a cog in the social machine by behavioristic social science, it has sought in desperation to find the truth about existence by looking to existence itself.

That is why it has made such essential use of phenomenology, the fundamental analysis of the structure and meaningfulness of consciousness that was inaugurated by Edmund Husserl in our century. Husserl's great slogan, "To the things themselves," was a liberating outcry of simple honesty and truthfulness. There is nothing in human experience that can be dismissed under the contemptuous title of "meaningless," not even meaninglessness itself; for it is precisely the meanings and the meaninglessnesses of lived experience that have to be understood if the task of philosophy, to help change the world rightly, is to be fulfilled. Knowledge, truth, freedom, law, art, religion can be understood only by studying them as they are, that is, as they show themselves to be. G. E. Moore, who was much influenced by the early phenomenology of Brentano, sturdily resisted the reduction of goodness to anything other than itself. He thought of himself as following Bishop Butler's maxim: Everything is what it is, and not another thing. The gains due to phenomenology could be said to flow from following that maxim implicitly. Nothing is just nothing and not another thing; terror is terror and not another thing; freedom is freedom and not another thing; therefore it behooves us to look at them in the most careful way and to disentangle their structure and meaning in the most scrupulous way.

When philosophy does this, it becomes possible for it to move ahead to its great task, namely, to find the key to the problems of meaning and existence faced by man just because he is human. The men I have mentioned have worked as individuals or in small groups. They have been the few creative ones of whom Heidegger speaks as the ones who initiate profound transformations, not by direct action on the world but by the indirect and pervasive spread of their ideas through the intellectuals to the great masses of men. It is with his eyes on this indirect mode of influence that Heidegger views philosophy as a path-breaking thinking that discloses the perspectives of man's historically necessary knowledge of norms, values, meanings, and their hierarchies.

In its inaugural function philosophy works to institute a new mode of being that belongs to its people. It is, in the field of thinking, the sister to art in the field of the creative imagination. Petty thinking is not philosophy; not even scientific thinking reaches the philosophical level; thinking must go beyond the condition of truth as correctness—the mere scientific conformity of statement to fact—to truth as disclosure of the possibilities of being itself. Within our own selves as we exist here and now in this world of ours there are possibilities of existence waiting to be born, new and strange possibilities which are our very own, the realization of which is the only thing we can properly call our vocation, our destiny. So far as we realize these possibilities, we are able to come to the truth of our own being, to authentic existence as the beings that we are, fulfilling our deepest impulse.

Such an achievement of human being cannot be attained merely by planning and willing. It is not a merely technical feat but a process of growth and creation. As the artist must wait for his inspiration so man must be patient, waiting for the right question, the right answer to come.

> To know how to question (writes Heidegger) means to know how to wait, even a whole lifetime. But an age which regards as real only what goes fast and can be clutched with both hands looks on questioning as "remote from reality" and as something that does not pay, whose benefits cannot be numbered. But the essential is not number; the essential is the right time, i.e., the right moment, and the right perseverance.[1]

And he points out in another place:

> We never come to thoughts. They come to us.
> That is the proper hour of discourse.[2]

Petty art, even correct art—art of amusement or of representation—does not reach the level of the establishment of truth. Great art is art that reaches this level, and here truth happens in the art work for the men to whose life it belongs. Suddenly, in the obscurity of the dense forest of things that surround us, a clearing occurs. It is as though there had descended upon the great art work a transfiguring light that reveals, through the work, a new world in which our life belongs and into which we are summoned to enter. Such a work is, for example, the great temple.

> A building, a Greek temple copies nothing. It simply stands there in the middle of the rock-cleft valley. The building en-

closes the figure of the god and, in this concealment, it lets it stand out in the holy precinct through the open portico. It is by means of the temple that the god is present in the temple. This presence of the god is itself the diffusion and delimitation of the precinct as a holy one. The temple and its precinct, however, do not soar off into the indefinite. It is the temple-work that first fits together and at the same time assembles around itself the unity of those paths and relations in which birth and death, disaster and blessing, victory and disgrace, endurance and decline take on for the human being the shape of his destiny. The all-governing expanse of this open relational context is the world of this historical people. From and in this world the nation first returns to itself for the fulfillment of its vocation.[3]

As Greek art articulated in the media of architecture, sculpture, painting, music, and poetry the framework of the nation's world and its historical vocation, so Greek philosophy articulated that framework in the medium of conceptual thinking. Parmenides and Heraclitus brought out into the open of the language of thinking the vision of being and of man that finds equal expression in the poetic language of the tragedy of Aeschylus and Sophocles. The thinking of the philosophers was a poetic thinking as the poetry of the dramatists was a thinking poetry. In both of them the poetic element was the creative element—of *poiesis,* making—which was the source of their power of inaugurating the shape of a human world.

It is true, then, to affirm that philosophy inaugurates. It not only inaugurates the major branches of science but also, by the indirect effects of its ideas as they pervade men's minds, it inaugurates transformations in their historical world. But its reference to the future can be meaningful and effective only as philosophy is at the same time a reflection on the past and a thinking that is part of its own age. Philosophy is and can be only where it belongs —now, not yesterday, not tomorrow.

Among the branches of knowledge whose origin can be traced to philosophical thought, conspicuous by its absence is . . . history. Herodotus did not derive his *History of the Persian Wars* from the Ionian philosophers or the Sophists, though his worldly attitude manifests an enlightenment of spirit similar to theirs. Philosophy is possessed by the spirit of thought and it seeks comprehension, the universal. History, not an enemy of thought, will consent to comprehension where the facts are intelligible. But it insists first and last on finding out what happened, whether or not it is explicable to man. A miracle is as historical as a battle. What history searches for is the particular and the individual. It describes the human world, its coming into being, its passage through time, and its passing out of being, by means of its own power of historical apprehension and insight. It discovers that philosophy too, and precisely as it inaugurates, is historical: it comes out of the past, and what it is at any time is a function of what it has already been.

The thinker who saw most acutely the essentially historical character of thought was Hegel. Indeed, so intense was his sense of the historicity of philosophy that he placed the emphasis here on the side of the present in its relation to the past rather than to the future. For him, philosophy does not inaugurate a new world; it only thinks and knows its own world. Philosophy is not the thought of the future; it is the thought of its own time. It does not exist in the abstract as an isolable and isolated system of eternally true propositions, like geometry; not even geometry can exist in that way; it is the form in which the spirit of a people and an age becomes conscious of itself. As in any period a people has its own constitution, its institutions and forms of government, morality, social life, achievements in art and science, religion, warfare and foreign relations, so too it has its philosophical ideas. In the introduction to his lectures on the history of philosophy Hegel compares the mind of a people with a cathedral, divided into numerous vaults, passages, pillars, and vestibules, and he describes it as possessed of such unity that all the parts have proceeded out of one whole and are directed to one end. One form of these many aspects is philosophy, which Hegel calls "the fullest blossom, the notion of mind in its entire form, the consciousness and spiritual essence of all things, the spirit of the time as spirit present in itself." It reflects the multifarious whole as in a single focus, the notion which knows itself.

Just because the philosophy of an age is the age's own thought, comprehending itself and its world, it cannot overstep the limits of the age; it cannot also be the thought of a new age. Even when it is a thought that is prospective, preparing for change, it is the prospective thinking of the present and will be different from and not viable as the actual thought of the new age. Greek philosophy, no matter how much it was used, was transformed into something entirely different in Roman thought; the latter's destiny was the same when the European world became Christian and needed its own form of thought; and so it has been down to the present. Roman thought could not have formed itself without Greek thought, Christian thought without Roman thought, modern thought without Christian thought; yet each such necessary predecessor is only a transformed ingredient in its successors.

Philosophy cannot stand above its time in content, because its own time is exactly the substance of its own self. It stands above its time only in form. It is the thought, the knowledge of its time and of the substantial spirit of its time. It therefore makes that substance into its own object, standing apart from it as seer to seen, thinker to object thought about. But it transcends its object only in form and standpoint, not in time, history, and reality.

And this means, too, that the philosophical thinking of a period cannot formulate itself fully until the period has already shaped itself and produced its own substance. For philosophy meditates on the content precisely of the constitution, institutions, morals, sociality, art, science, war, and peace that belong to the age. "When philosophy with its abstractions paints gray in gray, the freshness and life of youth has gone."

A consequence is that philosophy is hardly equal to the task of giving instruction as to what the world ought to be. As Hegel says:

> Philosophy in any case always comes on the scene too late to give it. As the thought of the world, it appears only when actuality is already there cut and dried after its process of formation has been completed. The teaching of the concept, which is also history's inescapable lesson, is that it is only when actuality is mature that the ideal first appears over against the real and that the ideal apprehends this same real world in its substance and builds it up for itself into the shape of an intellectual realm. When philosophy paints its gray in gray, then has a shape of life grown old. By philosophy's gray in gray it cannot be rejuvenated but only understood. The owl of Minerva spreads its wings only with the falling of the dusk.[4]

So we come full turn to the position exactly opposite that of American pragmatism and German existentialism, of Dewey and Heidegger, who attribute to philosophy the essential role of giving imaginative shape to the growing world. The difference is related to a difference in philosophical persuasion. Neither Dewey nor Heidegger shares the absolute rationalism of Hegel. Hegel's thought was the thought of its own age, an age that had a profound faith in growth, evolution, and the spiritual meaningfulness of life and history. Hegel could believe in the romantic vision of history as theodicy of the spirit and of the historical process as the unrolling of the divine nature in time. Consequently, for him, every age and every nation had the spiritual substance needed to unfold the divine history, and no matter how barbaric its institutions, they were to be grasped as a necessary stage in the development of the spirit. In the same way, no matter how irrational a past epoch may look to us, it itself contained all there could be of rationality at its time; whatever was, was as reasonable as its stage permitted; and in general the basic conviction motivating Hegel's thought is the philosophical dictum: What is rational is actual and what is actual is rational.

Because of his faith in the rationality of reality Hegel could declare that the task of philosophy is to comprehend what is, because what is, is reason. And he added:

> Whatever happens, every individual is a child of his time; so philosophy too is its own time apprehended in thoughts. It is just as absurd to fancy that a philosophy can transcend its contemporary world as it is to fancy that an individual can overleap his own age, jump over Rhodes. If his theory really goes beyond the world as it is and builds an ideal one as it ought to be, that world exists indeed, but only in his opinions, an unsubstantial element where anything you please may, in fancy, be built.[5]

So hardheaded a view of the opposition between the ideal and the real might at first hardly be expected from the chief of all idealists, yet it follows from his view of the absolute necessity with which history develops its stages of the spirit. A similar kind of hardheadedness appears in his chief materialist disciple, Karl Marx, because of the latter's equally absolutistic view of the necessity with which history develops its stages of class struggle and its ultimate overcoming.

But neither American pragmatism nor German existentialism could believe in the already-determined fixity of historical process or in the necessary development of either spirit or matter. Our age's terrible experiences of conflict, violence, and death, greater than ever in the past and less human because more mechanized and automated, do not let us so easily grant that it contains within itself, just as it is, the seeds of a fuller rationality which is one day destined to arrive by its own power. The thinking of the few, the thinking of the individual, philosophical thinking is today in a weaker position than ever, just because it is so much harder for the philosopher to experience the saving thought and to be heard when he speaks it by a world so full of business and so loud in its universal talk.

Is it not perhaps much easier to believe in the opposite of Hegel's maxim: What is irrational is actual and what is actual is irrational? Yet that would be equally untrue. The age is not more one of violence than it is full of the deepest and strongest yearning for reconciliation and peace. The very ones who preach and practice violence can do so only by proclaiming themselves to be the champions of justice, harmony, and peace.

The more modern science extends its grasp of the

mechanisms of things, even into the biological and behavioral realms, the more definitely do modern thought and art lay hold of authentic human freedom and spirituality. Modern art's greatest triumphs have come with its turning of ugliness and dissonance into the purity of an affirmation of the truth, the validity, the integrity of the human spirit and its possibilities of existence. And so too modern thinking has looked to the conflicts, the discords, the ugly realities of our life, and its endeavor has been to think the saving thought and speak the saving word.

What is it to think and speak in this way? What is the core of philosophical thinking, the substantial content that must fill the heart of the present-day thinker and that it must be his sole effort to articulate in appropriate language?

Philosophy inaugurates, to be sure, in the sense of initiating; yet it does so not by being before its time but by being of its time. Its initiating power comes from its own historical placing. Hegel's rationalism may be rejected, but one cannot so easily reject the view that living philosophy belongs to its age, is the age's own thought, by which it comprehends itself and its world.

To every time there belongs its hopeful or dreadful vision of the future, its ideals and dreams and plans and determinations, just as much as its remembrance of the past and its apprehension of the present. These three orientations of human time cannot exist without one another; they interpenetrate and determine one another. Every act of perception is at the same time an act of recollection and forecast, and every recollection and every forecast is rooted in its own present perception. What we remember, we remember now, at this time, from this perspective, in this mood, and what we look forward to is seen from this point, this angle, in this quandary. The present moment becomes and is what it is not just because of what we confront and observe within it, but because everything in it, on the side of the subject as well as that of the object, partakes of the nowness of the now—that is, issues as such from its own past and projects forward into its own future. The present moment is historical in a genuine and essential sense. It is not abstractly separated from the preceding moments and the moments to come, but is constitutively present in the real ongoing processes of time and becoming, belonging of its own self to the process of the very making of reality.

The consciousness that belongs to an age is the age's own. It is the age's own way—complex, containing many inner conflicts, oppositions, contradictions, vaguenesses as well as determinatenesses, blindnesses as well as insights, errors as well as truths—of being aware of itself and its world. Philosophy is only the most general and comprehensive articulation of this consciousness. It brings out and gives to its age an explicit frame of thought within which it first becomes possible for the age to do its explicit thinking.

The history of philosophy is not an autonomous development independent of its cultural context. Every philosophy, to be sure, learns from the past; but it forgets much of the past, too, namely, that which in its eyes does not belong to its own task. Current analytic philosophy, for example, has deliberately forgotten almost everything in the history of philosophy, rejecting it as irrelevant to its task. Heidegger has argued that most of the history of philosophical thought in the West has been a forgetting —perhaps even a culpable one, since it involves a covering up of what once was—of the pristine closeness of the pre-socratic Greek thinkers to being, in an authentic way, so that what we have to do is leap back over much of that history to the origins to pick up the true thread once more. These are two extreme views; more moderate, and more adequate in the end, is the approach that finds in the actual history of thought means of suggestion and stimulation toward the performance of the contemporary task. To shut oneself off from the past is the surest way to lose sight of essential needs and possibilities; to lose oneself in the past is an equally sure way of shutting oneself off from present needs and possibilities.

Philosophy changes in part like the sciences; earlier modes of thought are understood and superseded; we can never make a literal return to Plato, Aquinas, or Kant, not even to yesterday's philosophers like Dewey, Wittgenstein, or Heidegger. The fact that they have been means already that they belong to their own moment in the process of the age. We should be able to see better the features of existence in our time because of the philosophical experience through which they have gone, the experiments they have made.

On the other hand, philosophy changes also in part like the arts. Later philosophy is not necessarily truer just because it is later. Rembrandt may represent an advance on more primitive Dutch painters of color and light in a process of the gradual conquest of those phenomena, but he does not necessarily represent an advance upon the great art of Greece or Rome or Byzantium, or upon the Renaissance masters like Leonardo, Raphael, and Michelangelo. So too, Descartes advanced beyond the imperfect formulations of seventeenth-century thinking to fashion an initiation of modern subjectivism in philosophy, but his thought does not necessarily represent an advance on the great philosophy of the Greeks, Romans, or Christians who preceded modern times. He no more, and perhaps no less, adequately outlined the framework of thought in the Baroque era than did Plato that of post-Periclean Athens.

Philosophy is in part like science since it tries to be a way of knowing things; but it is in part like art, because what it has to know is things in their human meaning, importance, and significance. It is knowledge not at the level of the logical understanding alone, the level of science, but at the level of the human mind's height, the height of its spiritual dimension. What art intuits and what religion believes has to be comprehended by philosophy. Philosophical concepts must have incorporated within themselves the power of artistic intuition and of religious symbolism, and yet remain concepts of human reason, by which human reason comprehends the fundamental realities of its existence. Philosophy is the rational structure of the human mind's consciousness of the life of its period, as art is its intuitional structure and religion the structure of its representational symbolism and faith.

We owe our understanding of the role of philosophy in the history of consciousness to the labors of post-Hegelian thinkers like Wilhelm Dilthey, who recognized the variety of types and styles of philosophical thinking as being analogous to those of the arts and of other life-phenomena generally, and as being inseparable from the historical process of life itself. Human reason not only thinks historically, and therefore is historical in its attitude; it is essentially a historical phenomenon itself, as the mode of rational consciousness of its own period, and therefore it is historical in its substance as well.

Philosophy belongs to its time; but its time belongs, too, to its philosophy; for philosophy is inaugural in making its time what it is, in giving it the shape of its reason. Greek thought gave to its epoch the essential concepts of measure and the mean, being as *physis* or nature, form and matter, the essential and the accidental, the idea and the ideal, the end and the means, cause and principle, potentiality and actuality—I mention only some of the most decisive of its metaphysical thoughts. Earlier modern thought gave to our epoch the essential concepts of the ego and its *cognito,* the subject and the object, self-consciousness, theoretical, practical, and critical reason, experience, the *a priori* and the *a posteriori,* the finite and the infinite mind—one notices the great contrast, well-known, between the older objectivity and the more recent subjectivity. Greek reason was directed outward, seeking the ground and content of rationality in objective being. Modern reason has become more self-consciously aware of its own participation in determining the rational structure of the world. When Kant first discovered the human mind's constitutive role in determining the coherence of the world he spoke of it as philosophy's Copernican Revolution, for it changed the center about which reason could now revolve. We are still far from having emerged from the period of subjectivism in thought, despite the struggles of realism, empiricism, and phenomenology to break out of the circle of the subjective and that which is relative to the subject.

But there has been one great gain from thought's experience with subjectivity. That concerns the form in which we are now able to conceive of the unity by which philosophy attempts to think in its comprehensive manner. To comprehend is to hold together a manifold in a unity, in such a way that the manifold is genuinely known for what it essentially is. One way of putting the eternal challenge to philosophy is that of the problem of the one and the many. The search for comprehension leads ultimately to the search for what unites the disparate into a coherent whole, what makes cosmos in chaos, order in disorder, measure in the measureless, peace in war, harmony in discord, resolution in tension.

So long as our view turns primarily outward, our concept of unity—our concept of the being-together that makes a being out of what is not yet a being—has to be determined by relationships that contain something external about them: spatial, material, dynamic. The highest form of unity that can be discovered in mere objectivity is the unity of the organism, organic unity. In its ideal concept, organic unity is the unity of organs with one another and with the organism as a whole. Each organ is what it is, and does what it does, only under the influence of each other organ and of the whole. The purpose of the whole thus becomes effective in the whole and in each part, and the function of each part is effective in every other part and in the whole. This is an abstract definition, indeed, but it makes explicit the idea of purpose, insofar as purpose can be thought of as belonging intrinsically to an objectively existent being, like a plant, or an animal, and eventually the human organism itself.

The Greek understanding of life and existence, from which we have inherited one major part of our Western understanding of things, was primarily organic, guided by the comprehension of organic unity. Greek ethics is the ethics of the organic *polis;* Greek aesthetics is the indwelling principle of its greatest art, the art of classical organic beauty; the Olympian religion is the religion of organic unity; and we owe the explicit philosophical formulation of the idea of organic unity to Plato and Aristotle. Every one of Plato's heavenly Ideas and of Aristotle's actual Forms is a principle of organic unity and of nothing but organic unity.

Greek thought has so permeated the West that we are still partly confined within the framework of organic thinking. But Christianity and Judaism did not first think of the divine in organic terms. They understood God as essentially subject, to whom a bodily form is a contingent cover, of whom no images other than man's own spirit can give a proper hint. They understood him as person and persons, and therefore as spirit related to other spirits, including men as finite spiritual persons. The relationship of man to God was not that of an organ to an organism, or of an organism to a principle of organism, but of a person to a person. God called man by his name and required him to respond to the call. The essential being of man lay not in the organic unity of his body or his mind or his body-mind. It lay in his responsibility—his being able to be called upon to respond, to acknowledge and take upon himself the obligations that belong to a spiritual person, and eventually to participate in the unity of loyalty and love that stands at the height of human and spiritual possibility. Man is the being who can be responsible, and therefore who alone can sin and be justified.

The unity that philosophy understands when it finally achieves the thought of the person and the person's dimension of spiritual existence is the unity by which persons participate in a community or a communion of persons, by which an I, a thou, a he, a she, all participate in a we. The individual comes to be genuinely an individual precisely as he participates in relationships open to a person. The highest and most evolved forms of such relationships are those of the participation of free men in a free community. But they occur in differing ways and differing degrees in all the diverse kinds of community—in the family and friendship, the state and culture, school and society, law and morals, and eventually in the religious communion of men with one another and with their God.

Characteristic of personal and social unity is the inescapable presence within it of disunity—discord, tension, opposition, strife, evil, sin. It is a dialectical unity that emerges from its opposite. Its forms of innocence do not last, any more than Adam and Eve could inhabit the Garden of Eden forever just as they did in the beginning. Innocence leads to experience; the joyful simplicity of the songs of innocence and the tender being of the lamb turn into the more somber notes of the songs of experience and the fearful symmetry of the tiger. Only an understanding of such disunity and its conquest in the unity of participation in loyalty and love can give man a concept of unity that is adequate for the purposes of philosophy today.

What is this unity? What is the concept by means of which we are able to think it? I have already made use of several words to describe it. It is the unity of participation, responsibility and responsiveness, acknowledgment, loyalty, and love. At the core of all of them is the recognition, acceptance, possession, enactment of, devotion to *what is our own*. To participate with an other, to be an I to a thou and a thou to an I in an embracing we, is to accept the other as our own and to give ourself over to the other as his own. To be a responsible and responsive member of a group is to belong to the group in an authentic way, acknowledging it as one's group and oneself as a member of it. To revolt against a tyrannical power is to declare, on pain of one's own self-sacrifice, that that power overrides what is its own and that one oneself belongs elsewhere. Loyalty is the acknowledgment of those to whom one belongs and the acceptance and practice of the responsibilities entailed by the relationship. Love is the ultimate relationship of persons in which each is own to the other, in which mine and thine become indissolubly one. It is no accident that mysticism makes use of love as one of its most favored images of the relationship of the finite to the infinite.

The challenge to philosophy at present is precisely this: to let this personal and spiritual concept of unity permeate its conceptual sphere, purifying and transforming it so as to make it fit to do what now needs to be done. An age of profound sinfulness and of deep anxiety about the future of its own spiritual being can have as its fundamental philosophical problem only this: to take possession for itself of the concept of what is own—of participation, belonging, responsibility, loyalty, love, and devotion—and to make it into the consciousness that stands over the present moment telling it its own truth.

When consciousness reaches the ultimacy of its knowledge, in the shape of philosophy, it enters upon its most essential historical vocation, as the inaugurating, reflecting, and presently active thinking of what is own and not own to existent man.

2

The Vocation of Consciousness

The theme of ownness echoes throughout human life. It does so because it is no mere accident, not even a mere property, of our life, but its pervasive and ruling *motif.* Something analogous to it already exists and operates in all of life, the most primitive as well as the most advanced. When an organism feeds, it appropriates a part of its environment and assimilates it to its own body, throwing off the remains as not suitable to itself, not its own. When a mother cat protects her kittens against their enemies she makes clear to all and sundry by the lashing of her tail, the motions of crouching or of striking out with her claws, the yowls and other warning cries, what is and what is not own to her. All purposive behavior, even down to the tropisms of primitive plant life, consists basically in this, that the organism acts so as to impose its own aim on the material being dealt with. A bird that builds a nest impresses on the twigs, as it weaves them together, a form deriving from its own self; it makes them into a brooding-place for its own young, for the perpetuation of its own kind, and shows by its subsequent behavior how intensely it treats the nest as belonging to itself. Adjustment of organism to environment and environment to organism, which is the central feature of life-behavior and ecology, is the determination of how the two are to belong to one another so that the environment should become the organism's world and the organism that world's inhabitant.

When the life-process rises to the height of human being this theme of ownness and belonging, appropriation and participation, rises as well and becomes the single *motif* that runs through all the variations of our thought, feeling, and action. It appears in highly diversified ways, from the most elemental of physical acts, like eating, breathing, moving, copulating, defecating, to the most spiritualized, like sacrificing, praying, or entering into mystical union. It is able to exhibit these variations because it is the most universal of all possible *real* relations. It determines what the reality of a relation is, because it constitutes it. Real relation is belonging; real negation is not-belonging. How the electron is related to the nucleus of its atom is how the two belong to one another, a mode of mutual participation whose measures are expressed by the laws of physical particles. So, too, how the individual thought is related to the thought-pattern, the individual feeling to the mood and disposition, the individual intention to the will and plan, the individual human being to the group—these relations are forms by which realities belong to one another, participating in one another's being. To understand something is to apprehend it in its character of belonging and being belonged to, its real relations and negations.

If human being is to be understood, it must be understood from this viewpoint. When we see how a form of life is the manifestation of the impulse toward ownness, we understand it, for we understand the indwelling aim which leads it to take the shape that it does. The very being of an aim, its aimfulness, is the actualizing of ownness. To have an aim is, by its very nature, to intend to make something one's own. That is why the ability to grasp ownness is the same as the ability to understand an aim and the actualizing of it. The aim need not be a conscious one; most aims are not conscious. What is essential, however, is the impulse toward ownness, toward the reality of belonging and excluding—being with as one's own, being separate from as not one's own.

Consciousness, however, has a special role in human life. It does not belong exclusively to man; in some degree it extends throughout animal life; but in man it develops a human role, and it is this role that is of interest to us here. What is the role of consciousness in man's being? What is its vocation, the task to which it is called? The answer lies in the way in which consciousness functions to bring to light, in human life, the meanings of own and not-own. Through his consciousness, man stands in a special relationship to things: he becomes conscious *of* them. To grasp human consciousness for what it essentially is, is to understand how man's consciousness-of things functions in the process of his appropriation of and participation in reality.

The expression "consciousness-of" recalls immediately the phenomenological view of mind. Phenomenology approaches consciousness by way of its so-called *intentionality.* Consciousness, says phenomenology, has the unique characteristic of being consciousness-of. It is an act directed toward and intending something other than the act, as a perception of a cloud is directed toward the cloud, a recollection of a concert is directed toward the recollected concert, a wish for good news is directed toward the wished-for good news, or a resolute will to perform a certain deed is directed toward the deed to be performed. Even if not all consciousness can be said to be explicitly intentionalistic—as, for instance, it is a question whether a mere sensuous feeling of comfort or a feeling-state of elation or gloom is or need always be explicitly intentionalistic—nevertheless the modes of consciousness that unfold in cognition, practice, and affection all develop an intentionalistic structure.

One could even say, perhaps, that consciousness is susceptible of degrees, and that the degree of consciousness is just the degree to which the characteristic of intentionality has developed. When one is merely sensuously comfortable, the tendency is to lose the sense of oneself in contrast with something other. Sensuous discomfort makes one more aware, more conscious; one's attention is drawn to the source of discomfort, one's mind is directed toward it; that is, intentionality gets articulated and one becomes aware of the discomfort and the source as such. It is similar with affective states of the psyche sometimes referred to as moods—generalized and non-objectivating feelings that spread throughout the psyche and pervade the atmosphere of the whole self-world structure. When one is in a state of pervasive gloom, the gloominess does not direct itself intentionally toward a definite object; it tends, rather, just to settle down like a dark mist and soak through everything. Only when something particular attracts our attention as a source or focus of the gloom does the state begin to pass over into an intentionalistic act of the psyche—it is, perhaps, a piece of bad news that, we say, "makes us gloomy," on which our gloom focuses in such a way that we can now say that we are gloomy *about* the subject of the news. We hear of killings in the war and our gloom concentrates on that topic; we become gloomy about the present state of the world, about the political possibilities in our country, etc. This "about" is an intentionalistic preposition descriptive of the directedness of the emergent gloom-consciousness.

If, then, we think of consciousness as susceptible of degrees, and in particular think of it as present in the degree to which there is present an articulation of intentionality, then intentionality becomes an esssential characterizing attribute of consciousness. But whether or not we view consciousness in that light, it remains the case that it is the peculiar prerogative of consciousness that it should be able to develop within itself this unique characteristic of intentionality.

What we describe by the word "intentionality" is a certain relationship that can also be described in other terms. It refers to the act in its relationship to the object; it says, consciousness consists of an act intending an object. Viewing the matter in the inverse direction, we could say that consciousness consists in an object becoming manifest to an act or to the agent of the act. Manifestness, overtness, showing, seeming, appearing—these words characterize consciousness from the side of the object. Only in consciousness can there be the unique characteristic of the overtness, openness, lighting-up of something *for* someone. If we think of the ego as the agent in the act of consciousness, so that the ego is that which intends the object, then, looking at the scene from the side of the object, we can say that the ego is the being *for whom* the object is. This feature of being-for-one is as much a unique aspect of consciousness as is the characteristic of intentionality; it is just the other side of intentionality.

Consciousness is that peculiar actuality in which something is *for* one, something *appears to* someone.

The essential feature of consciousness is not just the one side alone, intentionality; it is the whole, including the other side as well, the side of evidence or appearance. Consciousness is essentially two-sided, a unity of intentionality and appearance. We have to use different words for the two features because the relationship between the act and its indwelling agent, on the one hand, and the object, on the other, is asymmetrical. The act intends the object, but the object does not (as such) intend the act. The ego is aware of the object, but the object is not (as such) aware of the ego. The object appears to the subject, but the subject does not (as such) appear to the object. It is the ego that reaches out toward the object so as to be aware of it; but it is the object that stands out over there so as to appear to the ego.

This asymmetry of consciousness is referred to in our use of different names for the two terms in the relationship: ego and nonego, subject and object, self and other. Consciousness is an ego's experiencing of its nonego, a subject's experiencing of an object, a self's experiencing of something other than itself. The objects in this room, the furniture, the room, the building, the people outside, the world stretching to the horizon—all these I experience as other than myself and other than my particular mode of being aware of them. Experiencing something other than the self is a fundamental structure of consciousness. Even when consciousness is fictively imaginative, as when I imagine a green sun and a yellow sea, I experience these as other than myself or my imaginative vision of them.

Consciousness is in the first place called upon to be and to develop this peculiar duality. The first part of the vocation of consciousness is to be the coming to light of the difference of ego and nonego, subject and object, self and other. This difference is a special kind of difference. In it, one constituent is there *for* the other *as* being other than the latter. In an ordinary difference, the two entities are, as it were, indifferent to one another. This chair is different from this table. The one *is not* the other. But that is all there is to the story of their difference. To be sure, they affect each other, by gravitation, electromagnetic attraction and repulsion, heat transmission and absorption, etc.; but neither of them—presumably—is there *for* the other in its difference from the latter. In consciousness, on the contrary, the one constituent—the nonego or object—is there precisely *for* the other constituent—the ego or subject—*as* other to itself. Only in consciousness can there be such a thing as an itself *for* which another is there *as* other.

The whole of consciousness and its every act as consciousness can be viewed correctly as consisting in the articulation of this duality as such. What is the point of it? Why should there be such a strange actuality as this duality of self and other and its articulation in the shape of consciousness? The question is not meant to elicit a causal answer. I am not asking by what genetic process consciousness has come about, or what are its chemical and physiological conditions. I am asking for the point of it; what is the psyche driving at in emerging into consciousness? Why should the psyche—that is, the total man, body-mind complex—work itself up into the light of awareness? What is it doing?

We may discover the answer by consulting consciousness itself in its own inner purposiveness. We are able to understand this purposiveness because we exist inside consciousness, participating in it in the manner of our own being.

The other, of which I am conscious, is in the first place not I. Its otherness is its difference from me. It stands opposed to me, beyond me, and I stand on this side of it, confronted by it as something that is not I.

At the same time, the I which is conscious of this other emerges here as an ego that is aware of itself as being in this relationship to something other. Consciousness essentially involves self-consciousness. I know myself as the ego at work in this consciousness. I know myself in the very act of intending the object as other than myself, as being for me.

This knowledge that I have of myself is immediate self-consciousness. It does not have the same structure as my awareness of the object. Even in the most immediate consciousness of something other as object, there is the difference experienced between myself and the object. This difference lies in the very nature of objectivating consciousness. But as being immediately conscious of myself, I do not pose myself as an object, an other which is supposed to be different from myself and for myself, alongside the object of which I am conscious. Rather, by an immediate participation in my own being, I am self-possessed in the very act of intending the object as other.

As the object becomes explicitly and actually for me in my consciousness of it, so my own self differentiates itself from it as the one for whom it grows explicitly actual, and my self emerges to that degree as a self in consciousness. A self is a being that is thus immediately aware of itself in the very act of being explicitly aware of something as other than itself. This could be taken as a definition of selfhood as seen from the particular perspective of the theoretical component of consciousness. It is not a complete definition, but it is one that gives a valid partial approach to the self.

This self-awareness of the ego in its consciousness of the object is the primary form and the foundation of all genuine self-consciousness. The grammar of our language tempts us into thinking about consciousness of self in the same way as we think about consciousness of objects. But the preposition "of" in these two phrases does not have the same use. When I am conscious of myself, my self is actually present to me. But it is not present in the manner of something that stands over against me, an ob-ject, such as occurs in sensation as a visual other, an auditory other, etc., or in perception as a thing with properties or an event proceeding in space and time, etc. It is, rather, present to me precisely as *not* an object, *not* something that is there for me as other than myself.

It is often said that the intentionality of consciousness consists in the directedness of the conscious act toward objects. But this should be taken only as an approximation. Not only are psychical states of a purely or predominantly sensuous sort, where meaning plays no part or virtually no part, non-intentionalistic (see Husserl on the "sensile hyle"),[1] but, as we have seen, psychic conditions in which a unitary quality pervades the whole situation, such as non-objectifying moods, are, though in a sense meaningful, nevertheless not object-constituting. The consciousness we are now concerned with, immediate self-consciousness, is also full of meaning, and can be said to be consciousness-of in one sense of "of"; but it is not the sense in which what the act is conscious of is an object for it. If we stress the sense that intentionality is the meaningfulness of consciousness, then immediate self-consciousness is intentionalistic; if we stress the objectivating function, or think of all meaning as being object-directed, then immediate self-consciousness is not intentionalistic. It depends on how one wishes to understand the notion of intentionality.

In any case, what remains true is that my immediate self-consciousness is not an object-consciousness. I am conscious of myself by inhabiting my own acts, and I am present to myself by my being my own self. Rather than having to observe what I am doing when I think, or act, or feel, I know within my very thinking that and how I am thinking, within my very acting or feeling that and how I am acting or feeling. I do not have to separate these acts from myself so as to pay attention to them as differentiated from the observational act and the observing self. They come to light without such differentiation.

I am able, on the other hand, to become conscious of myself also in a different way, making myself into an object for my observation, thought, feeling, and will. So I can turn inwardly and reflect upon my conscious acts and self, as when I try to watch myself perceiving or remember what it was like to make a certain choice. In this mode of inner observation or reflection, the self and its acts become objects somewhat like objects in the external world. They are amenable to a kind of inner perception, and thereupon to explicit thinking, doubting, believing, wishing, etc. In this role, the self is much like a theoretical entity; it is a structure hypothesized by thinking as lying at the ground of the observed acts, and is susceptible to the hypothetico-deductive methods of science. It is the self which serves as the object of the scientific psychologist.

The self that I know directly and immediately, because it is what I am and is the form in which I am presently existing, does not appear to me as such an object of reflection. It remains on this side of the conscious relationship as not-other and it never can become an other, no matter how much and how adequately I think about myself in an objective manner. What is other than me in consciousness remains always other, and I remain always not-other. If this difference between the self and its other were to vanish, consciousness would vanish. Such vanishing occurs in mystical experience, where self and other are transcended in the *unio mystica*. But consciousness remains in the sphere of difference, where the other is indefeasibly other. The object functions as a limit and a barrier to the ego. It is as though it were saying to the ego: "Thus far you extend, but not further; here, on the other side, you encounter what is not yourself, a piece of the fence of being that encloses you by its difference from yourself."

There occurs here a peculiar paradox, which may well be called the paradox of consciousness. Ego-awareness depends on nonego-awareness and conversely. The two come to explicit being at the same time and in essential relationship. As I become aware of the other, as object, as limit, I become aware of myself as ego, as subject, as limited. My consciousness is always twofold: a transcending consciousness of what is other and beyond myself and an immanent consciousness of my self. To be conscious is just to function as this twofold awareness: an outward-directed intention toward a transcendent object and an indwelling awareness of selfhood. The intention toward the object has to span a gap, the gap of otherness and difference, and therefore must be transcending. The immediate self-awareness has no gap to span; the subject is directly with itself as ego.

Now because of this intimate dependence of ego and object on one another, they belong to one another, in the manner of consciousness. Here too, as in the case of difference, so in the case of belonging: it is not an indifferent belonging, but one that matters to the conscious self, in an asymmetrical manner. The object is my object and I am its subject. In this relationship the minimal condition is that I should be functioning as a person. A person is a being who can be aware of himself as an I, an ego, in relation to something other as belonging to him, as being his own. In consciousness the object is my object and I am aware of it as such; only thus could I be at the same time self-conscious. As the object comes to light in its appearance to me, I come to light in my appropriation of that appearance. Whether in sensation or reflection, imagination or conception, belief or supposition, wish or repudiation, hope or despair, if the object is to show itself as other than I, that very appearance must become mine. That other and transcendent being must, to show itself as other than I, become my object.

This is not idealism; it is quite the reverse. Idealism said: in order for something to be an object for me, it has to be a part of the whole of me, it has to become a content of my own being: the nonego has to show itself to be the ego. That is the doctrine of the ideality of the nonego—of space, time, matter. It is the necessary contradiction of idealism that forced it to become dialectical in a logical rather than a spiritual way. But the life of consciousness says something other than idealism. In it, the object defines itself as being something other than myself, refusing itself to me in its strange and alien being, transcending my own being, whereas, at the same time, that very same object defines itself as being just my object and indeed, as the being which, by being strange and alien, by transcending my own being and being a limit and a barrier to me, defines me as its subject and thus brings me out into overt being as an ego and a person. The very otherness of the other is something that is essentially mine. It could not be other except by being mine. Already, in the most elemental emergence of otherness, ownness has also emerged.

No matter how opposed the object is to the subject, no matter how estranged and alienated it is from me, nevertheless, so long as it remains my other and therefore so long as I am conscious of it, so long does it remain mine and I remain its. It is mine as belonging to a person; I am its in the way in which a person belongs to—i.e., owns—what is his own. This is the paradox of consciousness and the root of its living and ultimately spiritual dialectic. I am conscious and can exist as an ego and a person only insofar as I can reach beyond the barrier that separates me from what is other than me and have it as my own. In order to be as a conscious being, and therefore as the possibility of a knower, a free man, and eventually a loving and devoted spirit, I must exist in a condition of difference and otherness with what is nevertheless mine and to be mine.

Now this ownness that exists in consciousness is not

just a nonconscious appendage of it. It constitutes the essential character of consciousness. The primary and overriding meaning in consciousness is the meaning of ownness. I am conscious of the object not merely as an indifferent different, but as my other, i.e., as the other which is my own. I am immediately self-conscious not as observing or reflecting on an entity which is my self; rather, I am self-conscious within my conscious act, and in the form of the act as being *my* intending of the object. My consciousness is the unity of these two different ownings, the owning of the object and the owning of the act; it is itself a single consciousness that diverges in these two directions. It is a single consciousness by virtue of being the consciousness of the act and the object as belonging to each other in just these diverse ways: owned to owner and owner to owned, his belonging to the person and the person to his belonging. The two—the personal act (itself appropriated by the person) and the other that is appropriated by the personal act—are appropriate to one another, not just as an indifferent fact of which consciousness could be unaware, but as the essential quality of consciousness itself. Consciousness *is* own-consciousness. It is the awareness of ownness as it radiates out into the person's act, and through that toward the person himself, on the one side, and toward the being that transcends the person on the other.

The vocation of consciousness is to be own-consciousness. In being called upon to be, consciousness is called upon to be the witness of ownness. It is the ownness-relation that makes possible the three features of consciousness: subject, object, and subject-object, or self, other, and self-other. We could say: the subject is the own that owns, the object the own that is owned, and the relation between the two, or consciousness, is the owning of the owned by the owner. This is not mere word game or trivial play with concepts. It lies at the center of human being. It is a formulation of the meaning of being when being becomes meaningful to itself.

The ownness that belongs to consciousness simply as consciousness is, however, only the beginning of true ownness. For it is the ownness of the other *qua* other, the ownness of otherness. To be this ownness of the other as other is the immediate, but not the ultimate, vocation of consciousness. Or more accurately, to be conscious, as dwelling within the ownness of the other *qua* other, is man's immediate, but not his ultimate, vocation.

It is necessary to return to fundamentals if we are to understand the role of consciousness in life. Man's basic and universal need is to be with what is other than himself —and this includes himself as other, too—as with his own, or even more fundamentally, to transform other into own. Every mode and form of human life and activity is a particular way in which this basic and universal need is satisfied. All substantive philosophy has recognized this need as fundamental to the being of man, beginning with the Platonic Eros, Aristotelian entelechy, Christian love, Indian bhakti, Confucian harmony of heaven and earth, Taoist Way, and Buddhist Nirvana, and coming down to the concepts of freedom in German idealism and its offshoots, will and will-to-power in Schopenhauer and Nietzsche, appropriation in Marxism and existentialism, the I-Thou relation of Buber, the behaviorist adjustment to environment, the Freudian libido, and the Jungian integration. Everywhere that man tries to formulate for himself, whether in abstract concepts or in concrete images, the fundamental impulse of his being, it takes the shape of an overcoming of estrangement between himself and that which transcends his self, a transformation of his relationship to other into a relationship to own.

Man is a being who, in order to exist, must exist in a world. The world is what the environment becomes for man insofar as it becomes *his* surroundings; it is the environment as own to him. The world is not a reflection of man, as though he were seeing merely his own self in a mirror when he looks out into his world. The notion that the world is a reflection of mind was a fiction developed in the idealist theology, which tried to explain God by an extrapolation from man's being. The world does not only express man's inner being, although it undoubtedly contains such expressions. It is and expresses the ownness that belongs to his vicinity in the universe, what surrounds him as belonging to the sphere of his life activity, immanent and transcendent. The world changes with culture and history. It even changes with individual development. Man belongs to his world and his world belongs to him; they are own to each other.

In the world, man encounters what is other to him. This includes his own self, his body and his mind, when and as he encounters them. He is in the world along with others, which are also other to each other, in a mutual extraneity. Consciousness is that phase of mind in which this otherness of things in the world comes to light and appears as such. In so far as man is conscious, what happens is that something shows itself to him as other. His consciousness of space is a consciousness of the simultaneous extraneity of things including, especially, their being outside and alongside himself. His consciousness of time is—or at least includes at its core—a consciousness of the continuing extraneity of himself in his world to himself in his world, the repeated othering and re-capturing of himself and his world. His consciousness of causality is a consciousness of the actual existence of the other, which makes itself felt by imposing constraints on his own existence, acting as obstacle and opportunity to his power of being.

At the very heart of consciousness there lies an impulse and an endeavor to articulate itself until it reaches its own fullness. Man is not and can never be satisfied with the mere otherness of what he encounters as other. That other must become his own, or else an exclusion must be set up between himself and it, by which it is kept off from him as not-own—whether by forgetting and ignoring it, i.e., becoming unconscious of it, or by exercising force to defend his own against it, to repel it, to dominate it. He cannot be satisfied with the other's merely being his own in the mode of simple consciousness, i.e., his own other simply as other; it has to become his own in a more thoroughgoing and pregnant sense, in such a way that ultimately all its otherness is, not so much cancelled or simply negated, but lifted up and transfigured into ownness.

The search for the determination of the other as own leads through the entire structure of human experience—of being at home and wandering; one's country and the foreign land; friend, stranger, and enemy; the family; property, individual and social; crime and law; history; religion; art; philosophy.

Conventionally we distinguish three main spheres or dimensions of human mentality: theoretical, practical, and spiritual. In all three the fundamental intention is the same: to transform the relationship of man to reality from the merely immediate stage of relation to other as other to the consummatory stage of relation to other as to own. Theoretical activity tries to make the world as other over into something comprehensible, i.e., it tries to give it the shape of intelligibility, what is own to man's intellect. Practical activity tries to make the world take the shape of man's designs and ideals, i.e., it tries to give it the shape of the good and the ought, what is own to man's will. Spiritual activity unites the two directions of the theoretical and the practical into a living unity. It tries to establish a relationship with reality in which man experiences the latter as being own to him, and himself as being own to it, in the concreteness of feeling of the whole personality, with all its powers, knowledge, and ideals. Such a relationship occurs in varying degrees in the affective dimension of experience and reaches its most comprehensive and profound form in *religio,* in man's linking of himself to the transcendent, the ultimate, the unconditioned.

In its higher reaches the affective relationship allows man to find the other as his own only in the very process of giving himself to the other as its own—a relationship possible only among persons—in the mutual bond of an ultimate connection. The height of love is reached only where the height of devotion can be engaged in.

What lies at the heart of consciousness, then, is the aspiring endeavor toward freedom and truth of being, namely, the fullest possible being with other as with one's own. As freedom and truth are realized, consciousness itself undergoes a metamorphosis. It becomes more extensively and more profoundly permeated by ownness. It becomes more extensively and more profoundly the appearing and evidence of ownness, the witness to ownness.

It speaks ever more articulately the language of ownness. It becomes ever more truly describable as own-consciousness. The vocation of consciousness is to be the articulate own-consciousness that belongs to the freedom and truth of man's being.

Man is the being who hears from within the depths of his own being the call to raise otherness up into ownness, to attain to existence in such a relationship to what transcends him that the two are as fully as possible own to each other. His actual experience of entities in the world is an experience of things which constantly challenge him to be with them as with his own. Man's hunger for food represents the need to assimilate the other materially to his body. His sexual desire expresses the need to join with the other person in a bodily giving and taking. His desire for children is an appetite to people the world with his own. His architecture, as environmental design, represents the need to transform his natural surroundings into a living space of his own. The story is one that extends to the highest reaches of mind and spirit, ultimately to religion, which expresses man's need to join with the transcendent infinite, namely, with that reality to which he can give himself completely and utterly and from which he can receive the uttermost—that final stage of being in which own has come to own without remainder, in the face of multiplicity, change, space, time, history, causality, constraint, and death.

Philosophy formulates this story in a conceptual way. Art brings it to intuition in an externally constructed figure. Religious symbolism, philosophical thought, and artistic imagination—all three are indispensable means toward the understanding of the vocation of consciousness. For it is in them that consciousness formulates itself in the shape of the ultimacy it strives toward. They show us the vocation of consciousness because it is the vocation of consciousness to become them.

The relationship between consciousness and ownness may be stated as follows, and along with it the vocation to which consciousness is called. In consciousness the ego, as mental being, relates overtly to its other. Consciousness is the stage of mind in which the difference between ego and nonego, the self and its other, comes to appearance. The difference is already a connection, for the nonego belongs to the ego as its own nonego, the other to the self as its own other. Yet the connection is at first merely immediate, and it is the difference of the two that is constitutive for consciousness as such. Consequently it belongs to the basic nature of consciousness that it should be in its origins a predominantly negating activity. Consciousness exists in order that the ego should be able to differentiate its other from itself so that it can thereupon proceed to establish the intimacy of ownness between the two. It establishes an estrangement between the self and the not-self in order that the self should be able to confront the not-self as such, its own other as other, having it there before itself as an object for knowing, a challenge for acting, and an appeal to caring. In consciousness the mental being opens his eyes upon that other which is to become his world, his reality, the partner of his destiny, so that he may first of all behold it and encounter it in its indefeasible otherness.

But the differentiation of nonego from ego is only the transitional or dialectical stage of mental actualization. Negation exists for the sake of affirmation. The intentionality by which my consciousness exists as consciousness-of its object—this differentiative negation, by which my consciousness determines concretely for itself the otherness of its object—comes about on purpose that I should be able to execute a further integrative act of affirmation, an act by which I determine in the object what is mine and what is not mine. The whole purpose for the sake of which consciousness has come into being is just this: that the positive integrating act by which the ego determines what is its own as over against what is not its own should be able to be performed.

This is not a merely contingent purpose of consciousness, which it might pick up and let go at odd intervals. It is the immanent purpose that makes consciousness what it is. It is the essence of consciousness in the way in which freedom is the essence of will or attraction and repulsion the essence of magnetism. To intend the other as other—and along with it, the other as own other—this is itself the purposive intent that makes consciousness what it is. It is the very intention of consciousness to be intentionalistic.

More concretely, consciousness is the medium of the person's intention to realize what is his own. He must first be able to differentiate himself from his own other and his own other from himself so as, secondly, to be able to discover and appropriate in that own other what is more and more profoundly his own. Life generates and inhabits consciousness in the course of its essential search for its own. Intentionality exists by the indwelling intention of life itself. It belongs to the dialectic through which life must pass to reach its own.

3

The Touch of Art

Art touches things and, as by a touch of magic, changes them. Eventually it changes the world and man along with it so that what is outside man should show itself as being own to man and man as own to it. An indifferent nature touched by art turns into a genuinely human world and man becomes an authentic dweller within it.

Technical art makes things in the world into man's tools, clothing, food, habitations, streets, concourses. It transforms the natural environment into man's neighborhood and his home, in which he exists as in the place that belongs to him and to which he belongs. At the same time it makes man into a domestic being, one who has a culture and a home.

Expressive art quickens this environing neighborhood with eloquence, so that it declares its own immanent meaning as a region of human life. In expressive art the appearance of a thing acquires a sudden significance just because it is the means of expression. It becomes more important than the mere literal nature of the thing.

The Gothic cathedral for instance, as at Amiens, was built of glass and ponderous stone but it ascends into imponderability. It was made to make present, in a local-ized junction of meaning with being, the true relationship between the earthly and the divine, the natural and the spiritual, the ponderous and the imponderable. It ex-presses the yearning of the human spirit to reach upward from out of its finite nature in a transcending gesture toward divine infinity, and it does this by means of the transition in appearance upward from the heavy encum-brance of earthly matter to the weightless color of the heavenly light.

In the cathedral the finite was to come into touch with the infinite, the human world with its divine author. As in Michelangelo's vision Adam, dimly forefeeling the life that was to flow to him from God, lifts his hand in search of the divine touch, so the cathedral lifted itself in the line of the divine communication and offered itself to be touched. The cathedral existed at the horizon of the natu-ral and supernatural worlds. As in a prayer, so in this architectural figure, man could enter into a thing which by the magic of its expressive power acted as a vehicle of his spirit's effort to relate itself to the eternal. The need for expressive power gave to appearance, the means of ex-pression, a signal importance, as the effort to reach an adequate relationship with his own gives to man's con-sciousness in art an equally signal importance. It is by means of consciousness that man is able to reach own-consciousness, and it is by means of the consciousness of what is his own and not his own that man is able to guide himself with appropriate feeling, insight, and determina-tion in the living of human life, so as to be and remain in valid touch with reality as his own in actual existence.

Therefore, although the full nature of art is not defina-ble solely in terms of consciousness, the latter, and especially own-consciousness, is fundamental in art. Art is a functioning part of life in which man uses his powers and skills to transform the world, including himself, and to bring out in the appearance of that world the meaning it is supposed to have. Art does this because man, in order to live as man, must live through the mediation of mind and spirit. He must relate to what is other than himself in terms of what in it is his own and not his own, what he is own to and what he is not own to. His world must show itself to him in this light. Consequently it must appear in its meaning of ownness and not-ownness, familiarity and strangeness, belonging and not-belonging, as object of the consciousness of man's ego. So, although it is not the whole of art, consciousness is indispensable to it, just as consciousness is indispensable in human life generally without being the whole of it.

The function of art, its essential intention and its ultimate value, is to make immediately evident to the human mind the meaning of things as being own and not-own to man. I refer to expressive art, not to an isolated technology as such. Art shares this task with religion and philosophy, but does it in its own way, the way of concrete figural intuition. Religion interprets reality by means of symbols and rituals that depend only in part upon their expressive appearances to communicate their meanings. The consecrated wafer does not need to look like the body of God. Its religious potency and meaning depend more on representational connections in the mind, often quite independent of the symbol, than on its actual aspect. Philosophy interprets reality by means of concepts which, in their abstractness, purposely depart from the particular concreteness of appearance so as to be able to state literally, in language amenable to the logical processes of reason, the meanings that are figured in art and represented in religion.

Art's special vocation lies in making reality own to man by way of the forms of figural intuition. Figural intuition, the intuition that belongs to imagination, the consciousness of ownness by way of the image—this is the mode of consciousness which is specific to art as an expressive activity. What art does is to articulate an image which exists as the object of intuition and which gives to intuition an immediate grasp of meaning. This meaning has as its content an ownness, a fitness and adequacy within itself and to the human spirit, on account of which the artistic image can be a living part of the spirit's life and culture. This is what we have now to make out, at least in the brief form of an initiation of thinking about art.

Art consciousness is intuitive. The importance of this fact stems from the nature of intuition. Intuition is the name given to knowledge in which the object is immediately apprehended by the mind. The mind here appropriates its object directly instead of by way of an intermediary. The object comes home to the mind and the mind becomes intelligent of it. All the difference that is made by presence rather than absence enters into the relation of the mind to its object, the difference between actually seeing, hearing, feeling, immediately having the thing, possessing it, as contrasted with hearing about it, thinking of it, receiving information concerning it. Intuition is the mode in which the object of knowledge becomes the mind's own as known. It is the shape that ownness takes when it occurs in the mode of cognition. That is why all knowledge that has ultimate significance for the spirit must become intuitive; the spirit is with the known object as with its own only when it receives the object in the direct encounter of intuition. And this gives to art its special significance, since art is man's way of attaining to intuition. The strength of Croce's doctrine of art lay just in this point, that he understood how the processes of artistic formation and expression are one with the process of intuition.

Intuition is able to be what it is, the form of immediate knowledge, because it combines into a single unity two features that are otherwise separate, even antagonistic, in knowledge, namely, immediateness and meaningful content, the given and the meant.

Usually we think of the act of meaning as an act by which we refer or are referred from something immediately given to something else that is not directly present. The conventional symbol is a good illustration. In Egyptian mythology the falcon was the symbol of Horus, king of the Earth and ruler of the sky, son of Isis and Osiris. The bird, whether real or pictured, is present before us immediately, in sensuous form; the god is bodily absent, represented to our mind by the bird-symbol. (In strictness, in actual religious experience, the god is already actually present in the bird; but for us, outside the religion, the mythology loses a certain vitality and becomes mere symbolism.) Our relationship to the god is an indirect one, mediated by the falcon, which is the immediately given representative of him. In the act of meaning we are thus referred by the immediate symbol to the meant content, the latter being only mediately presented.

The immediateness belongs to the one thing, the falcon. The falcon's function of meaning is a reference to something else, the god. Such is the normal situation in signification: the sign or symbol is an object that is immediately presented and whose meaningful content, the object meant, is brought by it to consciousness through a mediating act, the act of referring, by which the sign stands as representative for the absent content it signifies. Whereas we find the falcon directly present to us in sensible feeling or concrete imagination, the god Horus is only thought of but not found in sense, only conceived by the mind but not felt in the direct presence of sensible or imagined being.

Now in intuition this gap, which opens between the immediateness of the matter that is directly present to the mind and the mediateness of its meaning for the mind, is closed, or is not yet opened, depending on how one looks at the subject. In intuition the meaning is given and had immediately. That which is meant is found and felt in its presence, if not literally as a sensible thing, nevertheless in a manner of concreteness analogous to that of sensation. Instead of having to orientate itself toward an absent content the mind finds itself immediately in touch with that content. It is as though the mind had bodily seized the content or the content had bodily seized the mind. Possession has been taken, in both directions at once.

The symbol itself serves as an instance. We have it in intuition as the symbol it is, while we do not have in intuition the object it symbolizes. The falcon is there before us, the actual bird or the picture of it, real or imagined. When it serves as symbol we see it differently than we do when we perceive the mere bird. We see it *as* meaningful, *as* the symbol that it is. We see it as representing Horus. The experience is very much like that of seeing the word "Horus" as meaning the god Horus. We do not have to look first at the bird or at the word, then carry out an act of thought by which we relate the symbol to its meaning. The falcon means the god. I apprehend its act of meaning immediately. That act of meaning is not absent and referred to, but is present and possessed. I read the bird directly as a symbol, intuiting it in its symbolical immediateness. Its meaning, as act, is present as if it were literally incarnated, embodied in the sensible matter.

In this case I have the intuition of a symbol. But we can have intuitions of things other than signs or symbols. If I look at a house, it comes to me in direct perception. It is immediately present to me as a house. To be sure, I do not see the other side of it, and that other side is not given intuitively in sensible presence. But the meaning *that there is the other side* is given intuitively in my perception; I perceive the house *as having an other side.* This is like the falcon's *representing the god Horus* being given intuitively, even though Horus is not. My perception of the house is an intuition of it as partly disclosed and partly undisclosed to direct sensible view. As I walk around it, observing it, the parts that are disclosed to sensible visual intuition vary, but the whole meant content, *house,* remains constantly present in a perceptual intuition. This intuition of the house as a house is not and cannot be solely visual, as if it were a visual sensation. It is a perceptual intuition, understanding by perception a more complex unitary activity of mind than simple visual sensation. But it *is* an intuition; in it a meaningful content is presented in immediateness as if it were embodied, incarnated, in the sensible matter.

In an analogous way we can have conceptual intuitions, propositional intuitions, and the like—that is, intuitions at the level of thought. If I think of the philosophy of Stoicism, I may at present have in consciousness primarily the name *Stoicism* with its large and somewhat vague representational power vibrating in my mind. In such a mental state virtually nothing of Stoicism as a meaningful thought-content is given to me immediately. But when I read and understand the statement "He is free for whom all things happen according to his will and whom no one can hinder," a part of the meaningful content of the Stoic philosophy becomes present to my mind. This meaning moves into a certain immediateness. I have it, grasp it with my mind, feel it as just the meaning I understand, here, now, present in the very speaking of the sentence, not merely absent and thought about. It is given to me as directly as any sensible object could be, only in a different way. It is not given as a sensuous content. I do not see it literally with my eyes or taste it with my tongue. But, as it is embodied or incarnated in the sentence, I touch and seize it with my mind. It has become intellectually palpable to me. Indeed, is it not just the immediateness with which meanings, concepts, and propositions can be apprehended that has led language to use the manual metaphors of grasping—to grasp, to apprehend, to comprehend, to conceive—in order to name appropriately what happens here?

Intuition, then, is the act in which meaning becomes immediate for the mind. Intuition is the mind's feeling, as mind that is able to grasp meaning. It is analogous to sensation as the mode of feeling by which we touch, not meaning, but the simple otherness of being, and it is analogous to the inner sensitivity of feeling by which, again, we touch, not meaning but the simple ownness of our own being. As an intuitive being I am able to function as an intelligence that immediately finds and has meaning-contents as its direct object.

Intuition occurs everywhere that intelligence is able to

operate immediately. There are logical and mathematical intuitions, immediate apprehensions of meanings, with which logical and mathematical minds are familiar. A well-known classification divides mathematicians into those with intuitive and those with analytical temperaments and habits of mind. An intuitive historian can bring together into an immediate unity for his intelligence a unifying interpretation of a large and complex historical occurrence, yes, even a great period in its essential character, like the Renaissance in Italy or the Victorian Era in England. A great general will have in his mind's eye, at once, immediately before him, his interpretation of the events of the battle and his scheme for defeating the enemy, a scheme that may extend in its anticipation over days, weeks, months, even years. Mozart is said to have grasped the whole of a symphony in his mind at once. Every composer, and every creative or performing artist, knows at first hand what it is to intuit the work with which he is engaged.

Art is intuitive, but in its own special way. The manner of its intuition is differentiated both in form and in content.

An artistic form is an external figure or construction. It is a carved stone, a painted wall or canvas, a building or a larger environmental setting like a neighborhood, a campus, a town. It is a composition of sounds, instrumental or electronic, a composition of words which can be read and spoken aloud, a complex movement of human bodies in a dance, or a complex interplay of human individuals in a drama.

This artistic form as an external figure is something that has been made by man, by the individual artist as individual or as representative of a prince, a wealthy donor, a church or business, the government, the party, a special group, and, eventually, as a member of his own living culture. It is made on purpose (or, if found, it is at any rate selected) as a meaningful figure. Its purpose is to articulate the meaning that belongs to it so as to bring it to intuition.

As a form that articulates a meaning for intuition, the artistic form is an *image* or *figure.* These words point to the twofold bearing of form: on the one side it is a particular concrete thing that offers itself to us in immediate sensuous or imaginary presence, and on the other side it is meaningful in its immediateness. It is an embodiment or incarnation of meaning. It is an image, first in the sense of being a sensuously concrete object, but secondly also in the sense of being an image *of* something not itself sensuously concrete. Similarly, it is a figure in the sense of being a sensuously concrete *gestalt,* but also in the sense of being a figure *of* something meaningful which it brings before us by means of its own immediate presence. It is like a word which, by its literal sense, develops a figurative sense which is brought before us directly by a metaphoric process.

Before we can ask how an image works as an image, a figure as a figure, an artistic form as artistically meaningful—that is, before we can ask how the content is related to the form—it is necessary first to identify the artistic content as such. There are many different ways in which an image can represent its meaning. The relationship between the two depends on the nature of what is to be represented, the meaningful content, and the medium of representation. For instance if a physical object is to be represented in the medium of a two-dimensional graphic art, such as painting, drawing, or photography, it has to be *pictured*. So the image of a mountain or a tree in graphic art is a picture of such an object. If, on the other hand, the content is inward and psychical, as the character of an individual who sits for a portrait, in the same medium, that inner content cannot literally be pictured. The reason obviously is that it does not itself have a visual shape. It has to be *expressed physiognomically*. Whereas the picturing of a physical object is a kind of copying, the physiognomic expression of character is not a kind of copying, but an expressing in outward form of what belongs to the inward reality. Again, if the content is a thought-content, as for instance the divinity of a god, then it cannot be literally pictured, since divinity as generally understood does not have its own literal shape; nor can it be expressed adequately by physiognomy, since it is a richer content than any psychological character. It needs a different kind of articulation, suited to its nature as a content, namely, one which while it reveals the quality of divinity does so by showing at the same time its indisclosibility to sensuous view. For this purpose *symbolical means* are used—a halo, a mandorla, a gesture of the hands and feet, the attitude of the body, the curling of the hair, the pitch of the eyes, the shape of the ears, whatever it may be. There are many forms in a painted or sculpted Buddha which symbolize his divine nature and which are neither pictures of it nor physiognomic expressions of his inner being.

If then there is a content that belongs to the art work as such, it is necessary first to identify it, before the nature of its mode of representation can be considered.

What is this meaning? What is the content of the artistic figure as a content that specifically belongs to art and for the communication of which art exists?

At first one is astounded and confused by the multiplicity of artistic contents. Everything that is in any way of interest to man, it seems, can be comprehended within the contents of art works. The artist will make a bowl of glazed pottery, or a vase, a bottle, a dish; but also he will fashion a horse or a bear, a dancing couple, or an abstract shape. There are paintings of gods and devils, of heaven and hell, of the land, the sky, the sea, of living things and dead things, of the soul's interior as of the world's exterior, and paintings of nothing, too. The poet will sing of love, sadness, fame, shame; the dramatist will write of conflicts and reconciliations in the life of man; the novelist ranges the world, factual and fictional, for materials to appear within the frame of the story he narrates. What can there be that is shared in common by all these contents?

It is helpful to distinguish between content in the sense of material or subject-matter included in the artistically constructed figure and content in the sense of the particular meaning of the work itself, for the expression of which the materials and subject-matters are brought into it. A landscape painter includes a rock, a pond, and trees in his painting. They are materials, subject-matters, introduced into the artistic composition for the sake of making the figure. The figure as a whole is the total composition itself —the landscape, as such, is the meaning that belongs to it as just that total artistic composition.

But multiplicity raises its head again. This landscape is different from that landscape; landscapes are different from portraits, which also differ among themselves; both are different from abstract paintings, which differ among themselves; and so forth. There are lyrical poems, dramatic poems, and epic poems; and among lyrical poems there are lyrical lyrics, dramatic lyrics, and epical lyrics; and so forth. Ultimately every individual work of art dif-

fers as a singular figure from every other individual work
of art, including all the other members of its genre, if
indeed there is a genre to which it belongs.

Can there be something, then, of the nature of meaningful content that is shared universally by all these works
and shared by them specifically as works of art? Can there
be a universal sort of meaning of which each work of art,
insofar as it is art, is a singular instance?

I believe that the answer is affirmative. I have already
mentioned it earlier in speaking of art's function as that
of making evident to the human mind the meaning of
things as being own and not-own to man. I would like now
to return to that idea and to offer the following considera-
tions leading to it.

The strikingly obvious and inescapable fact about art
works is that they are works and, indeed, works of art.
They are works—that is, products of an activity of man by
which they are selected, fashioned, configured, or as is
sometimes said in a hyperbole, created. And they are
works of art—and that means, first, works produced by
skill, craftsmanship, capacity, but secondly, works produced by an artistic impulse that works itself out through
the exercise of technical capacity upon the materials and
subject-matter chosen for the work. It is the intention
immanent to this artistic drive to which we must look for
the specific character of artistic meaning.

As in the case of the role of consciousness in life generally, so here with the indwelling intention of art, we have
to return to philosophical fundamentals if we are to reach
a genuine understanding.

Man is the being whose being consists in attaining,
maintaining, and enduring in a relationship with what is

other than himself (including himself) as with his own. When, therefore, he is faced with the business of being in and with an environing world of nature, it becomes his task to subject his being in nature to such a metamorphosis as to be there with the environment as with his own. Art—expressive, artistically meaningful art—performs this transformation by putting the touch of the meaningfulness of ownness upon the matter it takes as its medium.

The image in art is externally constructed as a figure whose essential function it is to articulate ownness in the immediateness of human intuition. It is an image or figure, a *gestalt* or shape given to sensuous-imaginative matter, in and through which is revealed a meaningful content of ownness, in such a way that we are able to apprehend the content immediately and directly in our sensuous-imaginative grasp of the image.

Man has a profound need to see his mark stamped upon things. Put a blank surface before a child and his first impulse is to scrawl something on it—a crude shape, his initials, a picture, a phrase. This is not yet art but it originates in the primal instinct that ultimately needs art in order to fulfill itself. For the child what matters, perhaps, is less the particular figure he inscribes than the miraculous fact of the inscribing itself. Suddenly a mark stands there, outside him, over against him as thing to self, object to subject, which nevertheless carries the meaning *mine*. It is not literally a piece of his self that he has placed out there. Rather, he has imposed his will upon the matter, stamping it with the attribute of belonging to him—not as property belongs to the proprietor, but as a manifestation does to the being it manifests. Like the *x* signed by one who does not write, it is the mark by which he manifests and attests to himself. He articulates himself by changing something in the world so as to give it the character of such a manifestation.

And the especially significant and important feature of the inscribed figure is that it has been placed there, and is there now, just as a manifestation of ownness. The importance lies in its being an intuitional manifestation or revelation, an expression whose essential and pervading content, though it cannot be literally pictured or physiognomically expressed or merely abstractly symbolized, yet is immediately and directly embodied in the figure, incarnated, and thereby brought out and given overtly to intuition.

What is manifested or revealed in bodily form in the scratch upon the wall or the scribble on the paper is: *ownness.* Ownness as made evident to intuition takes the shape of *the mark made,* which, when art is reached, becomes *the work of art* as product of the artistic mind, as made by art, as created. The core of the createdness that belongs to art as art is just this nuclear element of ownness articulated in an image.

In painting, one of the most evident characteristic features of ownness is exhibited by what is called "touch." Literally it is how the artist touches the paper with his pen, the canvas with his brush. In the comprehensive sense it is how he "handles" the whole work, the coloring as well as the drawing, the feeling of importance and significance as well as the representing of objects, the expressing of feelings, or the symbolizing of ideas. It is how he "manages" the elements, the relations, the subject-matters, and the contents.

It is through touch that the peculiar content of art, ownness, receives articulation in the image. Touch is not a picturing; it is not a physiognomical manifesting; it is not an abstract or conventional symbolizing of something other than itself. It is the touching, the reaching out, testing, feeling, tasting, palpating, even the caressing, as well as the forcing, of an external reality into the embodiment and incarnation of what belongs to the human spirit. The touching is a struggling with the object to quicken it, to affect it so that its willingness and unwillingness to belong to us and possess us are persuaded and overcome. Through touch, the ego and the nonego, self and other, man and world, are brought into the intimacy of an immediate contact.

An artist's touch may be highly individualistic, as it is in many Western artists, such as Leonardo, El Greco, Chardin, Turner, Van Gogh, Matisse, Picasso. It may be highly collectivistic, as it is in traditional art cultures, such as the ancient Egyptian, where the shaping process was so schematized that a single whole could be done by parts in different workshops, yet fit together perfectly at the end; recent art that falls into the genre called "minimal art" approaches the same condition. It may be in between, individual with strong collective features, collective with strong individual features, as in classical Greek architecture and sculpture and much contemporary urban architecture. When the touch has a strong collective component it is the touch, not simply of the individual artist, but also of the culture at work in him. He works as spokesman for the group. His handling is the handling that the group needs, wants, and demands.

In any event touch is not just the touch of the hands. It is the touch of the mind, the heart and spirit, for which the hands are the magic wand by which it reaches the paper or the canvas. As the child reaches out to a piece of the world to touch it, making its mark there, so the artist's mind, with its individual and its social features, reaches out to a piece of the world to touch it and make its mark there. Touch transforms the other into the own. Every art has its equivalent of touch—the attack, the handling, the sensitivity of the handling, the manner and mode of the handling of the subjects and the medium.

The fact that the specific content of art is ownness explains why style is a fundamental phenomenon in art. Style extends beyond art; it belongs to everything human. It is as much in evidence in our manners of thinking, willing, and feeling and our manners of behaving, ultimately of living—whence the expression "life-style"—as it is in art. It becomes more evident in art only because the function of art is to bring ownness out into evidence, as revelation or manifestation in an intuitional figure for the contemplating mind. Style is the form of ownness as it works out in the particular subject-matter. A man's style of walking is what characterizes the walking as his, not someone.else's. A man's life-style is his way of life, the way that imprints itself on everything that he is and does, from the physiognomic formation of his chin and ears to the way in which he engages in philosophical controversy. It is how he touches and comes into touch with reality. Hence when the artist turns to his medium, the style that develops in the work is the manifestation of the ownness that permeates his spirit, one which is ultimately individual and singular, holding only for this work, done at this time, in this mood, under these circumstances.

At the same time the work may, indeed must, incorporate a considerable amount of social and cultural style, i.e., of the ownness that belongs not just to an individual man but to a group, a nation, a culture, a world. The romantic style in Coleridge is noticeably different from that style in Wordsworth, but both reflect the character of the early-nineteenth-century English romanticism that contrasts with the romantic style in France of that time; but further, the French and British share in that provincial style—Western European romanticism of the early nineteenth century—that distinguishes them from Eastern European, African, Near Eastern, and Far Eastern art of the same time. Throughout art, style reveals the ownness that belongs to culture and constitutes its heart and lifeblood. Through it, too, the culture comes into touch with being.

I said above that the child's scrawling is not yet art. But is not the difference more a matter of degree than of kind? To be sure, lacking in the child's scribble is the discipline and maturity of the artist. The child has not yet developed adequately its own individuality and sociality. But the child is fascinated and absorbed in the shaping of the figure. The mere existence of the figure is already a matter of importance to him, as it is to every real artist. Therefore, although the ownness that shows through is of a rudimentary kind, it is nevertheless one that has come about through a genuine activation of the child's own care. It may be the ownness of what is still a merely childish being, existing outwardly in a largely inarticulate way, but it already begins to reveal an authentic ownness.

The artist invests the making of the figure with a discipline proportionate to the care it deserves: the greater the artist the greater the disciplined care and caring discipline. And although his own subjectivity is deeply involved in the act of production, in which his unconscious mind is engaged too, with its profound energies, his spirit is just as vigorously objective. He draws upon the contents of his world, its interests and its inhabitants, as his materials. He participates in the world's comprehension of what is its own and what is not its own, whether by accepting it or criticizing it or transforming it. His work speaks to others in his world as a comprehensible revelation of the ownness of things in which they can share partly or wholly, in actuality or in imagination. Consequently the ownness that belongs to it as a work is mature, developed in the course of the artist's and his culture's struggle with reality to reach their identity and to give it the articulate expression it needs in art.

The child has only begun this process on his own account. The artist stands for himself, his fellowmen, eventually for man universally, in the effort—as old as man himself—to find out and make evident to himself and others in the form of intuitive appropriation what is man's own and what is not man's own.

The artist's brush grazes the world and, by its magic touch, relieves existence of its alien otherness and grants to it the wondrous strangeness of what is truly ours. The work may be a picture, an expression, a symbol of something other, yes, but only as it is first touched by the spirit does it become a *witness* to the spirit's own.

4

The Voice of
the Dead Wife

Most contemporary artists are not interested in representing beautiful things. Much recent art—not only visual art but other art as well—looks for its subject-matter to fields far from the beautiful and uses for its forms the most striking kinds of deformity, distortion, asymmetry, and discord. If anything, one is inclined to say, recent art seems to seek on principle to move as far away from beauty as it possibly can. It searches even for effects opposed to beauty.

When Kafka wrote "The Metamorphosis"—that story, so terribly pitiful, enervating, and hopeless, of a young man transformed into a great insect—he was surely least of all concerned to bring to the reader a beautiful vision, to provide him with a picture of something that tends to arouse delight, fondness, joy, or the resting and uplifting satisfaction commonly associated with the experience of beautiful things. Or think of Picasso's *Les Demoiselles d'Avignon*, the *Three Dancers*, the *Girl Before a Mirror*, or the *Guernica*, all at the Museum of Modern Art in New York City. The artist's problems in these paintings were far from that of representing beauty in any form. It seems as though he felt himself compelled to choose exactly the opposite of beautiful elements and combinations to make his constructions: intensely loud colors, harsh color contrasts, ugly distortions of the human form and features, loud and jangling linear outlines, ambiguities and confusions in the placement of shapes and volumes. In the music of Schönberg and his followers, all effects of tonality and tonal harmony were in principle eliminated. The whole of the music was constructed out of musical elements chosen in such a way that they cannot but make an impression of extreme disharmony, cacophony, and tonal ugliness. As Kafka chose the ugly to write about, and Picasso the ugly to organize into a visual order, so Schönberg chose the ugly to make into a musical composition. Modern art is essentially, in principle and on purpose, an art of the negative: the unformed, the ugly, the absurd, the accidental, the discordant. The negative is the element in which it lives, breathes, and configures itself.

Now the use of negative elements, though extensively developed in the art of the twentieth century, is not altogether unknown to older aesthetics. Lessing compares the ancients and the moderns in the opening sections of his *Laokoon*. "The Greek artist," he says, "represented nothing that was not beautiful. Even the vulgarly beautiful, the beauty of inferior types, he copied only incidentally for practice or recreation. The perfection of the subject must charm in his work ... among the ancients beauty was the supreme law of the imitative arts."[1] As a result, the Greek artist was led to suppress or soften anything in the representation that might be incompatible with beauty. In this way Lessing explained (what he thought, wrongly, to be a fact) the absence of anguish in the face of Laokoon. Truthful expression of such a passion would have produced a hideous distortion of the countenance and this would have disfigured the work. The artist was led to soften the expression, sacrificing it for the sake of beauty. Winckelmann had thought that the artist expressed no violent emotion in the face because he wanted to represent a noble soul suffering great pain with Stoic endurance. But the true reason is that the law of beauty forbade it.

> The master was striving to attain the greatest beauty under the given conditions of bodily pain. Pain, in its disfiguring extreme, was not compatible with beauty and must therefore be softened. Screams must be reduced to sighs, not because screams would betray weakness, but because they would deform the countenance to a repulsive degree. Imagine Laokoon's mouth open, and judge. Let him scream, and see. It was, before, a figure to inspire compassion in its beauty and suffering. Now it is ugly, abhorrent, and we gladly avert our eyes from a painful spectacle, destitute of the beauty which alone could turn our pain into the sweet feeling of pity for the suffering object.[2]

Modern art, on the contrary, has, according to Lessing, a different law. It no longer sets the narrow bounds to itself with which Greek art was content. Its realm has been greatly enlarged.

> Its imitations are allowed to extend over all visible nature, of which beauty constitutes but a small part. Truth and expression are taken as its first law. As nature always sacrifices beauty to higher ends, so should the artist subordinate it to his general purpose, and not pursue it further than truth and expression allow. Enough that truth and expression convert what is unsightly in nature into a beauty of art.[3]

If modern art makes use of the unsightly and ugly, then, it is for the sake of truth and expression. But—and this is the significant point to observe—the artist thereby achieves a higher beauty, one that art attains through its expression and its truth.

Did Lessing go wrong here? Is the restriction to beauty, even if it be a higher beauty, a weakening and taming of the effect once more? Does it not represent still the search for harmony, repose, quiescence, the essentially unoffending? According to him, the artist, whether poet or painter, ought never to express the ugly simply for the sake of doing so. If he does, he disgusts and offends our taste for harmony and order, which excites our aversion to the representation. He may, however, make use of the ugly—certainly in poetry, where it undergoes a diminution of effect because of the successive enumeration of its elements, and where it can be combined with other elements to produce mixed sensations of the ridiculous and the horrible. Less certainly, the ugly may also occur in painting, where it may be similarly employed in attaining the ridiculous and horrible. But since in painting the picture is there for us all at once, and the effect of ugliness is not weakened, the painter must never express it for itself.[4]

So Lessing thought he could legitimize the ugly in art by observing that the aims of modern art—truth and expression—opened the possibility of its presence, leading to a new artistic beauty. When displeasing features occur in a work in the service of truth and expression, as in Homer's making Thersites ugly in order to make him ridiculous, the result is *a beauty of poetry*. The poet can use this ugliness because, through his description of it, it acquires a less repulsive effect; in a way, it stops being ugly. He uses ugliness not by itself but as an ingredient to produce mixed impressions, for instance the comical, which entertain us in the absence of beauty's more agreeable impressions.[5]

Lessing was still timid as regards the use of the ugly. There is a "beauty" still to be gotten, which reduces the ugliness of the ugly. This is an ambiguous position. Recent art moves beyond it, seeking to use the ugly precisely *as* ugly, without weakening it, and not merely for its shock effect but for something that takes the place of beauty. Truth and expression become even more predominant. But now a new problem arises. Of what nature is this truth and expression?

In justifying the use of disagreeable elements for the sake of truth and expression, and thereby ultimately for a beauty of art itself, Lessing sounded a familiar note, heard already in the time of Aristotle. The Greek philosopher had explained our pleasure in seeing imitations of disagreeable objects by stressing the enjoyment of the knowledge this gives us. Lessing rejected this theory. Such a pleasure of knowledge is only transitory, whereas the discomfort is permanent and essential; the pleasure can hardly overbalance the displeasure. The sensations of pain induced by ugliness are incapable of being converted by imitation into pleasurable sensations, and in consequence the ugly cannot be a fitting subject for painting as a fine art.[6] If, then, ugliness is used in any of the arts, it must in some way be reduced to the position of an element contributing to an artistic effect in which the original discomfort is overcome; and in achieving this effect, the work of art will have arrived at a beauty of a new kind —a beauty of art itself.

Lessing however makes little of this notion of an artistic

beauty that transcends the beauty or ugliness of its constituent factors. It appears that he had in mind hardly anything more than Addison had in speaking of "the beauties and imperfections of an author" that a man of fine taste in writing will have the capacity to discern.[7] The artistic beauty produced by the use of the ugly or the loathsome is nothing other than the truthful expression of the ludicrous or the terrible, needed as it may be in the construction of the work. It is not beauty in any more essential sense, in a sense close to the concrete beauty of form that Lessing attributed to Greek art as its ideal.

The question arises whether there is anything more to the conception of a specifically artistic beauty than this. If modern art is an art of truth, or of expression, or of any other comparable aim, what indeed has beauty to do with it? Is not the ideal of beauty one that is limited as an artistic effect and dated as an historical phenomenon? If one begins to speak of an artistic beauty over and above anything beautiful or ugly represented in a work of art, can the word "beauty" be used here in any other than the innocuous sense that makes it synonymous with "fine point," "goodness," "excellence"? Or is there indeed a beauty visible less to the eye than to the mind and soul, one that belongs to art as such?

> To a great many persons art is the special domain of aesthetic feeling. In the presence of works of art they feel a release from all that obstructs them from the enjoyment of beauty in looking at nature. They worship art as being for them a means of gaining pure beauty from nature. They glorify the artist who in his work is not only able to win from nature a pure content of beauty freed from all disturbing attributes, but also able to create out of himself a beauty that is not offered by nature. They immerse themselves in contemplation of beauty. Their

feelings rise from admiration through veneration to enthusiasm. They enjoy works of art with tense susceptibility and indulge themselves in this enjoyment. Who has not yet owed such pleasures to art, and who does not count such hours among the most beautiful of his life? But are we entitled through such pleasures to believe that we have caught hold of the essential, the really artistic substance of works of art?[8]

So asks Conrad Fiedler (1841–1895), German philosopher of art, friend of the painter Hans von Marées and the sculptor Adolph Hildebrand, and with them one of the important sources of the modern formalistic movement of "pure visibility." His answer is, No. Objects of nature are beautiful and afford us aesthetic pleasure as well as works of art. But the essence of artistic substance owes its origin to the spiritual power of man. How, then, can objects of nature have the same substance? It is impossible. The substance of art must lie elsewhere than in beauty and aesthetic sensation.

I mention this rejection of the connection of beauty with art purposely in order to set it aside. It is clear from the way in which Fiedler asked and answered his question that his desire was to turn directly to works of visual art without distraction from the constraints of aesthetic discussion. Supposing that works of art derive from man's spiritual power, why should not some natural objects nevertheless be similar in appearance, if not in origin, to them? The argument Fiedler offered had little cogency; it was not at the center of his concern. It is an instance of the obfuscation to which reference to beauty can lead, and is best ignored in favor of a direct dealing with the concrete experience of art and nature.

At the focus of Fiedler's vision was art itself. Art can be understood only in terms of art. We must see the world in terms of the artist's own interest if we are to grasp his concern with the visible world. Now the artist seeks, not the enjoyment of sensations of the world, but the perceptual comprehension of the world. As the scientist seeks conceptual mastery of the world's appearances, so the artist wishes to master the visible world by his powers of visual comprehension. By this means he subjugates the visible world to himself and is enabled to recreate it in a free act of configuration.

> Artistic activity begins when man finds himself face to face with the visible world as with something immensely enigmatical; when, driven by an inner necessity and applying the powers of his mind, he grapples with the twisted mass of the visible which presses in upon him and gives it creative form. In the creation of a work of art, man engages in a struggle with nature not for his physical but for his mental existence, because the gratification of his mental necessities also will fall to him solely as a reward for his strivings and his toil.[9]

The whole point of the artist's activity is the creation of visual form. He is not interested in copying the visible world simply for the sake of having a copy of it. He is not interested in copying at all, but in comprehending; and comprehension comes only in shaping. The act of creating form is at the same time the act of comprehension. Thus art is not concerned with forms ready-made, prior to its activity, independent of it. Its beginning and its end lie in its own autonomous creation of forms. Art does not create a second world alongside the world that exists without art, in order to imitate it. Art creates the world as it is made by and for the artistic consciousness.

And yet, although the only aim of art is to create form, to attain in this way to a mastery of the visual world, that very aim contains something more within itself. The work of art is only the outward aspect of an inner process which is the essentially artistic activity, the true artistic creation. This inner process is the production of *artistic consciousness.* Artistic consciousness is a form of spiritual being in which experience with visual appearances is the sole concern and in which everything irrelevant to this recedes. It exists, not for the sake of results, but for its own sake: the activity itself is the result. The artist's drive is toward the ever richer development of this special consciousness of the world. Instead of vision being in the service of other purposes, forces, passions, enthusiasms, the situation is reversed; all emotional forces, all driving forces, passions, enthusiasms must be harnessed in the service of this specific mental activity.

A work of art is the expression of artistic consciousness raised to a certain height. It is able to be such an expression by virtue of the form that has been created in it. Artistic form is the vehicle of expression of artistic consciousness. The form cannot exist independently of the consciousness, and the consciousness cannot exist independently of the form. The inner substance of the outer work of art is the artistic consciousness, that comprehending and configuring act by which the mind grasps and masters the visible world.

To the extent to which the world is mastered in this way, it becomes a visible reality for us; but, at the same time, because this reality is created by the artistic mind, it exists in the mode of ideality. Art is at once realistic and idealistic, and neither realistic on the one hand nor idealistic on the other. But what is important about it is that in and through it the driving forces of the artist's—hence, too, our own—nature rise to expression, in one work here, in another work there, though they are never exhausted. A work of art is a fragmentary expression of something that can never be fully expressed but that lies at the ground of our being and demands release. In the very act of striving to order the chaos of visual phenomena into a necessary whole, the forces of our being rise to a release in consciousness, in the form of a visual conception clear in all its parts, something that has attained a complete, necessary existence. This, for Fiedler, is the highest stage which the productive cognition of the artist can reach—one in which complete clearness and necessity have become one.

Thus far Fiedler. We must, however, go further. His reference to the union of clearness, completeness, and necessity in the visual form is of primary significance in understanding the artist's aim. The artist strives until, if successful, he reaches a perceptual experience that is developed into a visual form that has complete, necessary existence, clear in all its parts.

"Clear in all its parts"—this does not mean that all the parts have clear colors, clear forms, clear locations, clear relations. It is not a restricted ideal of art, like that of constructivism in general or of hard-edge painting in particular. A painting by Rembrandt in which light penetrates and pervades the dark body of space in one and another area, and in which by this means the sense of obscurity and profound mystery is realized, is also "clear in all its parts." The clarity we must have in mind is not superficial clarity of the visual materials but clarity of the visual-spiritual meaning. Rembrandt's obscure depths are among the clearest of all artistic achievements. The culminating point is reached where the form in which the visual conception is developed stands out clearly, is complete and necessary to the artist. The visual conception has been worked out and brought to the point at which "this way and no other" becomes a necessity for him. The unclarity, fragmentariness, and arbitrariness of the world of ordinary vision, because of which it is a chaos of un-related phenomena, have given way to a clear and coher-ent order, connected by means of a comprehension of the internal relationships of the visible world, complete in itself and pervaded by necessity.

What Fiedler has described here is the attainment of *a form that testifies, in its very presence and openness of being, to its own validity.* Not any arbitrary ordering of visual phenomena will satisfy the artist. He can easily achieve an "order" of visual phenomena by following the rules of the academies or the equations of analytic geometry. Either of them will bring the visual phenomena into an arrange-ment, introducing a kind of order into the chaotic visual materials. But there is more than mere order in what the artist strives to form. It is an order in which "this way and no other" becomes a necessity for him: the order is for him a personal necessity.

In art, necessity does not have the nature of the physical necessity with which events of nature blindly occur. That is a necessity without ideality, without the *ought* that ad-dresses itself to the mind. In its blind compulsion it ig-nores and brutally destroys all real value. On the other hand, art's necessity is not of the nature of the necessity of the moral *ought* with which the requirements of duty are addressed to the mind. For that is a necessity in conflict with actuality. The moral *ought* is merely ideal and, as such, opposes the actual and demands its change. In art, necessity has both the ideal accent of the *ought* and the actual presence of the *is.* It is an *aesthetic necessity.* The conflicts that appear in natural knowledge and morals are overcome. The visible form displays its own indwelling necessity, in complete and utter freedom: it is as it ought to be and it ought to be as it is. Artistic necessity brings the ideal and the actual into a harmonious union.

With this we come to a realization of what that visual conception must be of which Fiedler speaks, that mode of comprehending the visual phenomena not by abstract concepts but by the concrete power of artistic vision, and which we may well call the *artistic idea* that configures itself in the visual form. It is the idea of aesthetic necessity, and its content is: the union of ideality and reality, the ought to be that is real and the real that is as it ought to be. This content has become clear and has been expressed as completely as possible in the given visual form. The fundamental conception of the artist—the visual conception that develops for him in the visual form, and by means of which his visual comprehension of the world becomes possible—is no other than this: the identity of *ought* and *is*, the reality of the ideal and the ideality of the real.

Do not imagine that this means merely a kind of artistic idealism in which what exists factually is prettified to fit some ideal the artist has in mind. The artistic idea is not merely the abstract ideality of the real alone. It is not the transformation of the real in accordance with an ideal derived from elsewhere—religion, ethics, metaphysics, personal sentiment. It is also the reality of the ideal. It is concrete, which means that the ideal is not imposed from outside but uncovered as the indwelling ideal of the given reality, its truth and not its decoration or denial. Even the most extreme naturalism exhibits the artistic ideal *if—and only if—it is a genuine outgrowth of artistic consciousness.*

This unity of ideality and reality, necessity and fact,

ought and *is,* is conceived in visual terms, in the form of the appearance; its reality is exhausted in the showing of itself. The artist's basic aim is to realize the unity of ideality and reality in the purely apparent form of the phenomenon. It is the realization of *aesthetic* necessity, or the unity of real and ideal in the form of show, of semblance.

This realization takes place by means of the artist's intuition.

It is not an accident that art seeks to realize the unity of ideal and real in the form of semblance. Semblance, appearance, by its very nature, is that being whose reality consists in its being ideal. Semblance is the show of being, abstracted from physical reality and held by the mind in the position of mere show. In art, the work's being lies in its being abstracted from its physical existence as a mere thing and in functioning as a show. (This is all the more true when it is shown precisely as a thing; the showing of thinghood becomes the essence.) This abstraction is one side, the negative, of the so-called aesthetic attitude in its relation to its object; it is the excluding act by which the artistic mind separates the object from the surrounding actuality. The positive side of the aesthetic attitude is the impulse to behold the semblance, once it is abstracted, as the being in which ideal and real are identified. It is the drive toward the realization of the artistic idea. Only in semblance can the artistic idea be realized. Semblance is the necessary foundation, the elemental medium in which artistic thought and action germinate and dwell and in which *ought* and *is* find their unity.

Now the idea of the unity of ideality and reality is an idea of *valid being.* When we come to a form of being that is as it ought to be and ought to be as it is, we have arrived at an entity that is *right in its own being.* It has an intrinsic rightness, not derived from an abstract standard separate from itself. Moreover, because this rightness is intrinsic to it, and does not consist in its mere accordance with a standard outside itself but is its own autonomously determined rightness, it is a rightness in and of the being of the thing. In the sense in which truth consists in the accordance of a thing's reality with its own ideality and its ideality with its own reality—not, therefore, in the sense in which it is the accordance of a statement with a fact outside it or the even more general sense of the accordance of a thing with a standard of any sort outside it—the unity expressed by the artistic idea is the unity that constitutes truth, namely, *truth of being.* For this reason it is proper to speak of the artistic idea as truth of being and of the artistic product as being valid.

If we add that the validity which is arrived at in the work of art is validity in the form of appearance, we are thereby justified in describing the work as being *aesthetically valid.* In this sense, the artistic aim may also be described as the attainment of forms that are aesthetically valid.

Is the conception of aesthetic validity, which emerges so naturally from the notion of the artist's striving for visual comprehension, a mere product of philosophical speculation? Let us consult artists themselves, real and great ones.

Regarding his choice of colors in painting, Matisse spoke of an impelling proportion of tones that could induce him to change the shape of a figure or to transform his composition. Until he achieved this proportion in all the parts of the painting, he strove toward it and kept on working. He kept working until the moment came when every part had found its definite relationship, when the impelling proportion (the ideal, the ought-to-be) was fully established in the picture (the real semblance, the is). From that point it became impossible for him to add a stroke to the picture without having to paint it all over again.[10]

The form of the painting, with its "this way and no other," is the outcome of a process of striving. What is present throughout is the artistic idea, which has an individual shape in the individual process. For Matisse it is the impelling proportion of tones, the definite relationship which, once it is worked out into the whole picture, is now so fully as it ought to be that nothing can any longer be altered without upsetting the balance.

Arnold Schönberg spoke similarly of the idea of a piece of music. Begin the composition with a certain tone, say C, and add to it a second, for instance, G. Does this express C major or G major—or even F minor or E minor? To make the result more definite, add other tones, say E, or E flat, or B flat, or A. The problem may or may not be clarified, but it is not yet finally decided. A state of unrest is produced, a state of imbalance, which grows throughout most of the piece. Other features of the music, especially the rhythm, enforce further this growing unrest. How is the balance to be restored? The method of doing this, declared Schönberg, seemed to him to be the real idea of the composition.[11]

It is striking to notice how closely Matisse's and Schönberg's descriptions of the artistic process resemble one another. What the musician says about musical tones the painter says about colors. If on a white canvas, says Matisse, he jots down some sensations of blue, green, red, each new brushstroke affects the preceding ones, diminishing their importance. He wants to paint, say, a room, and begins with the cupboard, which gives him a sensation of bright red; so he puts down a red that satisfies him. Immediately, a relation gets established between this red and the white of the canvas. As new colors are added, a green near the red, a yellow floor, there must still be a relation between all these components which will satisfy the artist. The several tones weaken each other. Therefore he has to be careful in applying the colors, that they be so balanced as not to destroy one another. He has to organize his ideas, establish the tonal relations so that they sustain one another, carrying out the total interpretation. He has to change, repaint, transpose, bring out a new combination, continue adding and altering, until finally the picture may seem completely changed. But the result must be an ultimate relationship of all the tones that is a living harmony, a harmony, he says, not unlike that of a musical composition.

This striving to balance the elements so that they do not destroy but support each other, this impulse to modify and transpose, to organize and reorganize ideas, to change the composition and color relationships continually until the spirit of the picture has found its proper form—this is the drive toward a visual comprehension that, in its form, expresses the peculiar artistic consciousness. Notice how Matisse characterizes the quality of the desired form: a living harmony of tones, not unlike that of a musical composition. This living harmony is the form that, for Matisse, aesthetic validity assumes. He finds what is visually valid in a living harmony of tones—language that directly recalls the most ancient and most enduring of all characterizations of beauty.

It is the same when the poet Rilke describes the sculpture of Rodin. One could, he says, explain and illuminate most of Rodin's works by associating ideas with them. Such interpretations—noble, great, full of significance—could be helpful for those who are unaccustomed to approaching sculpture in its own terms as sculpture. But the figures themselves, more fundamentally, have an infinite rightness and trueness, a perfect equilibrium of all their movements, a marvelous inner justice of proportions, a way of being imbued with life—and it is this which makes them into things of "beauty" or, as we should say, constitutes their aesthetic validity. And, as Rilke indicates, it is as if this powerful inner validity, which makes them so infinitely right as forms, is just what also endows them with the power to be unsurpassable embodiments of the themes Rodin evoked when he named them.[12]

We may next call upon the testimony of Paul Valéry. There is, he maintains, a strange power in our inner life that causes us to seek after poetry or to produce it, a power which is an inexplicable demand of our being or its purest answer. What we feel the need of here is something that serves no ordinary purpose. It is merely, as it were, a kind of *rightness in certain arrangements of words,* which might to other eyes appear quite arbitrary. Having the experience of this need and its fulfillment, no one can teach us to love what we do not love or not to love what we do love—which past criticism used to aim at.[13]

This rightness in the order of words in poetry, like the rightness of colors in Matisse's painting or the rightness of tones in Schönberg's music, occurs within a harmony. The value of a poem, according to Valéry, lies in the indissolubility of sound and sense. His favorite image of the working of poetic language is the pendulum, oscillating between sound and sense, voice and thought, form and content. As the pendulum swings, from sound to sense and back again to sound, at each line the meaning and the form sustain and recall one another. Each is there for the other, as though the meaning present to the mind can find no other outlet than the word-form and the word-form no other sense than that meaning. It is as if each inevitably requires the other, so that between form and content, sound and sense, poem and poetry there is revealed a symmetry, an equality, which does not exist in the ordinary prose of everyday or factual communication. In prose, the sound and the sense are unequal. The essential principle of poetry is their equality, their harmonious interchange, the rightness of their indissoluble harmony.[14]

Those who practice prose as an art have the same thing to say about the prose work. Gustave Flaubert once wrote to George Sand that he would like to write a book which would produce the same effect as one of the walls of the Acropolis, completely bare. Independently of its content, the book's parts, composed of rare elements, with polished surfaces, would fit precisely, making a harmonious whole, because it would be the outward manifestation of an intrinsic virtue, a kind of divine force, as eternal as a principle. Because of this force, the right word is necessarily the musical word, and great compression of thought results invariably in a line of poetry.[15]

That this ideal of Flaubert's—which is more or less realized in *Madame Bovary*—is itself one-sided, looking for artistic validity to the form by itself, the semblance as such (for which reason he says that what seems to be outward form is actually essence), he himself understood, for he immediately added that to keep going for long on this track would lead the artist into a hopeless predicament. Art must also come from the heart; it has only the qualities we can give it, and we are not free—each follows his own path, determined by something deeper than his mere will. So Flaubert, too, acknowledged a kind of rightness, a truth to the heart, to the profoundest part of our being, more valid and more characteristic of great art than the specious rightness of preciosity that first speaks in his declaration.

Rather more simply Flaubert said also that a good prose sentence should be like a good line of poetry—*unchangeable*.[16] His disciple De Maupassant sums it up in the preface to *Pierre et Jean* with a classical formulation of the ideal of *le mot juste:*

> Whatever one wishes to say, there is one noun only by which to express it, one verb only to give it life, one adjective only which will describe it. One must search until one has discovered them, this noun, this verb, this adjective, and never rest content with approximations, never resort to trickery, however happy, or to vulgarisms, in order to dodge the difficulty ... One must discriminate, and with the utmost lucidity, all the modifications in the value of a word which are established by the position it occupies in the sentence.[17]

And André Gide only repeats the principle of his forebears when he declares:

> It is perfectly and obviously true that, in a fine line of verse, one cannot change or displace a word; but the same is true of fine prose. My sentences ... have to meet requirements that are as strict, even though they are frequently hidden, and as domineering as are those of the most rigorous prosody.[18]

Gide speaks elsewhere also of the "gait" of his writing and the "movement" of the ideas in it as even more important than the ideas, leading his translator, Malcolm Cowley, to remark that instead of trying to translate the interviews word for word, he tried to achieve the same sort of movement and rightness in English.

Not only is there an essential harmony between sound and sense in poetry, but the laws of harmony extend over everything in the poetic universe, and so Valéry speaks of a poem as a

> powerful and perfect work which transports [the reader] into a world where things and people, passions and thoughts, sonorities and meanings proceed from the same energy, are transformed one into another, and correspond according to exceptional laws of harmony . . .[19]

Moreover he connects this harmony of the poem with an exaltation of the self, as the continuation of the above citation makes plain:

> . . . for it can only be an exceptional form of stimulus that simultaneously produces the exaltation of our sensibility, our intellect, our memory, and our powers of verbal action, so rarely granted to us in the ordinary course of life.

This exaltation of the self comes about because poetry's harmony is exactly the harmony of the whole person, body and soul: Poetry must extend over the whole being; it stimulates the

> muscular organization by its rhythms, it frees or unleashes the verbal faculties, ennobling their whole action, it regulates our depths, for poetry aims to arouse or reproduce the unity and harmony of the living person, an extraordinary unity that shows itself when a man is possessed by an intense feeling that leaves none of his powers disengaged.[20]

Poetry makes man its own by its harmony, for this harmony is man's own harmony. And as human harmony extends over the whole being, bodily as well as mental, so the poetic harmony extends over the whole of the poem, sonorous as well as meaningful. Literature, says Valéry,

> never possesses me wholly unless I find in it traces of a thought whose power is equal to that of language itself. The force to bend the common word to unexpected ends without violating the "time-honored forms," the capture and subjugation of things that are difficult to say, and above all the simultaneous management of our syntax, harmony, and ideas (which is the problem of the purest poetry) are in my eyes the supreme objects of our art.[21]

Note that the harmony is placed between the syntax and the ideas, in the purest poetry, that is, between the sound and the sense, language and thought—rightly so, for is it not just their synthesis? Or should we say, perhaps even more accurately, that the ultimate poetic harmony is given in and through the simultaneous managements of syntax, ideas, and harmony? To make them all go together, belonging to one another—is that not the poetic problem exactly posed in its purity as such?

It is the same with painting. Paul Klee also remarks on the indispensability of the aesthetic validity which has been occupying our attention. In his lecture "On Modern Art," which he gave on the occasion of an exhibition, including works of his own, in 1924 at the Jena museum, he pointed to what he called the multidimensional simultaneity of a painting as a work of art.[22] In this multidimensional simultaneity Klee distinguished four dimensions: the elementary formal sphere of construction, the sphere of objective representation, the sphere of physiognomic expression of content, and the sphere of style.

"I often dream," he said, "of a work of great range, extending through the entire elementary, objective, contentual, and stylistic sphere." But we may consider here only what he says of the first dimension, which though elementary is also crucial—the construction of the form out of the elementary means of the art. This is the *pons asinorum* of painting. The elementary formal means are line, tones of light and shade, and color. When the artist comes to the first constructions with the elements of these three means, he comes to the point of decisiveness of the art of painting, where lies the center of gravity of the artist's conscious creation, and where his professional deed concentrates itself. Here, as Klee says, it is critical. This stage of conscious configuration is critical in two ways: for one thing, mastery of the configurational means gives the artist the possibility of consciously articulating objects with such carrying capacity that they can also extend into dimensions reaching beyond the conscious context, and for another, this is the place at which the greatest and most important contents become unreachable and founder, despite the most beautiful talents or gifts of a psychological sort, just because there is lacking orientation to the formal plane.

What I have been calling aesthetic validity—which, in this formal sphere, is a rightness, necessity, and completeness of a vital kind—is the governing consideration in the artist's work. Recognition of it makes the difference between understanding and not understanding the point of the artist's work. At a time when the battle for the freedom of abstract art had first to be won, it was still necessary for the artist to make clear to the viewer that he was looking at a work of art, not at a reproduction of a non-artistic reality. Klee explains:

> While the artist is still wholly a striving to group the formal elements so purely and so logically together that each is necessary in its place and none does damage to the others, some layman looking on from behind already utters the awful words: But it doesn't look much like Uncle! The painter, if he has disciplined nerves, thinks to himself: "To hell with Uncle! I must continue to construct. . . . This new building stone, he says to himself, is, to begin with, pretty heavy and pulls the whole thing too far to the left; I shall have to add a not insignificant counterweight on the right, in order to restore the balance." And he keeps adding in turn to one side and to the other until the scale's index points directly upward. And he is delighted if he had to make this purely initiated construction of a few good elements waver only to the extent that contradictions, contrasts belong to a structure full of life.

Once again, then, we see that the critical factor, which decides the difference between art and non-art, is aesthetic validity: the vital, living rightness that the artist, as artist, strives to produce. Klee's attempt to exhibit this validity first in the domain of formal construction, and later to add to our view of it the further dimensions in which it must also operate (presentation of the objective, expression of the subjective, and style or the concrete unity of the whole), gives a distorted picture, to be sure, since aesthetic validity must hold in all dimensions and in the whole multidimensional simultaneity, not alone in the configuration of the elementary means of the medium. Nevertheless the distortion sets us on the road to the truer account, provided we remember its one-sidedness.

I would like to cite also a few words of Kandinsky's written for *Eri Udstilling* (Copenhagen 1937) under the title "Approach to Art:"

> 2 herrings + 2 herrings = 4 herrings. There seems to be an eternal law that remains always unshaken.
>
> 2 yellow + 2 yellow = ? Often = 0.
>
> In art increase is not seldom attained by means of decrease. Where does calculation remain? Logic smirks in embarrassment. Mathematics holds its head.
>
> Who still wants to calculate a work of art?
>
> The artist "hears" "someone" saying to him: "Stop! Where are you going? The line is too long. Shorten it a bit, but only a bit! 'A bit' I tell you." Or: "Do you want to let the red ring louder? Fine! Then put in a little green. Thus 'break off' a bit, take a bit away. But only 'a bit' I tell you." What Henri Rousseau took to be the "dictation of his dead wife."
>
> "The dead wife" is the inexhaustible source of the "miracle of art." The path losing itself in infinity.
>
> One must only understand how to "hear," that is, when the voice sounds.
>
> In this way forms are "discovered," "measured" by the artist, and in this way "proportion," balance arise. "Construction"! ˙
>
> But all this doesn't help at all if the "beholder" has no "ear." He does not need to hear what has yet to come into being, but he must be able to hear the "clang" of the work that has already come to be.[23]

It is artistic intuition, not mathematical-logical reason, that governs the structuring of a work of art. The difference between mathematical mathematics and painterly mathematics is clear to every artist for whom the elements are living things. It shows itself even in color alone. Adding herrings to herrings, apples to apples, stones to stones, increases the number of herrings, apples, or stones; but adding more and more yellow to a given yellow does not increase, but only diminishes, the value of the yellow. If feeling and intuition are eliminated in favor of abstract mathematical calculation, the result must be artistic failure, for it overlooks the difference between the two mathematics—mathematical and artistic.

We may now return to the question with which we had left Lessing. Is there a beauty in art that belongs to the art in art and not merely to this or that represented subject? The answer is, Yes. The driving impulse of the artist at work is the striving to realize the artistic idea, the idea of the identity of *ought* and *is* in the form of the phenomenon. In any particular process this idea takes shape in a particular task. For Matisse, the task consisted in defining the character of the object or of the body he wished to paint. In another artist it might be that of expressing an emotion, representing a landscape, or constructing a purely abstract spatial volume. The forms of art, the types of artistic effect, the genres within an art form—all of these represent specializations of the generic artistic task of realizing the idea of the identity of ideal and actual in the form of the phenomenon. Understanding of the concrete structure and systematic relationships of forms and types of art rests on seeing them in their character as specializations of this sort. Whatever the particular content that the idea takes up, however, its essential core is always the same: to make something true-in-itself, valid-in-itself, in the form of semblance.

When the result aimed at is attained, a form has been created that is, as far as possible, clear, complete, and necessary, all of these in an aesthetic sense. In it, because the actual is ideal and the ideal actual, there is attained a harmony that belongs to the very being of the semblant form and its constituents. As in Matisse's painting it is a harmony of tones, so in every successful work it is a harmony of its ingredients. The parts and contents do not destroy one another but mutually sustain each other, all submitting to the spirit of the whole. Though we grasp this harmony in and through the semblance, and thus in and through what we see, hear, or imagine, it is yet nothing merely sensible as such. It is not like another color sensation, sound sensation, or image, nor is it like another body or act that we perceive. It is, rather, something apprehended only through artistic consciousness by a kind of spiritual eye or ear. It is apprehended as a condition of being into which the visual, auditory, or imaginative form has been brought—a condition of harmony of being, in which ideality and actuality are at one. Such a condition can be apprehended only by a concrete spiritual act, not by a purely visual or auditory perception. The mind that apprehends it has to be able to grasp both *ought* and *is* and grasp them in their unity in the individual semblance. This act of apprehending the necessary and the actual, and the unity of them in the individual semblance, is not an act of sensation or perception, not even of ordinary discursive understanding. That is why no amount of scientific information about art approaches it. It is an act of the spirit that alone can comprehend truth of being in the semblance: the act of aesthetic intuition.

Once we have attained to the idea of aesthetic validity, or truth of being in the semblance, we no longer need to make use of the ambiguous word and concept of *beauty.* We begin to see, instead, that behind the formation of the concept of beauty was the impulse to grasp the idea of truth of being in the semblance, so that having arrived at the latter concept we have indeed realized what the concept of beauty strove to fix. Truth of being—or the unity of ideality and actuality—in the semblance represents the universal essential aesthetic fact in art. Wherever art occurs, there occurs a realization in some degree of this artistic idea. The degree of its presence and emphasis is a measure of the degree of the presence of the unique feature of art. When we find it realized in a work we know at once that we are in the presence of a product of genuinely artistic capacity, to whose higher reaches we give the name of genius. Its presence makes the difference between art on the one side and rhetoric and technique on the other.

Let us recall Fiedler's remark on the finality of the consciousness of the realized form in art—all the emotional forces, driving forces, passions, enthusiasms, are useless to the artist unless they are harnessed in the service of this specific mental capacity. In artistic activity and in our comprehension of the artist's work, all capacities of the mind are ordered to the one end of the creation and apprehension of truth of being in the semblance. So, equally, all materials that can enter into the semblance—directly or indirectly, as immediately present or as connoted or symbolized—are subordinated to this one end. The fundamental question is: Can these materials become functioning parts of the semblance in which the unity of *ought* and *is* is realized? Can they be the medium in which the artistic idea is expressed? If so, then their presence is validated.

If art today finds that it must make use of materials that are negative, discordant, ugly, meaningless, in order to build a valid semblance, this does not show that the human spirit is breaking down, that man can now affirm nothing but nothingness itself. It begins rather to indicate the particular shape in which the human spirit in each of us is able to survive and grow and affirm itself in a world that is in fact shadowed by nonbeing and pervaded by discord. Of discord itself the challenge is to make a harmony—not one that denies discord, or covers it up, but one that raises discord into its own essence and becomes a harmony in and of discord, not a resolution of tension but a harmony in tension, not a negation of strife but a peace in strife.

The Greeks made harmony obvious so that all the world could see it. We hide our harmony under the cloak of the negative. It becomes invisible, perceptible only to the spirit that penetrates the semblance by aesthetic intuition. Our beauty is no less a beauty than theirs, but we are so intent on hiding it—in order to make it all the more authentically visible—that we even refuse to use the name, and are impelled to such an ugliness as the word "validity."

These remarks on the art of the negative are only preliminary and are not to be understood as offering a full view of the nature of this art. We discover in this art the answer that life itself gives to Hegel's claim that art had no significant future. Art today is more alive and freer than it ever has been, even in Greece or in Renaissance Europe. It has found renewed sources of energy in a life that has renewed its own energy in a realization of its situation as clear-sighted as any had in the past. It is a task of the philosophy of art to express the principles in terms of which this phenomenon becomes intelligible.

Thus we obtain a general answer to the problem left by Lessing. The existence of any and all elements—and not alone of negative elements—in a work of art is a function of the particular shape of the artistic idea at work, and this itself is a function of the life-situation, needs, and demands of the artistic sensibility in action in producing the work. The forces of our being are set free to pursue their own goals in the semblance. Semblance gives to the artistic spirit a field and an element free from the compulsions of actual necessity in which it can project the artistic idea as the goal of its action. If in this freedom it seeks to form the harmony that suits it out of dark rather than light tones, out of mysteries and negations rather than clarities and affirmations—this shows only the temper of the spirit at work. It defines itself by choosing its own harmonic style, the particular terms in which it is possible for it to affirm the validity of being.

The challenge of producing a valid aesthetic result out of the negative elements became a principle for recent art. André Gide, a master practitioner of the genre, formulated it thus:

> The work is more beautiful, the more the thing overcome was revolting to begin with.[24]

To understand aesthetic validity is to understand the crucial aesthetic fact in art, and the concept, as I have here tried to fix its general content, may serve in place of beauty as the idea by which the phenomena of art can be interpreted and related to each other in an aesthetically meaningful way.

We have only to ask now what are the character and meaning of the rightness that composes aesthetic validity. Who is the dead wife who speaks to the artist, the inexhaustible source of the artistic miracle? What is that strange power in the inner life of the poet that Valéry saw as causing poetry to be sought after and produced, a power that is revealed as an inexplicable demand of our being or as its purest answer? What is the spirit of the picture to which Matisse maintained the artist's interpretation of nature must be submitted and which demands that the relationship of tones must be a living harmony? What is the real nature of the idea which Schönberg described as the totality of the piece, the method by which balance is restored, an idea which is the composer's and which, being born, must be developed to its very end? What mental necessities are they which, as Fiedler claimed, must be satisfied in the struggle with nature that makes up the act of art creation? What intrinsic virtue is there, which comes from the heart and even compels us along our path—a kind of divine force, eternal as a principle—which Flaubert discovered in a work whose parts fit exactly? If Gide speaks of the "gait" of his writing or if Klee speaks of the artist as a striving to group the formal elements in a mutually supportive necessity, what reveals itself in the manner of the artistic walking or grouping?

All these questions point in the same direction and call for a single answer. The fundamental demand of man's being, which the artist experiences in its purity when he works with his medium, is the demand to be with what is other as with one's own. Things *are* together with other things in the structured process that forms their natural world; they belong to their world as its natural members. Man, however, has first to seek and find that in the other which is to be his world, his people, his sphere, his life. He experiences *ought* from within, not just as a moral ought, but as an ought that belongs to his very life and heart, as the ought-to-be of the world and his self and the relationship between the two, in which the self is his own and the world is his own and the two belong to one another, fitting together as they should—akin. When this happens, man is at home with his own, dwelling in freedom.

Freedom, indeed, is the name given to fulfilled being in the practical domain of life; for to be free is to be in such a way that what happens is identified by you as your own choice, as willed by you. What you accept as yours no longer stands as alien and opposed, but is just what is other than yourself which you find to be, and adopt as, your own, belonging to you and you belonging to it.

Another name for freedom is authenticity. An authentic act is one that is performed by the self, *autos,* of which the self is the author, and which is thus done on one's own authority. My act is authentic when it is truly my own act, such that I can say it was genuinely I who acted in it, and such that it is I who am responsible for it. Without ownness of the act, there can be no responsibility and hence no human authenticity. But the act must be truly my own if I am to have acted authentically, and this means that I must really do it and live it as mine.

What is mine and what is not mine, the own and the not-own, cannot be determined by merely abstract intellectual means. That is the truth behind Kandinsky's denial that a work of art can be calculated. For calculation omits the self. It tries to be objective, that is, the same for every self regardless of the self's own selfhood. But anything that could hold objectively in this sense—homogeneously for all selves—would be simply impersonal and selfless, own to no one, own only to the thin residue of humanity that is left when all individual selfhood has been removed from it. Science is objective in this way, but not art.

What is mine I can discover only by letting it work on me, my own self. I cannot tell beforehand who or what I am. I must wait to hear my self speak, telling me of itself and of what it discovers to be its own. This is the voice of the dead wife. The dead wife is my own, dearest of all, the one who belonged to me and I to her. Only when I open the path for her to come forth have I opened access at the same time to my deepest being to listen and respond. Thus do I let my own selfhood reveal itself; and it does so, not by projecting a representation of itself, an exterior copy, but by determining that in the object which is genuinely its own—the shortened line, the green to contrast with the red, the forms discovered and measured, the harmony, the balance. This is true artistic objectivity, the self owning its objective other, acknowledging the other as its own, recognizing the other as that to which it belongs and that which belongs to it—akin.

The harmony is real only if it can be felt. Feeling is the key here, because feeling is the process in which the self experiences what is other than itself as own or not-own to it. The feeling that belongs to love is the feeling of the other as mine and of myself as its. The feeling that belongs to aversion is the feeling of the other in its alien oppositeness. That is why the voice that speaks in art is that of the dead wife and not of the stranger and enemy. The voice in art is ultimately the voice of love, which tells about what belongs to what, which cannot be cleverly calculated beforehand, which must be waited for and, when it comes, speaks with the authority of authenticity.

We are lucky when we find someone else whose own is ours, too, and for whom ours is own, so that it becomes possible for us to belong to one another. It is that good luck which, when we find it in a work of art, causes our heart to leap with joy. The joy is the blessing of the rightness by which everything belongs to everything else in the work, a network of love which becomes ours as the work seizes upon our spirit, possessing it for its own.

5

The Kin-Consciousness
of Art

Art is a language by which the human mind gives utterance to its own integrity. It holds together the two main
sides of experience—objective and subjective—in their
appropriate unity and it articulates that unity in an image
for intuition.

One function of mind is theoretical, devoted to the formation of knowledge of reality. Here we try to make reality our own by submitting our intention to it. We
appropriate the real as real, cognitively, by adapting our
ideas to the real as it is. Theoretical mind attends
primarily to the object of consciousness and concerns
itself with determining the being and content of the object
qua object. Its aim is truth: the agreement of the subject's
intention with the object's being. In the whole economy
of life its role is the development of science, the illumination of reality. Within art, one-sided emphasis on it gives
rise to the tendencies known as realism and naturalism,
whose ideal is the truth of reality, as well as other tendencies, like symbolism, which seek to express a transcendent
truth and reality.

A second function of mind is practical, devoted to acting and doing. It sets its attention on the subject's appetites and goals and concerns itself with realizing his desire and his will in existence. Here we try to make reality our own by causing it to submit to our intentions. We appropriate the real, practically, by making it conform to our values. We call things, actions, and persons right and good when they agree with our norms. Practical mind thus reverses the direction of theoretical mind: it aims at the agreement of the object's being with the subject's intention. It makes being accord with thinking, rather than thinking accord with being. In the economy of life, therefore, its role is the reflected correlative to that of knowing. It is the development of man's governance over things, including himself, in accordance with standards he determines as being suitable for them—as, for example, in technology, law, morals, politics, and war. In art, one-sided emphasis on this aim—the aim at freedom—gives rise to counter-naturalistic, counter-realistic tendencies such as idealism, constructivism, expressionism, Dada, and surrealism.

Theoretical and practical mind are necessary for the integral unity of the psyche, just as objective and subjective are necessary for the unity of consciousness. What is the unity of the consciousness of which art is the language, and what is the psychical unity corresponding to it? The nature of these unities is already indicated by the language we use to describe the ideals of its two indispensable sides, the theoretical and the practical. One is truth, the other freedom. In one, intention agrees with reality; in the other, reality agrees with intention. In both, the union is one of agreement. The ideal of mind in its integrity is agreement—the mutual agreement of intention and reality. But the intention has to be not merely the one-sided cognitive intention of theoretical mind, and not merely the equally one-sided elective intention of practical mind, but the full intention of mind in its integrity, namely, the affective intention of the love that joins spirit to its affinity.

The third and unifying function of mind is the spiritual one, whose aim is to reach the mutual agreement of intention and reality. It includes knowing, but is not mere science. It includes freedom, but is not mere action; and it is no longer merely freedom, for it yields itself to its other in devotion to it. Its essential aim is to exist in the reciprocal devotion of love.

This is the ultimate and true form of ownness. It transcends and includes the validity of all cognitive and all practical appropriation of reality, for in it is realized the underlying aim that gives rise to both knowledge and practice, the desire to be together in a unity of belonging, the desire for existence in mutual appropriation.

The mutual ownness of the spirit overcomes the violence and constraint that are essential to the two one-sided forms, knowledge and practice. In knowing, the mind constrains itself to change, submitting to the nature of the reality it wishes to know. The mind has to make itself over in the image of the being that stands opposed to it. In practice, the agent constrains the matter he works on to alter its form, causing it to submit to his design for it. Here, he makes the opposed being over in the image his mind envisions for it. In both cases, one of the two factors of experience, mind or being, subject or object, is caused by the agent ego to be something other than it was. Constraint and compulsion have to be used. But in the mutual ownness of spirit, subject and object, mind and being, I and Thou agree with one another. Whatever constraints may have occurred earlier, in the final togetherness each has his own way. They do not make each other be or do anything. They give themselves to one another. Egoism vanishes. Knowledge knows the other at a distance; love knows the other in intimacy. Practice becomes free by its conquest of the other; love is free on both sides, of itself. The mutual ownness of spirit joins the qualities of knowledge and practice—truth and freedom—into a new unity: true freedom, free truth, the fulfillment of love, or blessedness.

The consciousness of this mutual ownness of love I call, by an obvious metaphor, *kin-consciousness.* It is the consciousness of self and other in their mutual belonging to one another, their mutual fitness, harmony, accord, kinship. The negative form of kin-consciousness—which fills most of life and affords most of the subject-matter of art —is the consciousness of unbelonging, unfitness, discord, disharmony. There are many modifications of it, complications of the positive and negative forms, among which are to be found notably the consciousness of the tragic and of the comic. Goethe celebrated it under the name of "elective affinity." Plotinus took it for the foundation of his view of beauty:

> Our interpretation is that the Soul—by the very truth of its nature, by its affiliation to the noblest Existents in the hierarchy of Being—when it sees anything of that kin, or any trace of that kinship, thrills with an immediate delight, takes its own to itself, and thus stirs anew to the sense of its nature and of all its affinity.[1]

Mutual ownness is the truth of being. The alienation of otherness is overcome. The self and other are reconciled in an at-onement which is not a mere quieting of otherness but an affirmative and reciprocally enhancing appropriation of one another in, through, despite the reality of opposition. Love forgives the finite for what it is and takes it to itself precisely in its finitude.

Art's language is the language of this mutual ownness, its negation, its modifications. In art, man's spirit utters its meanings as concrete unities of the subjective and objective. Unlike those one-sided meanings that are expressed in the prose of science and the rhetoric of practice, they reveal concretely the essential bond of true being. The one-sided tendencies in art must contain this concrete unity, since they are art first before they succumb to their own abstractedness. So, for example, expressionism, because of the tortured character of its love, must torture the object into a fitting distortion. Dada and surrealism, out of an indefeasible craving for perfect spontaneity and absolutely uninhibited freedom, must destroy every vestige of rational order in the object: only the nonsensical, absurd, irrational shows itself to them as their very own. Still, neither the one side nor the other reveals in art the true wholeness and purity of spiritual unity. Only those art forms that do justice to both sides of experience give an ultimately true expression of spiritual unity. These are the fulfilled classical forms of art, that come into being and endure as long as a culture comes into the maturity of its conscious life and endures —normally, perhaps, only after the great military, political, and economic achievements are behind it. They are the arts that belong to periods like the Gupta in India, the T'ang and Sung in China, or the mature classical period in ancient Greece and the Gothic, Renaissance, and Baroque in Europe. Consummate artists and works arise in these periods, because they are periods in which the spiritual consciousness of the culture arrives at its natural fullness and demands utterance, and the material means are available in power and riches to give the artist scope for his task.

To illustrate art as the language of the mutual belonging of kin-consciousness, I choose a relatively minor work, yet one that brings out clearly the character of this unity by a certain inner contrast. Written in a period of somewhat low key, it is a poem written out of a mood of melancholy, which realizes that it has lost the golden splendor of the great classical age. Though it has to come to terms with an austerely natural world, it realizes for itself, in its very utterance of itself, the unity whose loss it deplores. It is Matthew Arnold's "Dover Beach."

> The sea is calm tonight.
> The tide is full, the moon lies fair
> Upon the Straits;—on the French coast the light
> Gleams and is gone; the cliffs of England stand,
> Glimmering and vast, out in the tranquil bay.
>
> Come to the window, sweet is the night-air!
> Only, from the long line of spray
> Where the sea meets the moon-blanch'd land,
> Listen! you hear the grating roar
> Of pebbles which the waves draw back, and fling,
> At their return, up the high strand,
> Begin, and cease, and then again begin,
> With tremulous cadence slow, and bring
> The eternal note of sadness in.
>
> Sophocles long ago
> Heard it on the Aegean, and it brought

Into his mind the turbid ebb and flow
Of human misery; we
Find also in the sound a thought,
Hearing it by this distant northern sea.

The Sea of Faith
Was once, too, at the full, and round earth's shore
Lay like the folds of a bright girdle furl'd.
But now I only hear
Its melancholy, long, withdrawing roar,
Retreating, to the breath
Of the night-wind, down the vast edges drear
And naked shingles of the world.

Ah, love, let us be true
To one another! for the world, which seems
To lie before us like a land of dreams,
So various, so beautiful, so new,
Hath really neither joy, nor love, nor light,
Nor certitude, nor peace, nor help for pain;
And we are here as on a darkling plain
Swept with confused alarms of struggle and flight,
Where ignorant armies clash by night.

What is the artistic form by which the kin-consciousness of art shows itself to the intuitive imagination? The particular dimensions of the showing are two: the presentation of objectivity and the expression of subjectivity.[2] Their essential connection lies in the fitness, the kinship, by which they belong to one another.

In all art something has to be presented objectively as that to which the self in the work attends. Most familiar of the modes of objective presentation is the representation of objects. The work will be a painting of figures, animals, a landscape, a city scene; it will be the sculptured image of a god or a man, the story of an event, the dramatic enactment of a conflict, a lyrical evocation of the self's world. But objective presentation also operates in other ways than literal representation. Art uses for this purpose a symbol of an abstract concept, an allegory of a universal meaning, a metaphor, a simile, or other figure for an objectively thinkable content. It can present objectively that which transcends all finitely thinkable meaning, the mysterious, the infinite, the transcendent, by means of inscrutably suggestive images.

Even in the most subjective kind of art, the lyrical, or the most subjective of the arts, music, there is present an indelible objectivity. I do not merely mean that musical tones, fleeting as they may be, stand forth for themselves and build the strongest structure out of the gossamer web of their relations in time—a Bach fugue, a Mozart sonata. That is the objectivity of the utterance itself. I mean rather to point to the fact that when music is at its most lyrical and subjective, as in the romantic melody of Schumann, Chopin, Brahms, Wagner, and Bruckner, it remains at the same time, however strangely and mysteriously, evocative of an unheard world, a world unnamed and undescribed, toward which nevertheless the subjectivity in the melody is turned; and this merely adumbrated objectivity, the ghost of objectivity that remains with subjectivity when the latter retires into itself, is more truly representative of the function of objective presentation in art than the actual sounding of the tones.

Lyrical art is the self pouring forth its utterance; but it utters its feelings in tones, words, verses, images, which are themselves powerful in the presentation of objectivity.

Red lips are not so red
As the stained stones kissed by the English dead.

Wilfred Owen makes his speaker express the poetic irony by an image as objective as any image can be—the contrasting vision of the living, pulsating, warm red lips of the beloved kissed by the lover, and the stone stained red with the blood of the slain lover of his fellow.

Abstract art shows this feature of objective presentation most clearly. In its extremest form, so-called *non*-objective art, it is precisely the presentation of a pure objectivity, and therefore the most purely objective of arts. It abandons the representation of objects familiar in the world outside the work and it concentrates on presenting only objects that are imagined purely through the medium of the work. The whole of the objectivity in the work is absorbed and exercised by the work itself, in its own purity of medium, freed from having to bring into itself objects from the external world. A pure design by Mondrian is stunning in its objectivity, just because it disdains to copy trees, mountains, rivers, cows, men, buildings, and other such ordinary objects.

Objective presentation is essential to the constitution of the art work. But it is only a necessary condition, and it is not sufficient of itself to fulfill the artistic function of showing ownness and love. It is in itself indifferent to artistic ownness—as is evident, for example, in non-artistic photography and in scientific illustration, from maps to electronic circuit diagrams. Objective presentation is a phase of theoretical activity; consequently, it betrays the merely formal, abstract ownership practiced by the theoretical mind. Once it has appropriated the object in its abstract manner, cognition is indifferent to what remains over and above the prosaic objectiveness of the thing. The indifference extends to everything in the object except its objectness. Once objective presentation has made the object intuitable, it is finished with it, whereas love has only then begun with it.

The second dimension of showing is subjective expression. This is as essential a function of art as objective presentation. If presenting the object may be called the epical function in art, expressing the subject is art's lyrical function. A painting has to be made as something envisoned, a piece of music as something sounded, a poem as something spoken. A subject sees, sounds, speaks.

> The sea is calm tonight.
> The tide is full, the moon lies fair
> Upon the Straits;—on the French coast the light
> Gleams and is gone; the cliffs of England stand,
> Glimmering and vast, out in the tranquil bay.
>
> Come to the window, sweet is the night-air!

There is someone speaking here, from a personal point of view, bringing out in the imagery a visual scene from the window, speaking with a surface calm that, as the poem proceeds, proves to be a transparent medium for depths of disenchantment, and appealing in the end to his companion for the mutual trust of love. The poem is a short dramatic monologue. Through the role it assigns to the speaker, it lets him express a complex attitude, containing within it a vision of the present actuality, an understanding of the state of modern man's deliverance from religious illusion, the deep sadness that accompanies disillusion, and the hope for, and will to find in finite human love, something of a finite answer to an infinite problem. The speaker expresses his own subjective experience—his perception, imagination, thinking, feeling, aspiring, his character and temperament—while he is at the same time presenting an aspect of the world objectively in his language.

Everywhere in art something similar happens. Art articulates both the objective and the subjective components of human experience. It does this in such a way as to keep the objective objective and the subjective subjective. Objectivity is presented—pictured, symbolized, suggested, designated—and subjectivity is expressed in its role of viewing, thinking, feeling, desiring, willing. The visual arts construct not simply objects, but visions of objects and objects envisioned; music makes not just sounds, but sounding expressions; in a poem or other literary work, there is articulated an experience of something, a concrete consciousness that utters itself in words. In a drama, a mind broods over the struggles of men in their world; the audience, sitting with that world presented before it in immediate presence, is given the opportunity to participate in that silent contemplation, full of complexities of thought and feeling, as the pathos of *Romeo and Juliet,* the satirical contempt of *Tartuffe,* or the profound understanding of the human in Euripides' *Electra.*

As subjective lyrical art makes essential use of objective presentation, so objective epical art makes essential use of subjective expression. Every story has its narrator or narrators; every object seen has its seer, every thought its thinker, everything presented presupposes the emotion that feels it. The supposed pure objectivity of *Madame Bovary* is only the inverse side and reflection of an in-

tensely passionate observation, insight, and moral judgment passed upon Emma, her husband Charles, the phar-
macist Homais, and their bourgeois world and life—a
complexity of attitude that is as much a phase of the composition of the novel as any objective situation it represents.

Of the dimension of subjective expression we must say
also that taken by itself it is a necessary but not sufficient
condition for artistic revelation. It, too, is in itself indifferent to the artistic content of ownness, as is evident in
forensic rhetoric, passionate argument, cursing, and
blessing. There is, to be sure, a formal element of appropriation in expression, since the subjective attitude has
been made accessible to intuition and so appropriated by
the mind as an intuitional content, part of an image. But
this appropriation is, so far, limited just to the formality
of becoming an image. It has not yet extended to the
fullness of being an image of mutual ownness.

We begin to approach the articulation of kin-consciousness only with the union of subjectivity and objectivity.
For here, if the artist is successful, the objective material
presented and the subjective attitude expressed belong to
one another, joining together into a unity of essential
appropriateness. If in Arnold's poem the mood of disenchantment and muted consolation in human love is to be
veritably expressed, the vision and thought of the world
given to the speaker must work by being suitable to the
attitude. The sea, with its ever-recurrent surf, has to work
as an image, and indeed it does so in this poem. The
calmness with which it is presented at the beginning will
belong to the subjective attitude at the end. The slow

tremulous cadence with which the sounds of the waves make themselves heard—drawing back pebbles and flinging them at their return up the strand, beginning and ceasing, beginning and ceasing, again and again—is telling in its ability to

bring

The eternal note of sadness in,

without a let-down into sentimentality.

This sound that Sophocles heard long ago, that master of insight into human suffering, brought into his mind,

the turbid ebb and flow

Of human misery,

and we northerners, far in time and far in space from that golden age,

Find also in the sound a thought.

The thought is of the vanishing of faith in the reality of beauty, joy, love, light, certitude, peace, help for pain, in the real world. That faith was once a sea, like this, which

at the full, and round earth's shore

Lay like the folds of a bright girdle furl'd.
But now I only hear its melancholy, long, withdrawing roar,
Retreating, to the breath
Of the night-wind, down the vast edges drear
And naked shingles of the world.

The objectivity that is seen, thought about, and presented for feeling, acts to bring out with distinctness and vitality the dominant mood. Dover Beach becomes an effective figure for the world—that darkling plain

> Swept with confused alarms of struggle and flight,
> Where ignorant armies clash by night.

Here, where art does what it is able to do, the two dimensions of its configuring action, the objectivity presented and the subjectivity expressed, join together in a relationship of mutual belonging. The symbol of the sea, its tide, its surf, the rhythm of its recurrence, the coast, the cliffs, the beach, the vanished light, the whole content of the history of faith—all work to give a stand for the sad consolation, and the mood itself works to hold them all together in the unity of its own meaning.

The poem articulates a certain truth. By this I refer, not to the thought that the world is no longer a habitation of the divine, but rather to truth of a unique sort, an agreement between subject and object of the kind that occurs here between expressed mood and presented matter. There is a rightness of each to the other, a reciprocal accord. They feed on one another, being true to each other. They are kin. The mood lives, flashes up into a vibrant response, through the shape of the objective matter; and the scene and world that are imagined live, flashing up into an equally vibrant resonance, through the inspiration of the mood.

Here, in this inner truth of presentation and expression to each other, is our first glimpse of the ownness that is constitutive for art. The objective matter is own to the mood, the mood to the matter. The matter does not copy the mood, nor does it express the mood; it is the *words* of the poem that both present the objective matter and express the subjective mood. The matter and the mood stand in a special relationship, of own to own, mutual kinship. Here we encounter a relationship of spiritual content to figural form, inside the work, which can begin to show us how ownness finds its outward form.

The question is how the poem as words, the outward poetic image or figure, the shape of the words as a poem, is able to reveal the content of ownness, the mutual kinship or truth of presented objectivity and expressed subjectivity. The words, shaped into the poem, are the poetic image in the most literal sense: the image that is, and is not merely in, the poem. The content which this image signifies, the poetic content as such, is the unity of the objective and subjective constituents within the poetic meaning. How does the linguistic shape do this?

It is not a copy of it. That is evident. The verbal structure does not look like a union of the two dimensions of consciousness, nor does it sound or smell or taste like it.

It is not a physiognomic expression of it. The verbal structure is not like, for example, a man's face as it expresses an inner feeling or character. It cannot be so, because the reciprocal truth, which is a union of the two dimensions of consciousness, is not a suitable content for physiognomic expression. It is not something merely subjective, but is a union of the subjective and the objective, at once a truth and a freedom.

The poem is not a symbol of the ultimate unity, in the sense in which a symbol represents the symbolized as something different from itself, separate from itself, in place of which it stands here to point there to the absolute content. The clearest example of such a symbol comes not from art but from science, as when the physicist uses the letter *G* to stand for the force of gravitation. But the poem does not just stand for the truth, to remind us of it as *G* reminds us of gravitation. In this sense, then, *the poem is not a symbol.*

If the poem symbolizes the truth, it does so by participating in it: the truth it symbolizes enters into the very speaking as such. As the sentence "Burlap is made from jute" says what it does, uttering this flat piece of information, so the poem more than merely says, it speaks in its own way, it poetizes its meaning, the truth it exists to utter, by being *of* that meaning, participating in it, belonging to it as its own. In this sense, *the poem is a symbol.*

The sentence is not a symbol that only stands for something else, even though it is made of such symbols. It is a piece of language that speaks in its flat way of saying, and in its speaking already participates in and belongs to that which it says. The poem speaks in its full way—intoning, singing, weaving its rhythmical way through its utterance. As the truth which the sentence speaks is spoken *in* the sentence, so the truth which the poem speaks is spoken *in* the poem. It is not spoken by one or other of the words in the poem. It is not in the poem as a word or words.

In the poem, a man speaks. Presumably he is speaking to a woman. This man's perceptions, memories, thoughts, wishes, moods receive expression, and his world comes to objective appearance, in the poem. Through his voice, the poem speaks as it does. He begins:

The sea is calm tonight.

Both the sea that he perceives and the mood in which he perceives it begin to come to utterance. He reaches out with his words and brings to view the sea, calm tonight. By his noun he discloses to our imagination a marine image, which he stills by an adjective and brings to time by an adverb.

At the same time, by the same words, in the same sequence, he discloses to the same imagination, not an outward picture alone, but also an inner consciousness, a disenchantment, a disconsolate consolation, which now just begins to be felt, but will grow and gain definiteness as the reading of the poem continues. We who understand his language are able to imagine this subjective phase in a manner appropriate to subjectivity. This happens not by looking at the mood, as though we were turned toward it as an object, but by participating in it empathically. As we are conscious of our own mood, not by looking at it objectively but by being in it and being inwardly and nonreflectively aware of it, so are we conscious in imagination of the mood of the poetic speaker. Our own mood is conscious of itself not as an object but just as itself, in itself, by means of itself. It is self-knowing in being what it is. That is the basis for our knowing the mood expressed by the poetic speaker.

At the same time, by the same words, the speaker brings to imagination the unity of subject and object. The disenchantment intends the calm sea. This is an essential constituent both of the disenchantment and the sea. The disenchantment is of and about the sea, and it permeates both the seeing of the sea and the sea as seen. So, later, we hear the tremulous cadence of the grating roar of the pebbles, which brings in the eternal note of sadness. The sadness is out there in the moaning of the surf as well as in here in the breast of the man. The words of the speaker make us understand this essential unity by which the sea and the mood belong to one another. They give it to our intelligent imagination.

Why does the disenchantment choose the sea? Why not something else, somewhere else? Why do you choose the city in which you live? Why not a village, in another country? In and through the sea, which the disillusionment chooses and by which it is itself chosen, it lives its own being, comes to articulated shape by an intentional congruence with it, as you come to be what you are by your living dwelling within your city. The sea is own to the disenchantment because the sea is the object of which the disenchantment is the subject. The sea is the disenchantment's own other—its elective affinity, its kin—which the disenchantment has been able to make its own in the way in which disenchantment can own things. The sea has captured the disenchantment, by capturing the disenchantment's imagination, fascinating it, casting a spell over it. Is it not through the power of this spell that the disenchantment comes to spell out the name of the sea, calling upon the sea so that it may tell its own story by telling the story of the sea? Is it not this spell, permeating the sea and the disenchantment, that reaches out into man's language and seizes upon the words—its elective affinity, its kin—that spell its own name and story? This spell is the magic of art, that gives to art its magic touch.

What makes sea and disenchantment own to each other makes the language of sea and disenchantment own to them and to itself. The symbol shares in the symbolized by appropriating it and being appropriated by it—by essential affinity and kinship.

But this is only half the story. It tells only how the mutual ownness of the disenchantment of this poem and the sea of this poem find the verbal form of this poem to be its very own utterance. It is therefore the story only of a particular poem, but not of poetry, and only of a poem, but not of the art work as such. The question is: What happens not just with this poem, and not just with poetry, but with art and with every art work?

Wherever there is a work of art, there is an utterance of some particular union of subject and object in their concrete being own to each other, as in our example the disenchantment and the sea are to each other. The way in which the objective matter is presented and the subjective matter expressed varies from art to art, genre to genre, work to work. Dancing is in some respects a more objective art than music, and in some respects a more subjective art than architecture. Lyric poetry is more subjective than dramatic or epical, and poetry in general is more subjective than drama, epic, or novel. Chopin is more subjective than Haydn, Keats than Dryden. Architecture makes an external world, painting represents it, music adumbrates it, poetry imagines it through meaning, drama presents it in a semblance. The self in lyrical poetry utters itself, in drama it looks silently on, in the novel it narrates. Music does not make use of the sentences of the intellect's language, literature is full of them. Music is auditory, painting visual, literature verbally imaginative. And so forth. The changes can be rung on all the different ways in which subject and object figure in the arts. But throughout the arts, and in all the works, one essential universal prevails—the reciprocal ownness, the kinship, of subjective and objective, the inner truth to each other by which they join together to form a true unity. As with "Dover Beach" so with every other work: given the means of investigating and understanding, one could discriminate the objective and subjective components in the intention-structure of the work, and in the same process bring out for awareness the way in which the two belong to one another and to the whole, and the way in which the whole finds its own utterance in the external shape, the existence of the work in the world.

El Greco's *View of Toledo,* in the Metropolitan Museum in New York City, transforms hills, buildings, river, clouds, people, and sky into an image full of mystery and foreboding, as though some awful miracle is about to happen. It is seen with an intensely passionate concern that transcends everything merely earthly, looking beyond to the infinite for the meaning of what happens in time and space. We learn to live our way into an understanding of the transcending concern by learning to see the tremendous image, and conversely. As we accomplish both at the same time, we rise to a concrete intelligence of the interior truth by which the two belong to each other. We are able to partake of this truth in imagination, because the painting itself partakes of it, in every inch of the canvas. The painting, like the poem, is able to stand for all works. Each stands for all and all for each.

What makes the work a work of art? The interior truth, which takes the outward shape as its vehicle of utterance and articulation, giving itself to it as own to its own. Art is the uttering of just the intimate belonging to one another of subject and object, an uttering which itself belongs to that belonging and is true to that truth. The artist is the medium in whom this intense appropriative process takes place, in and through whom the poetic content finds its language and the language articulates its content. Through him the spirit of the work speaks.

Art is a way of being possessed by ownness, or, as we may say, by love. The artist is the creature of love, and art is love's way of uttering itself by finding the language that belongs to it—its own beloved language. Deeper than the disenchantment and the sea, deeper than the truth that unites them in the poem, is another kind of attitude, object, and unity. For the poet, the disenchantment is not the final mood—not so long as he remains a poet. The mood of poetry itself is more profound. The disenchantment is a constituent in a poem. Other poems, other attitudes—enchantment, gaiety, terror. For the poet, again, the sea is not the final image. The poetic image is more ultimate. Other poems, other images—eagle, shipwreck, bridge, West Wind. These, too, are constituents in poems. The unity of disenchantment and sea, elation and eagle, transcending piety and miraculous mystery—these, again, are constituents in poems, unities of content that have, belonging to them, the unity of the outward shape of poem, painting, work. It is this ultimate unity of inner content and outer shape, total meaning and external vehicle, that casts its spell over the artist, making him an artist.

Here is where art becomes something real, something that exists in the world, and where the artist is at work in the world as an artist. The meaningful totality that consists in the unity of subject and object—the concreteness of full consciousness—needs to be given utterance. Indeed, it needs to find utterance in order to articulate itself. The spirit needs the world to give shape to itself by finding and shaping the world as its own kin, of which it can truly say, "That is mine and I am its." Art is the spirit's attaining to its kinship with the world.

The artist is seized by the spirit of ownness—that is, of truth, freedom, and love—in search of its own utterance. Every poem he makes, or every painting, sculpture, dance, or building, is one sound in the grand utterance. In each of them the ultimate subjectivity, the love of truth, freedom, and love, reveals itself, not by casting itself forth into the world, but by speaking its own language. The concealment by which the speaker says what belongs to him is the revelation by which he gives himself to us to have as our own. As we receive this gift, we come to our own self, giving it to him, and in that gift coming at the same time to possess it for ourselves.

6

The Poem Is Not
a Symbol

Itself
Is time, apart from any past, apart
From any future, the ever-living and being,
The ever-breathing and moving, the constant fire,

The present close, the present realized,
Not the symbol but that for which the symbol stands.[1]

Is the work of art a symbol? Is symbol a category—not to speak of *the* category—which will uncover the structure and meaning of art as art?

A symbol is something that stands for something else. For instance, the speaker in Yeats's "Sailing to Byzantium" explains that because his native land is one of youth and generation, neglecting the monuments of unaging intellect, he has

sailed the seas and come
To the holy city of Byzantium.[2]

This journey, mentioned in the title and explained in regard to its motive and significance in the body of the poem, is a symbol. It symbolizes the search for the spiritual life, making use of the historical fact that ancient Byzantium had been, as Yeats put it, the center of European civilization and the source of its spiritual philosophy.[3] The journey is but one of a whole group of symbolic images in Yeats's two Byzantium poems: birds, salmon, mackerel, seas, countries, wall mosaics, artificial birds, the Byzantine emperor, Hagia Sophia, the starlit golden bough, a ghostly mummy, dolphins, smithies, the fire dance on the Emperor's dancing floor.

The Byzantium poems cannot be read comprehendingly unless these symbols are read as the symbols they are, with the definite significance and the indefinite suggestiveness they possess. The mummy, for example, is a symbol of death that comes into life or life that dwells in death and that, by its linking of the two, is able to be the conductor of the spirit to the eternal. The dolphin is the "fish whereon souls ride to Paradise," according to an early draft.[4] Consequently the soul's ride on the dolphin's back is itself a symbol of the speaker's journey to Byzantium, and conversely, the journey is a symbol of that ride, and both the journey and the ride symbolize the invisible, unspatiotemporal translation of the spirit from the natural (the country of the young, the mackerel-crowded seas, the fury and the mire of human veins, the dolphin's mire and blood, the flood, the dolphin-torn, gong-tormented sea) to the supernatural (the holy city, the miraculous golden bird on the starlit golden bough, the artifice of eternity, Hagia Sophia, the dancing floor).

These symbols stand for something other than themselves. But does either of the poems, "Sailing to Byzantium" and "Byzantium," stand for something other than itself ? The question can be repeated for every work of art, wherever symbols occur in art. Even when the total work of art appears as a single grand symbol, as the Great Stupa at Sanchi in India, the question recurs. The function of the stupa was to enshrine a relic of the Buddha, some of his ashes, within a structure that symbolizes the total structure of the universe in the form of a cosmic diagram.[5] But does the art of this work consist in the symbolism?

Anything that exists—or even that does not exist—can function as a symbol. A tree can be a symbol—a phallic symbol, a symbol of life, a symbol of aspiration, a symbol of the god. But what of the tree itself ?

The dolphin—its name derives from the Greek *delphus,* womb—is one of the complex, highly charged symbols in the second of the Byzantium poems, "Byzantium." (It figured in the drafts of "Sailing to Byzantium" but vanished in the final version.) The dolphin, then, is a symbol. It enters into the poem. It also enters into the first sentence of this paragraph. That sentence contains the dolphin-symbol, as well as other symbols, as *e.g.,* the symbol "name" which stands for names, the symbol "poem" which stands for poems, etc. Is the sentence itself a symbol?

The sentence tells us about the dolphin being a symbol in "Byzantium." If the sentence were a symbol, then presumably what it stands for would be what it tells us. But what need is there for it to stand for what it tells us when it has already told us what it says? The dolphin in it helps the sentence to say what it says. The sentence finds the dolphin-symbol useful, because it wants to be a sentence about a symbol in a poem. But as a sentence it takes up the dolphin-symbol within itself and sweeps along in and by means of its other symbols as well in the act of doing what it is trying to do—to say something in the form of a statement, to speak declaratively.

If the sentence itself were to be a symbol, it would first have to be taken as the literal thing it is itself—the speaking declaratively about its subject-matter—so as to be able to stand for something other than what it says. A symbol first has to be something in order to be able to stand for something else. What makes the sentence a sentence is not its standing for something other than itself, but its speaking for itself, its declaring of that which it sets forth as the fact.

So it is with the poem. It has first to be the poem that it is in order for it thereupon to be able to stand for something that it is not, if indeed it stands for anything else at all. The poem also speaks—no longer, to be sure, in the shape of the prosy declarative sentence, but nevertheless in the shape of a genuine saying. "Sailing to Byzantium," for instance, describes and explains and prays and declares a fixed resolve, and it does these in a connected way, in the sequence of its four stanzas, so that the declaration emerges from the prayer, the prayer from the explanation, and the explanation from the description. The question is whether, having said all this in this way, the poem needs in addition to stand for something else, or whether, on the other hand, it is not sufficient, of its own self, in saying what it does.

Or, perhaps, having said what it says, it stands in a relationship other than that of standing for something else.

What do the Byzantium poems say?

The person who speaks in both is the same. "Byzantium" was composed in order to meet a criticism of "Sailing to Byzantium" by Sturge Moore. Moore had written to Yeats that the fourth stanza did not come up to the magnificent level of the first three. The goldsmith's bird, he had complained, "is as much nature as a man's body, especially if it only sings like Homer and Shakespeare of what is past or passing or to come to Lords and Ladies." Yeats speedily produced "Byzantium" in order, as he wrote to Moore, to give an exposition of the idea of the golden bird.[6] "Sailing to Byzantium" is spoken by the traveler who has recently arrived in Byzantium; in "Byzantium" he seems already to have settled into the mood and spiritual ambience of the holy city; his prayer to the sages has already begun to be answered—"Byzantium" is a result of their teaching, one stage of his heart's being gathered into the artifice of eternity.

The speaker is an old man—an old poet—who has sailed from his original homeland to take up final residence in Byzantium. The old homeland is no longer his own: it is no country for old men. It is a world of birth and death and of the passage from one to the other. The constant theme of its life is generation and corruption, with the emphasis on the act of reproduction—the young in one another's arms, the salmon leaping the falls, the seas crowded with mackerel. In the drafts the speaker had begun by pointing even to his God, as Christ, an infant on his mother's knees, and to the spirits of Irish folklore, his fathers' gods, as making love in the shadow of the twilit trees, hunting, at gallantries under the hills. It is the world of nature, in which everything is young and grows young day by day; but this youth is also spiritual youthfulness, i.e., that condition of spirit in which it is caught in the sensual music of nature, sick with desire, fastened to a dying animal, ignorant of what it is. Nature is the realm of becoming; the things in it are things becoming. Byzantium is the realm of the thing become.

The old homeland, from which the speaker journeys toward the new, refused itself to him just as much as he found himself alienated from it. Caught in its sensual music, its inhabitants neglect true art; at any rate, they neglect the art that he believes to be eternally valid. A type of it is Sato's gift—a changeless sword; Chaucer had not drawn breath when it was forged—which lies on the poet's table alongside his pen and paper that it may moralize his days out of their aimlessness:

> only an aching heart
> Conceives a changeless work of art.[7]

The mankind that lives in the old homeland of nature think they know the truth; they cry that his tale is told, his story sung. Their own song is a song of Plenty's horn, praise of the finite and temporal and transient and of the spawning energy that casts up and takes back again the thronging generations of nature. But the aged man, with his inexpungible memory of the furious surge of natural life, knows better that soul has to look elsewhere for its true home and its true song. An aged man, simply as the worn-out shell of the young being of nature, is a paltry thing. He has come to the end of the line; nothing remains for him to be but a scarecrow, a fraud to frighten the birds, those dying generations. Nothing, that is, in nature; but having exhausted the natural, having attained to the nothingness of the natural, he is first able to send his soul to school where it may learn to sing the true music.

> But now I travel to Byzantium
> . . . . . to unwinking wisdom's home
> The marvel of the world and gardens where
> Transfigurations of the intellect
> Can cure this aging body of defect.[8]

The paltriness of age is redeemed by the marvel of art. True art extols the eternal, makes a monument to praise the unbegotten intellect; in the singing school of eternity the unborn and undying soul and its unbegotten wisdom take the place of nature as object of reverence and praise.

Byzantium, the new land to which the speaker sails, is to be his true home. His prayer to the sages—they are not just images of saints in the wall mosaic, but eternal sages who stand in God's fire like the images in the golden mosaic—solicits them to descend from their holy height, unreeling the winding flight that leads to their heaven, to teach him the upward path and to help him rise by song to the eternal. That eternal sphere, transcending nature, contains in place of the natural body the body of the work of art. The soul that rises to eternity itself undergoes metamorphosis from being the ignorant, desire-infected soul of a dying animal to being the clairvoyant soul of a living artwork, the poet who can sing of what is past, or passing, or to come. The poet takes for his own the bodily form of the golden bird made by Grecian goldsmiths to stand on the golden bough of the golden tree to sing to the Byzantine nobles or, beside his bedside, to keep the Emperor awake. His heart has been consumed away, the ache of natural existence and experience has been lifted up into what Yeats was later to describe as the essential poetic gaiety that transfigures all dread:

> All things fall and are built again,
> And those that build them again are gay.

The poet in the artifice of eternity is like the Chinamen carved in lapis lazuli whom Yeats delights to imagine seated at the little halfway house on the mountain:

> On all the tragic scene they stare.
> One asks for mournful melodies;
> Accomplished fingers begin to play.
> Their eyes mid many wrinkles, their eyes,
> Their ancient, glittering eyes, are gay.[9]

The holy city of Byzantium is the new homeland. If in nature the soul does not know what it is, in the land of the spirit it arrives at self-knowledge. It belongs to eternity and, conversely, eternal being belongs to it. That is why it can transfigure all suffering and dread into gaiety. All the content of natural life—of what is past, or passing, or to come—has become the stuff of the song, lifted up out of time into timeless form. As the golden bird is deathless, being artificial and not organic, so too the mummy is deathless, being preserved forever in his winding cloth; and as the bird's song has the gaiety of essential poetry so the mummy's thought, the thought of him who preserves in timeless form the life that he has left behind, is sad in its gaiety and gay in its sadness:

> I have mummy truths to tell
> Whereat the living mock,

Though not for sober ear,
For maybe all that hear
Should laugh and weep an hour upon the clock.
. . . . .
Such thought, that in it bound
I need no other thing,
Wound in mind's wandering
As mummies in the mummy-cloth are wound.[10]

What "Sailing to Byzantium" says is this: I have left the old birthplace in time and come to the new home in eternity. Here is where I belong, forever. It tells what the old birthplace in time is, and why, as an aged man, I have to leave it. It pleads here in this new homeland with the native dwellers to help me to become one of them. It promises and resolves on my role here, in my true home, where I shall sing the joy that belongs to being here, raising this little monument to unaging intellect.

The poem is about where I belong and to whom I belong, what belongs to me and who belongs to me. It says: my true home is the eternal world of art and my true being the eternal (sad) gaiety of the poet. Saying this, is it a symbol of something else? Does it mean something other than it says?

"Byzantium" is replete with symbols, saying what it has to say by means of them. The traveler now dwells in Byzantium. He is out walking at night, when silence has fallen upon all the day-sounds—quarreling soldiers, robbers, harlots, gong of the cathedral bells. Lit by star or moon, the cathedral dome rises in disdain of man, his existence in nature, and ultimately of all natural existence itself. The sleep of night, brother to death, leaves behind it, by its silence, the brawls of life; the night-dominating dome, image of the dome of the heaven that gives to it the light of stars and moon, lightly soars over the complexities and brawling urgencies of human thought and desire. The dome, like the poem, is also a work of art, as is its bell whose gong, resonating, puts a coda to the din of the natural day.

The traveler treads the emperor's town, all his intricacies grown clear and sweet.[11] Images of day have given way to images of night, unpurged images to images cleansed and shriven in the light of the night-dome. First there is the mummy-image. The mummy stands twice removed from natural man; he is man who has died to nature and become a shade, a ghost; that ghost, hallowed, has thereupon become a purged image. Having left behind the moisture and breath of natural life, he breathes with no breath, speaks with a voice that is soundless, fit to articulate the clarified mystery of eternity. This mummy is the bobbin of Hades, wrapped in the windings of the mummy cloth. As the sages were petitioned to perne downward in a gyre, the winding path from heaven to earth, so the mummy may, by the winding of its vesture of eternal life (death-in-life and life-in-death), grant guidance along the upward path, unwinding from earth to heaven. For this reason the mummy is the image that floats before the dweller in Byzantium, guiding his steps along the complexities of its streets, enabling him to tread among the dark intricacies, to traverse all the town's intricacies; for, though wound in the intricate mummy cloth, it knows the winding of the path.[12] At one point Yeats had even written

Limbs that have been bound in mummy cloth
Are more content with a winding path

A mouth that has no moisture and no breath
May better summon me
To adore.[13]

The silent night-lit dome disdains the complexities and mire of natural life; the silent mummy shows the thought that illumines them and liberates from them. The golden bird, planted on the starlit golden bough, breaks the silence. The dome, a silent miracle of art, floats above the earth; the mummy, a silent mystery of spirit, floats before the walker, beckoning and summoning him to follow the winding path. The silent disdain of dome and mummy for the earthly breaks forth aloud in the glittering scorn of the artificial bird. Sharing the secrets of the birds of Hades— knowing the truth of the death of life and the life of death —this bird is the sounding miracle of the poetry of Byzantium. Made by the smithies of the Emperor, the artists of God, the golden bird sings the truth of spirit. Does it sing in symbols? It crows like the cocks of Hades; it scorns aloud

In glory of changeless metal
Common bird or petal
And all complexities of mire or blood.

Its song is the very scorn of natural life; it mocks man, bird, leaf, petal, and man's intricacy of mire and blood.[14]

Dome, mummy, bird—and now, the dancing floor. Led by the mummy to the Emperor's palace, where the golden bird has been planted on a golden bough to keep the drowsy Emperor awake or to sing to his lords and ladies of what is past, or passing, or to come, the walker has stopped at the Emperor's dancing floor. Here above all is the place to which the spirits arrived in Byzantium come to be cured of the furious complexities of life. It is through dancing on the magic pavement that they purify themselves. They are made pure by the agony of a fire-sacrifice in which they themselves are the sacrificial victims. The rite is a fire-dance, performed in the mystic flames of a fire lit by nothing material and fed by nothing material; undisturbed by anything material, its flames are born of flames, the pure fire of the spirit, in which spirits suffer as only spirits can, burning away the dross of life, falling into the trance of spirit, dying into the dance of eternity, a dance in which we cannot know the dancer from the dance.[15]

The dome disdains the complexities of natural life; the mummy unwinds the winding path of life; the golden bird scorns aloud the intricacy of the living mire; but only by the dance in which they themselves engage can the unpurged spirits leave all their blood-begotten passion.[16] Tracing out the simplicity of the intricacy of the enchanted marble, enfolding themselves in the tall flames that wind and unwind on the square, they burn away in the agony of measure the blood's imagination and blood's fury with which life had infected them.[17]

The Emperor's golden smithies, those divine artists who made the golden bird—did they not also create the dome, and design the whole holy city?—made this magic square for the saving dance. By a fiery enchantment the floor's marbles burn away the filth and mire. It is the smithies who do the Emperor's work. It is they who break the flood on which spirits, desperately clinging each to his own dolphin,[18] are carried as they tear through the sea toward the holy city. The image grows confused, complex; images overlap; the dolphins break the flood into spray as their fins torture the tide; the marble of the dancing floor breaks the flood as the crowds of spirits approach; the simplicity and integrity of the dancing floor break the bleak glittering intricacies, the aimless flood of imagery, the bright flood, the bleak complexity where images beget yet worse images ... Yeats struggled here to find the image that by its own integrity might break the intricacy of the poem's image-complex.[19] The breaking became multiple and the image of breaking a collage: the smithies breaking the flood, the marbles of the dancing floor breaking bitter furies of complexity, the dolphins breaking the sea surface. All three constituent images point toward the common content: the spiritual principle breaking the unholy body of nature, reaching an ultimate simplicity of true being through the agony of conquering the complexity of impure existence.

If Byzantium is the holy city, the dome its holy place of worship, nevertheless its holy center is the dancing floor on the Emperor's pavement, for it is finally there that the spirits are purged. Impure images burn away that element in them that makes them ever beget fresh images; the blood-blindness that causes them to beget ever blinder offspring is purged in the light of the burning flames. Spirits struggling on their dolphin-backs in the sea of life, tormented by the gong of the dome that summons them from afar, yearn to reach a goal they do not yet know to be the magic square on which they can dance out their life-fury. That dancing floor is where they belong in the end of ends. It is the hearth and sanctuary of the home of the spirit.

"Sailing to Byzantium" tells of the journey made in search of home; "Byzantium" tells of the home ultimately found.

Is the journey in search of home a symbol? Or the telling of it? Is the ultimate home and its ultimate center, the dancing floor of the spirit, a symbol, or is the telling of it such? Is the purging dance a symbol, or the telling of it? The poems use symbols to tell of the journey, the home, and the dance, and so they use symbols of journey, home, and dance. But this poetic telling—what is it?

The poems do not make the connection explicit; but may we not ourselves identify the sages of "Sailing to Byzantium" who stand in God's holy fire with those spirits of "Byzantium" who have danced into the fire to purge themselves? What purged spirit would deign to leave its flame—one thinks too, perhaps, of the mandorla that envelops a saint—except to serve as master to a needy soul, to teach it how to sing in the Emperor's castle and how to dance its way into its own flame on the dancing floor? The smithies make the bird and the flaming floor, but the speaker aspires to the singing of the bird and the dancing of the spirit.

The speaking of the poem is the singing of the bird and the dancing of the spirit. What song could the bird sing that would be better suited to keep the drowsy Emperor awake, to tell the lords and ladies of Byzantium of what is past, or passing, or to come, than the song that tells the journey of the pilgrim to Byzantium and his ultimate entry into the magic square? What dance would be better suited to purge the spirit of images than the dance of the poem that breaks its way through all the bitter fury of image-complexity to the pure insight of its own vision of the holy city? Beyond images that yet-fresh images beget, beyond symbols that breed symbols, is the dance that needs no further image or symbol, that is itself neither image nor symbol, but . . . a trance.

The symbol is an appearance that points to and stands for a reality that is not itself. The symbol of the song of the golden bird or of the dance of the fiery flame points to a reality, the trance of the enraptured soul. In a trance, the soul has made a transit. The boundary that separates it from its other has been overpassed. The veil of images, of symbols, that stood between it and reality, both disclosing and concealing, but in any case separating as well as connecting, has been pierced, broken through. "Breaking" is itself an image, as is "image." We cannot speak or sing without images; we must make use of them for the act of speaking and singing. But there can be a speech and a song, made of images, that break the whole bitter fury of complexity of image-existence.

Flame that cannot singe a sleeve is fire that does not burn. It does not reach out for material substance to transform. It has no effects, is not a cause. Its being transcends the relationship of cause and effect. It is contained within itself, by itself, in the condition of a trance. It is not the trance of mere inability to act, or of mere unconscious somnolence, but the heightened condition of agonized absorption. Like the mummy who is life-in-death and death-in-life, the dance-flaming-spirit dies into life and lives in that death. Sato's sword's moralizing knew that

> . . . only an aching heart
> Conceives a changeless work of art.

It aches because it knows the agony that must die into life to reach the shape of the sword, the tune of the bird, the winding of the dance. Agony is struggle as well as anguish. The agony of dying into a dance is the struggle against images. Images beget images, symbols beget symbols; the soul engaged with them is stranded in the midst of a dangerous sea. Tormented by the gong that sounds from the holy dome, astride the dolphin that can eventually bring it to the holy city, it suffers still from the bitter fury of the images of its life. Even the dolphin that is its sole vessel to safety may appear to it in its primal form, as the womb into which it must delve in the act of generating fresh images. The dolphin is a potent image: it leads back, in this one way, to the fury of living complexity, but it leads forward to the passage into Byzantium. In the former role, it is an image that multiplies images; in the latter, it is the image that conducts to the land where images are broken, the iconoclastic land.

The causal thinking of the genetic psychologist says: the dolphin as the fish whereon souls ride to paradise is only a sublimated form, a symbol of, a cover for, the dolphin as the real thing—the womb, riding on which is real ecstasy. It says: the poet seizes upon the image of the dolphin and the passage to Byzantium to give scope to what otherwise he is forced to hide: the womb, the sexual ride, the sexual ecstasy. The genetic psychologist can make much of all the images: the stick on which the old man is a tattered coat, the golden bird that crows like a cock, the dome and its gong that succeed the prostitute and her song, the stiff mummy that can unwind the winding path, the entranced dance in the fiery flame.

So long as these symbols are what he declares them to be, they are figures in the nightmarish agony that the poems describe as the bitter fury of complexity, the tortured tide, the blood-begotten passion, man's intricacy of mire and blood. They are then symbols, genuine symbols, of realities that belong to the mire and the blood. The whole poem becomes nothing more than an intricacy of images that stir the blood and stir up the mire. The crow of the cock is a mere liquid sputter, an ecstasy of transient energy, a trance-absorption that loses all meaning in the act because all the meaning it has produced has been ultimately only for the sake of the act.

The genetic psychologist has never yet understood the poem. He has not read it as a poem but as a symbol.

It is truer to say that the sexual relation symbolizes the poetic relation than that the latter symbolizes the former. Sexual unity is symbolic of the unity that the spirit seeks, that unity in which soul finds the other that is its own, which belongs to it and to which it belongs, to which it can say and hear in response: I am thine and thou art mine. The moment of the young in one another's arms fore-shadows this unity; but it does not last, it has no eternity in it, it leads only to the generation of new young to be in one another's arms. That, to be sure, is no small thing but a great one. The poet does not forget it. By 1940 the war had already flared and Thomas Mann had written: "In our time the destiny of man presents its meaning in political terms." To which Yeats appended this small, comical, and poignant note:

> How can I, that girl standing there,
> My attention fix
> On Roman or on Russian
> Or on Spanish politics?
> Yet here's a travelled man that knows
> What he talks about,
> And there's a politician

That has read and thought,
And maybe what they say is true
Of war and war's alarms,
But O that I were young again
And held her in my arms![20]

The poem is a sublimation of the sexual relation in the precise sense that it elevates what lies below. It raises to the height of sublimity the nethermost energies of existence. It lifts up the images that belong to the complexity of life into a unity in which they belong to one another forever, simple in their intricacy, purged—like the spirit enfolded in the flame of its dance—of all need to reproduce images. Nothing follows, nothing is to be inferred, nothing further is pointed to.

The height at which the poem soars is described by another modern poet, Wallace Stevens, in a poem about modern poetry, which is "the poem of the mind in the act of finding what will suffice. (It has not always had to find: the scene was set; it repeated what was in the script.)" The poetic actor, it says, is

A metaphysician in the dark, twanging
An instrument, twanging a wiry string that gives
Sounds passing through sudden rightnesses, wholly
Containing the mind, below which it cannot descend,
Beyond which it has no will to rise.[21]

The height is the plane of the right—the sudden rightness that every true artist knows about and seeks in the agony of the creative struggle to reach. It happens where every sound and every image gives itself over to every other sound and image for its safekeeping, and where the mind gives itself over to the whole and takes the whole for itself for their mutual safekeeping.

> How high that highest candle lights the dark.
>
> Out of this same light, out of the central mind,
> We make a dwelling in the evening air,
> In which being there together is enough.[22]

The height is the singing-place of the sound

> That clings to the mind like that right sound, that song
> Of the assassin that remains and sings
> In the high imagination triumphantly.[23]

What is, is the ground out of which grows the aspiration to attain to the clarity, simplicity, and sudden rightness of the poetic act of the mind. When these are reached, as in the actual poetry of "Sailing to Byzantium" and "Byzantium," the spirit itself reaches the stage in which it can make with its other

> . . . a dwelling in the evening air
> In which being there together is enough.

The act of finding what will suffice is the act of finding what is enough: the sudden rightness with which the mind dwells, in which being there together is enough.

As the poem says what it says, it speaks with the accent of that sudden rightness, with a sound that clings to the mind like the song of the assassin, triumphant in the high imagination. The dolphin, the golden bird, the mummy, the dome, the night-walker, the Emperor and his court, the smithies—all were needed, sublimed, to speak with

that sound. The symbols sound and resound in the rightness which does not symbolize but which *is* the belonging
together of all the images and all the sounds and of all with
the mind and the mind with all, in which the mind sees
what it has all along looked for, and is content.

After long silence, two aged lovers sit together again,
in a room at night darkly illumined by a lamp:

> Speech after long silence; it is right,
> All other lovers being estranged or dead,
> Unfriendly lamplight hid under its shade,
> The curtains drawn upon unfriendly night,
> That we descant and yet again descant
> Upon the supreme theme of Art and Song:
> Bodily decrepitude is wisdom; young
> We loved each other and were ignorant.[24]

The poem is not a symbol. It is the speaking of an
agony, the agony of the trance of the being there together
which is enough.

7

The Poem Is a Symbol

In the end, works of art are the only media of complete and unhindered communication between man and man that can occur in a world full of gulfs and walls that limit community of experience.—John Dewey.[1]

Every symbol opens up a level of reality for which non-symbolic speaking is inadequate . . . The more we try to enter into the meaning of symbols, the more we become aware that it is a function of art to open up levels of reality . . . Now if this is the function of art, then certainly artistic creations have symbolic character.—Paul Tillich.[2]

. . . at our end begins our endlesse rest.—John Donne.[3]

A symbol is something that stands for something else; like a sign, it points beyond itself to something else. If that were all that a symbol was, however, then we could not say that a work of art—a poem, for instance—is a symbol; for a poem does not merely point beyond itself to something else for which it is supposed to stand. A poem *is* something on its own account. To be sure, it opens up a level of reality for which non-poetic speaking is inadequate; to be sure, it is a medium of complete and unhindered communication between man and man, almost unique in a world full of gulfs and walls; but it opens up a level of reality and serves as a medium of communication only in and by its very being, and not just by the act of standing for or pointing toward.

Tillich tried to make the proper distinction by differentiating the symbol from the sign. Both symbol and sign, he said, point beyond themselves to something else. For instance, the red traffic light at the street corner, which is a sign, points beyond itself to the necessity of cars stopping; the nation's flag, which is a symbol, points beyond itself to the nation for which it stands. In this reference beyond themselves the sign and symbol agree. Their difference lies rather in the manner in which reference takes place. The symbol participates in the reality, meaning, and power of that to which it points, whereas the sign lacks any such participation. The sign is external to what it signifies, whereas what is symbolized is somehow present and embodied in the symbol. A flag participates in the reality, the meaning, and the power of its nation; hence our attitude toward it is quite different from our attitude toward a mere sign—we respond to the flag with the respect and awe due to the nation as such, because the nation's being is present in and revealed by the flag.

Dewey similarly tried to make the proper distinction by differentiating between expressive symbols and nonexpressive symbols. Signs, such as signboards or signs in mathematics, as also symbols like those used in mathematics, represent things by standing for them; their meaning consists in a purely external reference; they are nonexpressive. But in an expressive object, the meaning presents itself directly as possessed by that object. For example, flags can function in both ways. When used to signal another ship, they are used as signs or as conventional symbols, elements of a code, and then their meaning is that of a purely external, nonexpressive reference. But they can also function to decorate the deck of a ship for a dance. They then have a meaning also, but it does not consist in a merely external reference; they express the festivity, the spirit of joy, relaxation, gaiety, and conviviality belonging to such a party. These expressive contents are present directly as meaning in the flags themselves; the flags clarify and concentrate such meanings which are contained in less concentrated ways in other experiences, and—unlike scientific statement, which simply states its meaning—they express their meaning, they literally constitute the experience they mean.

It was because symbols participate in the being of what they symbolize that Tillich thought they were able to open up levels of reality otherwise ineffable; and likewise, it was because symbols possess their meaning in themselves that Dewey thought they were able to constitute experiences and to serve as media of full communication. Although "participation in the being of the symbolized" and "expression" are perhaps not exactly synonymous expressions, they are close enough together to make clear that both men were thinking along directions that have much in common. And if I did not believe that these directions, and what is common to them, point toward something fundamentally and radically true about art, I would not bring them together here in pursuit of the thought about the poem as a symbol.

If a poem—let us take the poem as a symbol of art in general—is a symbol, then it has to be so not by being a merely externally referring sign but by participating in the being of what it symbolizes, by having or being what it means. Now if a flag is also a symbol in this sense, it too will symbolize by participating in, having, being, what it symbolizes. Yet the flag and the poem are different. A flag is not—ordinarily, at any rate—an art work; a poem is *par excellence* an art work. So, if both flag and poem symbolize by participation, having, or being, it must be the case that *what* they participate in, have, or are is different. The flag symbolizes the nation, the group, the flag-owner; but what does the poem symbolize?

By this is meant: What does it symbolize as a *poem?* For, to be sure, the poem could symbolize the nation too, as happens in the national anthem. But not every poem is a national anthem; and it is not simply in virtue of its being a poem that the national anthem symbolizes the nation. We are concerned here with the poem as poem, the universal quality of poetry, so far as there is something universal in poetry.

Let us take our start from a poet's statement of this universal.

> What we call the beginning is often the end
> And to make an end is to make a beginning.
> The end is where we start from. And every phrase
> And sentence that is right (where every word is at home,
> Taking its place to support the others,
> The word neither diffident nor ostentatious,
> An easy commerce of the old and the new,
> The common word exact without vulgarity,
> The formal word precise but not pedantic,
> The complete consort dancing together)
> Every phrase and every sentence is an end and a
> beginning,
> Every poem an epitaph.

This passage is from "Little Gidding," the last of the *Four Quartets* by T. S. Eliot.[4] In a poem on the subject of poetry in wartime Eliot had written:

> . . . . . .
> Where is the point at which the merely individual
> Explosion breaks
>
> In the path of an action merely typical
> To create the universal, originate a symbol
> Out of the impact? this is a meeting
> On which we attend
>
> Of forces beyond control by experiment:
> Of Nature and the Spirit.[5]

A poem is a symbol, originated out of the impact of the forces of nature and spirit; in it, a merely individual explosion breaks in the path of a merely typical action to create the universal, the poem which is a symbol. As a symbol, it points to something beyond itself, which yet it embodies within itself, in which it participates, being itself what it points to beyond itself. This is true of every poem that is right: each is an end and a beginning, each is an epitaph.

What does it mean to say that every right poem is an epitaph? How can it make any reasonable sense to say, not just that poems inscribed on graves or tombs or monuments are epitaphs, but that all poems, insofar as they are right poems, are epitaphs? Pope's lines intended for Newton

> Nature and Nature's laws lay hid in night:
> God said, "Let Newton be!" and all was light

may be admitted as an epitaph; but surely we cannot also admit as one the epigram on epitaphs

> Freind,[6] for your Epitaphs I'm grieved,
> Where still so much is said,
> One half will never be believed,
> The other never read.

or the inscription "on the collar of a dog which I gave to His Royal Highness"

> I am his Highness' dog at Kew;
> Pray tell me, sir, whose dog are you?

You might say, these may perhaps be poems, but they are not right poems, they do not give those sounds passing through sudden rightnesses that emanate from the wiry string twanged by the metaphysician in the dark. But that would, I think, be an error. Pope may not have been a deep poet, a sublime poet, even a great poet, but he was a correct poet and more than correct, a poet with the undeniable gift of a highly sensitive taste and precise judgment. These verses, all of them, have the ring, are in tune, strike a lively accord: in them, the complete consort —modest as it is—dances together. If every right poem is an epitaph, then not only the first, but all three are epitaphs.

How so?

The poet wrote:

> And every phrase
> And sentence that is right. . . .

Every phrase and every sentence is an end and a beginning,
Every poem an epitaph.

Epitaph is imagined by him in apposition to *an end and a beginning.* An epitaph is an end and a beginning. How can an epitaph be an end and a beginning? By being a symbol of end and beginning, namely, by being the symbolic articulation of an end and a beginning, so that as a symbol it itself participates in and possesses as its own meaning the being of end-and-beginning. And is that not just what an epitaph—a genuine epitaph, and a right one—is?

An epitaph is an inscription upon a tomb, or grave, or monument, commemorating, epitomizing, passing final judgment upon the deceased. It is a symbol of the end of a man's life, and as a symbol—if it is a true and living symbol—it participates in that end. That is why it stands there, fixed upon the enduring stone of the tomb or the monument. It adorns the man's last earthly home, the home of his body's end. It calls the dweller to remembrance, keeping fresh the memory of his past life, serving as the perpetual ceremony of the daily anniversary. It commends him to us, giving in charge to us the memory of that past life as our trust to preserve. Epitomizing the life, it gives to it an ideal expression and embodiment in words. Judging it, it tries it and utters upon it a determining decision.

But: "to make an end is to make a beginning." Traditional faith thinks of the end as a beginning, the end of earthly life as a beginning of spiritual life. It imagines the soul departing from the dead body, leaving it behind on earth, and setting out for another embodiment and another habitation, inferno, purgatory, or heaven. The epitaph sends the soul on its way, ordinarily with an expression of hope that it will arrive safely at last.

> Even such is Time, which takes in trust
> Our youth, our joys, and all we have,
> And pays us but with age and dust;
> Who in the dark and silent grave,
> When we have wandered all our ways,
> Shuts up the story of our days:
> And from which earth, and grave, and dust,
> The Lord shall raise me up, I trust.[7]

The epitaph turns from time, the earth, the grave, and the dust to another region, the world above, to which it trusts the soul shall be raised. The epitaph is thus a mediating word: it stands between earth and heaven, time and eternity, the dark and silent grave and the bright and still mansion of the spirit, and it symbolizes both at once at the point of transition. The epitaph itself belongs to the earth and the grave; that is where it lies. But at the same time it belongs to the heaven, the eternal; for its meaning points ultimately there, and it participates in what it means. It is an expression of heaven, upon earth; and therefore it is, in its own symbolic way, heaven, upon earth.

The epitaph is the symbol of death and rebirth. Recalling the old life that belongs to time and the dark, it points to the new life of the ever-present moment and the light:

> Time past and time future
> What might have been and what has been
> Point to one end, which is always present.
> . . . . .
> At the still point of the turning world. . . .
> . . . . After the kingfisher's wing

> Has answered light to light, and is silent, the light is still
> At the still point of the turning world.[8]

As symbol of death and rebirth, the old life and the new, the epitaph participates in both of them—the right epitaph, that is. As words, as music, it moves in time; but as right, as true poetry, it reaches the stillness of the still point:

> Words move, music moves
> Only in time; but that which is only living
> Can only die. Words, after speech, reach
> Into the silence. Only by the form, the pattern,
> Can words or music reach
> The stillness, as a Chinese jar still
> Moves perpetually in its stillness.[9]

It is not because the epitaph is called one—*epi* + *taphos,* upon a tomb—that it reaches from the death of the tomb to the life of the still point; not every set of words that is inscribed upon the gravestone will rise up, reaching beyond the silence to the stillness. The form, the pattern, is needed. The burden is great and the words need the strength of form, the logic of the *logos,* the power to resist all the assailing forces, the temptations of earthly attachments:

> . . . . Words strain,
> Crack and sometimes break, under the burden,
> Under the tension, slip, slide, perish,
> Decay with imprecision, will not stay in place,
> Will not stay still. Shrieking voices
> Scolding, mocking, or merely chattering,
> Always assail them. The Word in the desert
> Is most attacked by voices of temptation,
> The crying shadow in the funeral dance,
> The loud lament of the disconsolate chimera.[10]

If the epitaph is to do its work, then, it must have the form, the pattern that belongs to a right epitaph. What is this form, this pattern? What makes an epitaph a right epitaph? Since an epitaph is at once an end and a beginning, its rightness is that which confers upon it this two-fold oneness. So our question becomes: "What enables an epitaph to be at once a beginning and an end?" And this question immediately calls upon us to say what a beginning and what an end is, for how shall we be able to say what enables an epitaph to be both at once if we do not know what either is?

Let us begin with the beginning. What is the beginning? Where is it found?

Home is where one starts from . . .[11]

We start from where we are, where we have been born, brought into the world, put in place, and have dwelt. Home is where we first find our lot, the portion of earth set aside for us as our allotment. The beginning of earthly life is in the earthly home, that region in which we first find our self in finding what belongs to us and what we belong to. We find our own body first there, with its features, its size, its powers; we find our parents, our brothers and sisters, friends and enemies, family and strangers, countrymen and aliens; we find our village, rivers, woods, and sky, the school to which we go, the field or factory in which we work. Finding all these, those that are ours as over against those that are not, we find at the same time and in the same act our own self, and are given the opportunity to grow into and take possession of that self. Here we first begin to find our identity, the name and meaning

by which our own self is denoted and constituted.
  But

> ... As we grow older
> The world becomes stranger, the pattern more complicated
> Of dead and living ...[12]

As the world becomes stranger, it becomes less and less
our home. What is strange is extraneous—outside, external, foreign. Where we were once set in place is now less
and less our place; we are losing our place, finding ourself
in another place, an alien land. The beginning begins to
show itself as the beginning of the end. The earthly home,
as the birthplace of life, shows itself to be the beginning
of the graveyard of death.

> In my beginning is my end. In succession
> Houses rise and fall, crumble, are extended,
> Are removed, destroyed, restored, or in their place
> Is an open field, or a factory, or a by-pass.
> . . . . .
> Houses live and die ...[13]

The house is the home; the home lives and dies. When you
return to your birthplace after a long stay in the world you
discover that the house in which you were born and in
which you lived as your childhood home has long given
way to a factory or a highway. Your beginning in space has
been buried there just as irretrievably as your beginning
in time has been buried in the past. Homes vanish.

> The houses are all gone under the sea.

Men vanish.

> The dancers are all gone under the hill.[14]

But

> In my end is my beginning.[15]

Home is where *I* dwell, not where the stranger dwells. Home is where *I* am, where the things are that *I* own, the people are with whom *I* am kin. The beginning of me, of the I who is truly I, comes only with the end of the I who is estranged from his own. The estrangement is necessary. Only through estrangement from what is strange to me can I arrive at what is own to me.

>   ... In order to arrive there,
> To arrive where you are, to get from where you are not,
>   You must go by a way wherein there is no ecstasy.
> In order to arrive at what you do not know
>   You must go by a way which is the way of ignorance.
> In order to possess what you do not possess
>   You must go by the way of dispossession.
> In order to arrive at what you are not
>   You must go through the way in which you are not.
> And what you do not know is the only thing you know
> And what you own is what you do not own
> And where you are is where you are not.[16]

Only when I find my true home do I find the place where I first find my true self, my self that is truly I. Home is where one starts from, to be sure, and therefore the true home, which I find at the end, is exactly where I begin and is my beginning. In my end is my beginning.

My end is not just where I finally arrive. My end is what I arrive at as something final. Where a process terminates, it ends; but its end, if it has an end, is its goal, the purpose which it had at the very beginning, to reach which is its own termination, in which what, for it, should be, is. The ought belonging to it, making it what it is, its own ought, is realized. The ought of my life, of which I was at the beginning ignorant, and which I did not possess, which I was not, which I did not know, which I did not own, and where I was not—if, in the end, I come to know this ought, possess it, be it, own it, be where it is, then in my end I arrive first at my true beginning, the being in which the essential intention that constitutes me comes out into actuality and is real.

What is this essential intention, the inner impulse and aim that from the very beginning of my life is in and with me and constitutes my essential nature, of which I am at first ignorant and which at first I have not yet appropriated as mine? How shall I know it, own it, be it?

Where is there an end of me? of my world, of my existence?

> Where is there an end of it, the soundless wailing,
> The silent withering of autumn flowers
> Dropping their petals and remaining motionless;
> Where is there an end to the drifting wreckage,
> The prayer of the bone on the beach, the unprayable
> Prayer at the calamitous annunciation?[17]

There is no end in and of time, merely as such. There is merely addition, the final addition of the moments or the years of the temporally finite being.

> Where is the end of them, the fishermen sailing
> Into the wind's tail, where the fog cowers?

Their temporal end is like ours and like that of everything temporal:

> ... the final addition, the failing
> Pride or resentment at failing powers,
> .....
> The silent listening to the undeniable
> Clamor of the bell of the last annunciation.[18]

The last annunciation is the announcement made by the bell that tells of the coming of death, the bell clanged by

> ... the ground swell, that is and was from the beginning,[19]

the ground swell which, unhurried, rings the tolling bell, under the oppression of the silent fog, which measures time not our time. Death's time is older than the time of chronometers or of anxious women trying to unravel and piece together past and future. The God to which the bone on the beach is a prayer is death.

There is only one end that is not mere addition, mere failure of power, mere death. It is the one end which is always present, the still point of the turning world, the place of the dance which is neither arrest nor movement.[20]

As the axis of the turning earth points to the pole star, the still star of the heavens, the seamark of the sky to lay a course by, so the axis of turning time points to the timeless; and like a symbol, it may participate in what it points to. This participation is the Incarnation of the timeless in time. I am a being in time; my home must be in time. I am a being who, in time, turns with the turning world. My being, too, has its axis, the same axis as that of the turning world. It points to the timeless, too, the sea-

mark of my being. Like a symbol, I too may participate in
that to which my own being points.

I am no saint

> ... to apprehend
> The point of intersection of the timeless
> With time, is an occupation for the saint—
> No occupation, either, but something given
> And taken, in a lifetime's death in love,
> Ardor and selflessness and self-surrender.[21]

For most of us the apprehension of the Incarnation of the
timeless in time can be only momentary, experienced in
hint followed by guess, the brief flashing moment of the
impossible union of spheres of existence which yet
becomes actual—

> the unattended
> Moment, the moment in and out of time,
> The distraction fit, lost in a shaft of sunlight,
> ..... music heard so deeply
> That it is not heard at all, but you are the music
> While the music lasts.[22]

The end that belongs to the finite human being is the
state and condition of participation in the Incarnation.
This is the end that is always present with us in the core
of our being, ever present because eternity is ever present
with time. Our birth is a being given over to time, to be,
and so to be born with the dead; our fundamental need is
to be redeemed from that same time, to depart with the
dying toward the end that is our home. Home is where we
started from, and home is where our end is.

> We shall not cease from exploration
> And the end of all our exploring
> Will be to arrive where we started
> And know the place for the first time.[23]

Redemption from time is not being taken out of time, with time left behind. We could not, as humans, bear eternity; it would destroy us. We need, not to be God, not to be in pure eternity, but, being in time, to be redeemed from time by the Incarnation of eternity in time. In our flesh, the changing body, the very enchainment of past and future protects us from heaven—and damnation.[24] Redemption from time is revolving around our axis, as the turning world revolves about its axis, but all the while pointing toward the unmoving star that moves the world.

> Only through time time is conquered.[25]

What is it that, at the still point of our turning being, we point toward? What is the timeless, eternal, that is the object of our pointing, giving point to our being? It is not anything moving. Nothing moving could be the unmoved point toward which being points. It is Love

> . . . itself unmoving,
> Only the cause and end of movement.[26]

Our beginning was in love, our ending is in love, love is the beginning and end, the timeless, whose touch makes the moment of redemption a timeless moment *in* place and time, "now and in England." To be in time, revolving in the movement of our world, and pointing with the axis of our being toward love—this is our human end, which was with us from the beginning, unknown, unpossessed, unowned, unlived, but yearning to come out of its hidden- ness into the light—yearning because drawn by love and called by its voice

> With the drawing of this Love and the voice of this
> Calling.[27]

To the question "What is a beginning, and what is an end, and what is it that can be at once a beginning and an end?" we may now answer: every beginning is in love, every ending is in love, and to be at once a beginning and an ending is to be a participant in love, an incarnation of it or a symbol of it. Love, which begins all and ends all, is itself beyond beginnings and endings; but the things of time, which have beginnings and endings, may find their beginning in their ending and their ending in their begin- ning if, while remaining in time, in the world-revolution, nevertheless the axis of their being, pointing through the still point of their turning, points toward and participates in the unbeginning and unending Love.

The being of the finite being, insofar as he reaches the point of the unity of his being and ending, is the being of . . . a prayer. Little Gidding is an Anglican chapel, de- stroyed in the civil war of the seventeenth century, rebuilt in the nineteenth century, visited by the poet during the Second World War. It could be visited in the dead of winter, or in springtime or summer, at noon or at night; but whenever visited, by whatever route, there would al- ways be the same truth to realize:

> you would have to put off
> Sense and notion. You are not here to verify,
> Instruct yourself, or inform curiosity

> Or carry report. You are here to kneel
> Where prayer has been valid.[28]

Here is England, and an Anglican chapel, where prayer has been valid. But here is everywhere and nowhere; it is Madras, too, or Moscow, or Boston, in a bazaar, a street, a museum. Whatever you are, you are there to kneel—standing, sitting, reclining—there where prayer has been, is, and always shall be valid.

> ... prayer is more
> Than an order of words, the conscious occupation
> Of the praying mind, or the sound of the voice praying.[29]

Prayer is the condition of being at the intersection of the timeless moment, at the still point of the turning world, giving oneself over to the drawing of this Love and responding to the voice of this Calling. This is the validity of temporal being, by which its temporality is elevated—"*Erhebung* without motion"—into the moment that, by its pointing toward Love the timeless, participates in the ever-present end.

We have now to return to the poem which, when it is right, is an epitaph; a symbol of end and beginning which itself participates in what it means and is consequently an end and a beginning, in whose end is its beginning and in whose beginning is its end; words which by the form, the pattern, reach the stillness of the still point of the turning world; words which symbolize the Incarnation by being an incarnation, mediating between time and eternity by the power of the logos; words turning on the axis of time which points to the timeless; redeemed words redeeming their time; words which, like a sea-bell, toll the annunciation of the love that brings end and beginning together into wholeness; words that are valid prayer.

What is the form, the pattern, the power of the logos by which the poem becomes this epitaph?

It is the form that belongs to being whose every part is an end and a beginning, namely, being which is itself the union of end and beginning.

The image which the poet uses to tell of this form is that of the dance. This image is closely akin to the dance image of Yeats's "Byzantium." The stranger whom the poet met in "Little Gidding(II)"—scrutinizing whom he

> ... caught the sudden look of some dead master
> Whom I had known, forgotten, half recalled
> Both one and many; in the brown baked features
> The eyes of a familiar compound ghost
> Both intimate and unidentifiable—[30]

this stranger, himself a master poet, as a compound ghost, is several poets, Heraclitus and Dante perhaps as much as any others. But he is also Yeats. With Heraclitus and Dante, as with every true and great poet, Yeats shared the concern with speech, and speech impelled them to purify the dialect of the tribe and to urge the mind to aftersight and foresight.[31] Yeats therefore also practiced the symbolic speech by which the truth of being is brought by participation into the verbal form.

The symbol of the dance in "Byzantium" is of the fire dance of the spirits on the Emperor's dancing floor, in which the complexities of fury of the blood-begotten spirits are burned away. Our poet meets the stranger

> In the uncertain hour before the morning
> Near the ending of interminable night
> At the recurrent end of the unending

. . . . .
> Over the asphalt where no other sound was
>> Between three districts whence the smoke arose[32]

. . . . .

The speaker of "Byzantium" was abroad during the silent night; he saw the fire dance at midnight. Let us then allow him to meet the speaker of "Little Gidding" in the hour mentioned. It will do no harm. The later poet receives the wisdom of the earlier:

> From wrong to wrong the exasperated spirit
>> Proceeds, unless restored by that refining fire
>> Where you must move in measure, like a dancer.[33]

But to be restored, our sickness must first grow worse; there is another fire, before the fire of the dance, through which we must pass:

> The chill ascends from feet to knees,*
> The fever sings in mental wires.
> If to be warmed, then I must freeze
> And quake in frigid purgatorial fires
> Of which the flame is roses, and the smoke is briars.[34]

The fire of the fire dance is purged of the smoke of briars; the exasperated spirit shall be purged and restored

> And all shall be well and
> All manner of things shall be well
> When the tongues of flame are in-folded
> Into the crowned knot of fire
> And the fire and the rose are one.[35]

---

*We remember the effect of the hemlock on Socrates who at that very moment requested his friends to make sure that Asclepius, the god of healing, receive his due sacrifice, a cock.

The refining fire of the fire dance is not the tormenting fire of the inferno, nor is it the purgative fire of purgatory; it is the saving fire of paradise, long lost and now found again, from which the diseased spirit has long ago been driven as from its forfeited home and to which now, in this moment, it suddenly finds itself restored—in this moment when, at the end of all its exploring, it has arrived where it started and knows the place for the first time.[36]

The condition of being of the spirit of the fire dance is one of complete simplicity—costing not less than everything.[37] It is nevertheless the complete simplicity of the complex movement of the dance, where the spirit must move in measure, the measure of the dance. We encounter here what seems at first a paradox but is in truth more profoundly true than any paradox, being an utterly simple truth, a single truth that embraces all the complexity without losing its simplicity. For the dance is danced at the still point of the turning world. The dancer is neither flesh nor fleshless; he moves neither from nor toward; his act is neither arrest nor movement; nor is it fixity either. It is not movement from nor towards; it is not an ascent nor a decline. It is the dance at the still point, where action reaches the truth of all movement, hence is *Erhebung* without motion. The reference is precise—to the Hegelian notion of the sublation of the finite in the infinite, the conflicting elements of an antithesis—motion and rest—in a synthesis that, while it transcends them, contains and preserves them in their true being.[38] The poet spells out the meaning: concentration without elimination,

> . . . both a new world
> And the old made explicit, understood

> In the completion of its partial ecstasy,
> The resolution of its partial horror.[39]

Deeper than the mere paradox of the existing together in one tensed stretch of flesh and spirit, movement and arrest, past and future, old and new, undergoing and acting, is the unity of the still point, the *Erhebung* in which the new world is the old made explicit, the spirit the flesh raised up, the arrest the movement perfected, the present the redemption of past and future. It is the unity of release from tension not by the subsiding of tension but by bringing the tensed forces into reconcilement—the unity of the reconciliation of opposites. It is an inner freedom from practical desire in which the power and force of desire have been preserved and raised up, a release from action and suffering (the inner and the outer compulsion) in which the power and force of action and suffering have been preserved and raised up.

> Garlic and sapphires in the mud
> Clot the bedded axle-tree.[40]

In the earthly life opposites exist with their full ambiguities. Garlic—precious herb and offensive smell; sapphire—precious jewel, cold and hard; and the two, in the earthly mud, clotting the bedded axle-tree, the circling world that carries us across the earth through its mud, at whose center too there is the still point of the turning world, neither arrest nor movement.

> The trilling wire in the blood
> Sings below inveterate scars
> And reconciles forgotten wars.[41]

That trilling wire is the "wiry string that gives sounds passing through sudden rightnesses, wholly containing the mind," the wire of the "metaphysician in the dark, twanging an instrument," twanging just this wiry string, in the dark of the blood, hidden below inveterate scars. The harmony of the trill, the power of harmony of the trilling wire, is what reconciles forgotten wars. Like a white light, still and moving, we move in the fire dance.

> ... above the moving tree
> In light upon the figured leaf
> And hear upon the sodden floor
> Below, the boarhound and the boar
> Pursue their pattern as before
> But reconciled among the stars.[42]

We, who were before the boarhound and the boar, fighting our forgotten wars, in this dance of light upon the figured leaf, remember the hunt and, looking up, see and hear its starry reconciliation, and are ourselves reconciled. We are not among the stars ourselves—mankind has to be protected from heaven—but in the space between heaven and earth we move and do not move, taking our stance on the world's axis, at the still point of its turning. Our deepest-lying impulses, by which we hunt the hunted and are hunted by the hunter, the deepest of desires and disgusts, fears and hopes, are not thrown away but purged of their dross, raised in their truth to the light dance in the space between earth and heaven. This dance finds its counterpart in two other dances, one earthly and the other heavenly:

> The dance along the artery
> The circulation of the lymph

> Are figured in the drift of stars
> Ascend to summer in the tree.[43]

The drift of stars is the turning of the heaven upon its own axis, around its still point; the dance along the artery, the circulation of the lymph, the rising of the tree's sap of life, are the turning of earthly things about their own axes, their own still points. We, who move above the moving tree and below the drifting stars, now move in the movement that belongs most truly to ourselves, participating in the movement of the universe by moving about our still point, the still point of our turning world.

The detail of the pattern is movement. In the aspect of time, man is caught in the form of limitation between un-being and being.[44] Unlike love, which is itself unmoving and only the cause and end of movement, man exists in the form of desire, that is, of love as it is caught in the form of limitation in time. It is in time that words move, music moves, the body moves, the dance can be danced. Yet if the words, the music, the body, and the dance were to remain in time and in motion, nothing would be saved. Time has to be conquered within itself if it is to be redeemed. Movement has to be conquered by a movement that, arresting itself, is nevertheless no arrest, for it has also to be movement: a movement that is no movement, an arrest that is no arrest, being out of movement in movement, out of time in time.

> ... Words strain,
> Crack and sometimes break, under the burden.[45]

The poet describes this act of the overcoming of time by the image of two ways, that of the saint and that of the dancer, i.e., the artist. The saint follows the way of descent

into the world of perpetual solitude, namely, the world of
complete surrender of the ego and even of the spirit itself:

> World not world, but that which is not world,
> Internal darkness, deprivation
> And destitution of all property,
> Desiccation of the world of sense,
> Evacuation of the world of fancy,
> Inoperancy of the world of spirit.

This is the way of darkness, to purify the soul,

> Emptying the sensual with deprivation
> Cleansing affection from the temporal.
> Neither plenitude nor vacancy.[46]

The saint moves out of the twittering world of everyday
life with its distraction from distraction by distraction into
the solitary world-no-world.

The second way, the way of light, and therefore a way
which makes use of sense, fancy, and spirit, is the way of
the artist—the poet, the maker of the Chinese jar, the
player of the violin, and in general, the dancer. This second way is, in essence, the same as the first:

> ... not in movement
> But abstention from movement,[47]

away from a world that moves by appetency

> ... on its metalled ways
> Of time past and time future.[48]

> ... the darkness shall be the light, and the stillness
> the dancing.[49]

It is the way of daylight, which invests form with lucid stillness, which turns shadow into transient beauty,

With slow rotation suggesting permanence.[50]

The form, the pattern, of the movement which conquers movement is the symbolic movement, movement as symbol of the motionless, that is, the slow rotation that symbolizes permanence. Rotation is the circling about of beginning into ending and ending into beginning. Abstention from movement which is not in movement can happen only by entering into the slow rotation, the movement that symbolizes eternity. As the rose-window wheels round its eternal center, the symbol of love, so the fire dance wheels round its still point, symbolizing love and doing so only by the power of participation in love.

Is the time, not our time, that is measured by the tolling bell of the buoy which is rung by the unhurried ground swell, such a time as conquers time in time? Is the ground swell, that is and was from the beginning, and that clangs the bell, such a slow-moving time as, by its eternal recurrence, lives the symbolic form of eternity—the tireless, resistless dance of the sea, the water first above the level of earth, under the influence of the moon's gravity? Is the grating roar of the surf's pebbles, beginning and ending and then beginning again, with tremulous cadence slow, bringing the eternal note of sadness in, which Sophocles heard long ago on the Aegean and which Arnold heard again just yesterday—is this roar, this one of the many voices of the sea, a symbolic annunciation of the eternity of love?

Reflection on it taught the one poet that the way of

redemption is truth to one another. What has it taught the other?

Our poet of the poetic symbol also has a vision of truth. It is of a wisdom that runs counter to the useless wisdom of the knowledge derived from experience, the useless wisdom of old men. Experience imposes its own pattern of ever-recurrent novelty, every moment a new and shocking valuation of the past; it is the pattern of time before and after, ridiculous by itself in its wasteness. So long as we think to find wisdom merely in experience we shall be burdened with receipts for deceit, formulae by which desire calculates the future, counting the time by the chronometer. Old men, rich in years and in the knowledge that time brings, are rich in folly—they fear fear and frenzy, they fear possession, belonging to one another, or to others, or to God.[51] So long as we exist in time, in our moving world, along with others, so long is our truth to be found in possession—not the possession of things, of the property of the foolish old wise men—but the possession that comes only in being possessed, in the frenzy of belonging, to another, others, God. Possession and being possessed, belonging to one another, in the only way in which persons can truly be each other's, is being true to one another, the reciprocal and mutual being-true of love. Poetry teaches each poet the truth it contains.

But the love whose truth is actualized in the being-true to one another of human beings, as in the first poet, is but one shape of the love, and truth, that the second poet glimpses, taught to him also by the poetry that contains it within itself because, as symbol, it participates in the being of the symbolized. It is the truth of eternal love and eternal truth, which redeems all of time, all of life, all of existence. The human being is finite. He exists in time, movement, desire, life, the turning world. Wisdom is, for him, the realization of his finitude: understanding it, willing it, loving it, giving himself over to the truth of it.

> The only wisdom we can hope to acquire
> Is the wisdom of humility: humility is endless.[52]

Humility is the acknowledgment and practice of one's essential finitude. Its opposite is pride, vainglory, the refusal of one's own finitude. In its purest form, pride is the desire to be God. As Nietzsche discovered first, and Sartre after him, the project of being God is doomed to failure, if you are not God. If you are not God, then you must bear not being God. Wisdom is bearing not to be God. How can we bear this burden? Not by being God but by participating in Him. As the symbol participates in the being of what it symbolizes, so the image of God may participate in the being of that which it figures forth. The saint lives in the solitary world between earth and Heaven, and in this solitude is folded in the bosom of his God. In the poem, the music, the dance, we move above the moving tree in light upon the figured leaf, moving in the space between earth and heaven and participating in the being of the timeless.

The timeless is love. How is it that, in the dance, in all of true art, the pattern of the movement is the pattern of Love? It is because love is the alpha and omega, the beginning and the end, which in going out of itself returns to itself and in returning to itself goes out of itself. Where this love is, there is a timeless truth, a rightness that is intrinsic to its time and that holds its time together, preventing its dispersion into distraction: *kairos.* In a poem that is right, the measure of the fire dance is also present:

> every word is at home,
> Taking its place to support the others,
> The word neither diffident nor ostentatious,
> An easy commerce of the old and the new,
> The common word exact without vulgarity,
> The formal word precise but not pedantic,
> The complete consort dancing together.[53]

Every word exists in its own, authentic finitude. It is not diffident, for true humility is not mere diffidence, but it is not ostentatious. It knows how to take its place and keep it, not because it is held in contempt by the others but just the opposite, because the others need it and they are given over to it to keep as its charge. Thus all is easy commerce: the elder with the younger, the exalted with the common, the precise with the informal. The consort is in concert. All dance together. The dance is the domestic festival in which all are at home with one another. It is the celebration of the homecoming and the being-at-home of all. The family that had been dispersed is drawn together with the drawing of this love and the voice of this calling.

The poet offers us a homely image of the dancing together of those who are at home with one another, drawn from Sir Thomas Elyot's dream of the dawn of a new age *(The Book of the Governour).* It is a magical image which you can behold if you do not come too close. They dance to the music of a weak pipe and a little drum around the bonfire. It is, thus, a fire dance. Moreover, it is the marriage ceremony

> The association of man and woman
> In daunsinge, signifying matrimonie—
> A dignified and commodious sacrament.[54]

The sacrament is the sacred ceremony that, by participating in the holy, has a saving power. This fire-dance marriage-ceremony has a redeeming effect on the man and the woman. They are brought into a "necessarye coniunction." A conjunction is not only sexual union and marriage of man and woman; it is also the meeting together of two stars in the zodiac; and this conjunction is necessary—saving the conjoined from the contingencies of time, reconciling among the stars the pattern of boarhound and boar. The reconciliation is the concord, which is betokened by the gesture of the dancers holding each other by the hand or arm. They dance in a circle, beginning to ending to beginning, round the fire as the still center (which yet, in its stillness, is ever in movement, the Heraclitean god),

> round and round the fire
> Leaping through the flames, or joined in circles,
> Rustically solemn or in rustic laughter
> Lifting heavy feet in clumsy shoes,
> Earth feet, loam feet, lifted in country mirth
> Mirth of those long since under earth
> Nourishing the corn.[55]

Here the heavy earth and those who live with the earth are lifted up in the joyous dance, and the dance itself is lifted up into a dream, the space of the poetic imagination between earth and heaven, moving in the roundness of the sacrament. The concord symbolized by the gesture of holding each other is the concord that comes of measure, the measure of the fire dance which restores the exasperated spirit, and it comes of

> keeping time,
> Keeping the rhythm in their dancing
> As in the living seasons.[56]

Keeping time, by the rhythm of the dance and the rhythm of the life, is being the keeper of time, taking time out of its destructive wildness and—not taming it but—giving it the measure of the dance's music. The keeper of time preserves and maintains it; he watches over it, holding it in its due course; he observes the time, commemorating it, celebrating it; he is the servant who redeems it from its passing. He knows what the time is for, and does what is appropriate thereto:

> The time of the seasons and the constellations
> The time of milking and the time of harvest
> The time of the coupling of man and woman
> And that of beasts. Feet rising and falling.
> Eating and drinking. Dung and death.[57]

Such is the time-keeping of the dance, through which, as in a dream of the new life, time is conquered and governed.

How is it that by the measure of the dance, keeping the time, time and movement are conquered? How is it that beginning and end, time past and time future, are brought into each other, pointing to one end which is always present, participating in what they point to? How is it that in the dance its measure grants a point for the intersection of the timeless with time, the incarnation of the timeless in time? Can we discover the power of the logos, the strength of the pattern by which words or music reach this stillness?

The first word, here, is consciousness. Consciousness is knowing together-with, *con-scire*. In consciousness, and in consciousness for the first time and only and ever, I know myself along with the other. Knowing the self along with the other, knowing this along with that, differentiating and relating I and not-I into own and own—this is consciousness, whose vocation is to be own-conscious-ness, to reach the ownness of each to each. Being with other as with one's own, so that one is own to that other just as the other is own to one, is the inner meaning of the logos, the word that is the clue to all. The power of the logos is the power of joining of own to own. It is through the work of this power that time and movement are over-come in the very midst of time and movement.

> Time past and time future
> Allow but a little consciousness.
> To be conscious is not to be in time
> But only in time can the moment in the rose-garden,
> The moment in the arbour where the rain beat,
> The moment in the draughty church at smokefall
> Be remembered; involved with past and future.
> Only through time time is conquered.[58]

This is the way. Time is the fluidity by which that which exists is ever separating itself from itself, becoming other than itself, negating itself, only to fall back into itself, in a hopeless endeavor to leave itself and find itself, never able to bring the leaving and the finding into one. Time is the mutual extraneity of moment to moment, hour to hour, day to day, eon to eon. Today is the death of yesterday and tomorrow will be the death of today—all tossed up, all drowned again in the heaving sea.

> Time and the bell have buried the day,
> The black cloud carries the sun away.[59]

The river of time is within us, the sea of time is all about us, its tolling bell measuring endless time, the endless ground swell that heaves forever.[60] Time, as time, has no end; there is only addition in it, that is, the next-to-next-ness of moment and moment as the moments file by. As it has no end, so it has—merely as time—no destination; even the concept of evolution is misleading, suggesting to the popular mind the notion that something like an inner consciousness is at work, enabling that mind to disown the past.[61] Genuine beginnings and endings can occur only where there is meaning, a meaning in experience which takes on historical character. Only history has beginnings and endings, and only in history can a beginning proceed to an ending which finds itself to be that beginning again.[62]

But the history must be genuine history, history that is authentically ours. History conceived as the mere course of events we read of in books as what has happened is as much an extraneity as is abstract time. Only lived history, in which man exists in the present appropriating his past and future, so that he lives in the actual experience that belongs to him, has real beginnings and endings which are able to connect themselves into their appropriate identity.[63] The time that is conquered has to be the time of consciousness that remembers its own past and that hopes and resolves its own future in the fullness of its present moment. Recollection, hope, resolution—let these stand for all the transcending acts of consciousness by which the dying past has been kept with us and the burgeoning future voyaged toward as ours, those acts by which we acknowledge and exercise our responsibility for the keeping of time. By means of them, the present moment, the moment which in its richest and most intense form is

> the moment in the rose-garden,
> The moment in the arbour where the rain beat,
> The moment in the draughty church at smokefall,

becomes

> ... involved with past and future.[64]

Involvement of present with past and future is the historical structure of living experience, brought about by the power of consciousness to join own to own. As in the present moment, remembering, hoping, resolving, I join my own past and my own future to this, my own present, the moment here and now becomes involved with the earlier and the later, and the incarnation of the timeless in time gets under way. For the involvement of past and future with the present is the act by which meaning is constituted, and it is the meaning of what is in time that makes up the content of the timeless.[65]

Further, history must be lived as history to be genuine history. Man is not just the human animal who involves time past with time future in a present remembering, hoping, and resolving. As such, he would be merely sunk

within time, the everyday human time of the life of plot-
ting and calculating. This is the time of the everyday journey:

> When the train starts, and the passengers are settled
> To fruit, periodicals and business letters
> (And those who saw them off have left the platform)
> Their faces relax from grief into relief,
> To the sleepy rhythm of a hundred hours.[66]

It is a time of man's appearance, not his reality. This time
is no healer, for the patient is no longer present. The
riders in the train are no longer the same people who
boarded it or who will arrive at the next station. The
narrowing rails slide together behind them. So Krishna
instructed Arjuna. The true self, the self that *is* in every
moment, that remains and endures as the moments pass
by, is not the self of the beginning station, the intermediary journey, or the terminus arrived at. For the true self
the past is not finished, the future is not "before us."

History genuinely lived as history is history realized to
be history, apprehended by the consciousness of its historical nature, and lived with that consciousness. In the
midst of the journey, at this moment (every moment),
time must be withdrawn, the future and the past contemplated with an equal mind, the past realized and appropriated as the own past and the future apportioned as the
own future. This consciousness is self-consciousness. But
it is not a merely abstract, introspective consciousness of
one's subjectivity as distinct from and separated off from
the objectivities of one's world. Such merely introspective
self-consciousness is radically incomplete and un-
wholesome; it tries to hold on to the self as a precious

content that must not be sullied by its contact with the world. It is the self-consciousness that, when it faces the world, becomes embarrassed and full of shame, because it has not gone out to the world as its own and it judges itself in that condition. The self-consciousness of historical experience is, rather, the consciousness that not only has, and has appropriated, its past and future but knows what it does. It sees the past as its own and the future as its own and the present moment and present place as the moment and the place in which it is serving as the body of the incarnation of the timeless within time.

> There are other places
> Which also are the world's end, some at the sea jaws,
> Or over a dark lake, in a desert or a city—
> But this is the nearest, in place and time,
> Now and in England.[67]

In this place and at this moment it *affirms* the past and the future as its own.

Nor is the historical experience affirmed the experience only of one's own single life,

> But of many generations—not forgetting
> Something that is probably quite ineffable:
> The backward look behind the assurance
> Of recorded history, the backward half-look
> Over the shoulder, towards the primitive terror.[68]

Affirmation affirms all: the moments of agony as well as of ecstasy.

> People change, and smile: but the agony abides.[69]

Genuine historical consciousness affirms time the destroyer as well as time the healer; and time the destroyer
preserves its destruction,

> Like the river with its cargo of dead Negroes, cows and
> chicken coops,
> The bitter apple and the bite in the apple.[70]

Affirmation knows the real destination: the moment, every moment, which is the time of death the ending, which
is the beginning, the moment which is neither of action
nor of inaction, in which the equal mind is poised in time
above time, owning all in its destitution of all property.[71]

Such self-conscious affirmation is what is taught by the
God Krishna to the saintly warrior Arjuna: Fare forward,
above time, in time, in the one action

> Which shall fructify in the lives of others:
> And do not think of the fruit of action.[72]

The second word about the power of the logos after
consciousness and self-consciousness is: measure,
rhythm, the measure and rhythm of the dance, the jar, the
music, of the words, phrases, and sentences of the poem.
For it is by measure that the fire dancers are able to keep
time, keeping the rhythm in their dancing as in the living
seasons. And as time is kept in the dance, so it is kept in
words, music, the Chinese jar, the violin.

How is it that measure is the means by which the refining fire restores the exasperated spirit, through keeping
the time and rhythm? How is it that, through measure,
consciousness is able to involve past with future, constituting its lived history?

Measure is not the principle of calculation, by which man measures the profits and losses of his possible actions; rather, it is the principle of action which does not produce fruits because it is its own fruit, fructifying in itself and in the lives of others. If it is to be so, it cannot, either, be a measure imported into action by a mere external artifice, like the imposition of rules by a power not one's own; it must be the measure that belongs to that which is measured as its very own. When what is measured arrives at its own authentic measure, then does it arrive at the one action of which Krishna speaks: the act of the moment which is neither of action nor of inaction, the moment of the poise of the mind in time above time, owning its own birth and death, circling in its own history.

Let us first say, abstractly, what measure is. The poet does not define it; he is writing the poem, not the philosophy of the poem. That he understands it, being a poet, is clear. For when he says that every right poem is an epitaph, the symbolic utterance of the union of beginning and ending, in which every word, phrase, sentence is end and beginning, every one at home taking its place to support the others, the complete consort dancing together, he has therein declared the essence of the matter. But philosophy wants to have the thing stated explicitly. So we say abstractly—informed by the exposition Hegel gives of it in his books on logic—that measure is that condition of being in which quality and quantity are united; it is the qualitative quantum, as over against the mere bare quantum of magnitude and number indifferent to quality.

Quantity, merely as such, is indifferent to the concrete being of the thing whose quantity is under consideration. This human being weighs 150 pounds. There are in him 150 pounds of flesh. So far as the thought of quantity is concerned, it does not matter whether these pounds are laid out separately in a line or joined together in a human frame; they are 150 pounds nevertheless, all the same, it does not matter. This couplet,

> We only live, only suspire
> Consumed by either fire or fire.[73]

consists of eleven words, a comma, and a period. The syllables of the first verse are eight, not counting the pause, nine including it; the syllables of the second verse are eight; the two verses are equal in the number of articulated syllables; the sound "–ire" is repeated—i.e., given a second time (after its internal occurrence)—at the end of the second verse. And so on. All this is quantitative talk about the verses, such as is found in books, and is like laying out the 150 pounds. As the counting of the pounds of flesh is indifferent to the man's being so the counting of the syllables is indifferent to the poem's being. The quantity is there, without a doubt, and it is there in an essential way; but to abstract it from the being of the thing whose quantity it is, separating it from that thing's quality, is to make it into a matter of indifference, i.e., a matter of mere counting, measuring, calculating.

Measure, on the contrary, is quantity understood as one with the being of the quantified thing, as in unison with its quality. A man's weight belongs to him as a living organism. He has a body which is more or less suited to his soul, his psychic quality and needs. This body attains its size and weight by the recurrent ingestion of matter and energy, in the form of food, and their appropriation by assimilation, with concurrent passage of waste matter and expenditure of energy. In the flow of matter and energy in time, the man's body keeps its being, its shape, its substance, by keeping the rhythm of its life. It does not do this perfectly, for it suffers from the weaknesses and failings that are the lot of all things finite. It can suffer deprivation and become too light, thin, weak; it can suffer excess and become too heavy, thick, and sluggish; in between there is a medial range, the range of health, in which the body becomes prosperous for the psyche. Within this medial range, the body's measure is observed. The size and weight of the body within the medial range are the size and weight that belong to the body in its quality, its character as living organism possessed of a psyche. They are quantities present in the body in the union of accord with the character and needs of the body as the organism of the psyche. The psychic-organic quality finds in these quantities the needed outward reality by which it can emerge into the world and be there, complete, perfect in the true form of its material existence.

Heraclitus wrote: "Most men stuff themselves with food like cattle." He also said—in regard to drinking as well as eating—"It is in the power of all men to know themselves and to practise temperance." Temperance is observation of the mean, of measure, the right proportions. To practice temperance is to live in accordance with Nature, with the *logos* of the *kosmos*. The kosmos is the universe in its right and beautiful order—the organism of the whole of things. "This kosmos, the same for all, was made by no gods or men, but it always was, and is, and ever shall be an ever-living fire, kindling and dying out in measures." It keeps the time, the rhythm of the fire; it is itself the fire dance. Wisdom is one thing: to know the *gnome*, the thought, by which all things are guided through all. The articulation of this thought is the word, the logos, the divine ordering agent—willing and unwilling to be called by the name of Zeus—which is everlasting and common to all, according to which all the transformations of nature keep their time, their rhythm, their measure. "The sea is dispersed and keeps its measure according to the same logos that prevailed before it became earth."

The logos unites opposites. "Opposition brings men together, and out of discord comes the fairest harmony, and all things have their birth in strife." Men are ignorant of the logos, but if they understood it they would understand how that which is torn in different directions comes into accord with itself: harmony in contrariety, as in the bow and the lyre. The bow, *bios,* is called by the same name as life, but its work is death. (But the work of the bow is the work of the logos, whose work is life and death and the union of the two in right accord.) High and low, heavy and light, wet and dry, great and small, day and night, war and peace, satiety and hunger—all join the rhythm of the ever-living fire, guided by the universal gnome of the logos, in the dance of its transformations, moving and resting in the hidden harmony of the whole. "The way up and the way down are one and the same." "One and the same thing are the living and the dead, the waking and the sleeping, the young and the old; the former change and are the latter, the latter change in turn and are the former." Earth rises through water and air to fire, and fire sinks through air and water to earth, and the whole process is the physiology of the living kosmos whose end is in its beginning and its beginning in its end, circling in its own timeless rhythm about its own still center, which consents and does not consent to be called by the name of Zeus. "In the circumference of a circle beginning and end coincide."

How does the logos unite opposites into a harmony? The logos is the guide of all things. It shows them their measures—the right time, the right place, the right accent, the right speed, the right effort. The logos is the knowledge of their essential being; it is everlasting wisdom, which knows the gnome by which all things are guided through all. As it tells the sea the rhythm of its tides and waves, so it tells everything its own rhythm. It speaks of the universal exchange, by which all returns to all in the endless circle—all things exchanged for fire, fire for all things, just as wares are exchanged for gold and gold for wares. The sun itself, the bodily exterior of the inner fire, is assigned its measures by the logos: "The sun will not overstep his measures, else would the Erinyes, the handmaids of justice, find him out."

How does the logos know these measures, the right time and place and all else right? "Men deem some things wrong and some right; to God all things are beautiful and good and right." That means, not that things men do are not wrong; it means, the logos knows the right because it is the life-principle of the kosmos itself, the God present and not-present in all the opposites, the principle by which all things belong to all things. The finite, deficient human body has within itself its own finite wisdom, by which it absorbs and rejects, appropriates and repels, the things with which it must stand in the transformative exchange. The homeostatic body is but an image of the ever circling kosmos. How is the quantity known that is not mere indifferent quantity but the quantity that belongs essentially to the quality of the being? It is known by the essential principle of the being involved in the process. The being involved in the cosmic process is the God, Zeus, the divine thought whose word by which it knows itself is the formula for the divine law that regulates the whole exchange according to measure. The logos knows the measures of things because it is the law of their measures, the wisdom of the law of measure. This wisdom is the justice whose handmaids are the Erinyes, standing watch even over the sun, to see that it joins in the rhythm of the fire dance. It is the universal wisdom, the one divine law "which prevails as far as it lists and suffices for all things and excels all things."

This is the wisdom of the Greeks, the wisdom of the kosmos which however is the folly of the spirit. In this measure, being is completed, but it is only being that comes thereby to completion. This measure is the principle of life, of the organic, the organism of the world. It is not yet the principle of spirit, which transcends organism. The unity of spirit is not just a unity of an organic law, a homeostasis of body that accords with the inner psychic principle. Spirit's unity is the unity of conscious beings, self-conscious in the very act of being conscious of what is own to them and what is not, and eventually self-conscious in the recognition and acknowledgment of their relation to the infinite. Heraclitus does not speak of freedom because he does not know the spirit. His logos is the wisdom of the necessary which is not yet truly free. Heraclitus is hailed as the prophet of becoming; but his becoming is only the form of movement and change by which being reinstates itself in its own eternal recurrence. Being remains with itself, a fire never-ending because always starting afresh, a tortured infinity of fire, a conflagration ever burning itself up—is it the Hell of being or the Purgatory of becoming?

There is another fire:

> The dove descending breaks the air
> With flame of incandescent terror
> Of which the tongues declare
> The one discharge from sin and error.
> The only hope, or else despair
>   Lies in the choice of pyre or pyre—
>   To be redeemed from fire by fire.[74]

This other fire is the fire of the spirit. The name of the spirit is love, the unfamiliar name

> Behind the hands that wove
> The intolerable shirt of flame
> Which human power cannot remove.[75]

And as there is this other fire, so also is there an other fire dance, and an other measure than the organic measure of the Greeks. This measure is also given by a logos who knows the measure of things because he is the spirit of their being, able to reflect on their being and make it into his own being. He is the wisdom of spiritual being, and he stands over justice to see that it joins in the rhythm of the fire dance of love, as the Greek logos stands over the sun to see that it joins in the rhythm of the fire dance of life. The Greek logos knows the thought that guides all things through all things, but this other logos is the word of the spirit that searches all things, not only the deep things of man but the deep things of God, too.[76]

The wisdom of human life was the spirit of the Greek: man's knowledge of himself as finite being in a world whose gods, too, were finite forms of infinity, overruled by a law—fate, necessity, Zeus—which was infinitely just in its own inscrutable way. The wisdom of our poet is that of divine life, hence of spirit, whose quality is love. This love

>   ... is itself unmoving,
>   Only the cause and end of movement[77]

so that it acts upon man not by compulsion but by the power of love, namely, the power to draw. It speaks to man not with the stern tones of the magistrate or the raving lips of the sibyl, but with the tongues of the flame of the dove, declaring the only hope, the one discharge from sin and error—its voice speaks with the accent of love, namely, that of calling. It calls to man to tell him of its gift and it draws him by this gift of its own self. The rose by any other name would smell as sweet; it is called the rose; the moment of the yew tree, of death, is the rose's moment of renewed life, renewed by the power of love. The tongues of flame are folded into the knot of the fire that is one with the rose.[78] The movement of desire mounts above itself into the dance that restores the spirit's exasperated being.[79]

The measure that belonged to Greek life and Greek art, and to the Greek poem, was the measure of the Greek logos. The measure that belonged to medieval life, and art, and poem, was the measure of the Christian logos. What is the measure that belongs to our life and art, and to our poem?

Our poet speaks the language of Christianity, but his language resonates also with that of Greece, of India, of the earth. His selected voices are those of Heraclitus, of Krishna, of the river god, and of the Holy Spirit. The spirit that draws him with its love and calls him with its voice whispers into his ear the measure of his verse. When he writes of thunder rolled by the rolling stars simulating triumphal cars deployed in constellated wars, working it up into a baroque vision of the heavens engaged in battle, his spirit warns him, and he returns to a level of prose that contains, even as prose, his own authentic poetry:

> That was a way of putting it—not very satisfactory:
> A periphrastic study in a worn-out poetical fashion,
> Leaving one still with the intolerable wrestle
> With words and meanings. The poetry does not matter.[80]

To everything there is its own measure, for everything has its own quality of being and therefore is required to seek its own quantity of being. The being of spirit, in itself infinite in its own way, has to seek for the quantity by which it realizes its meaning in the extraneity of time, space, matter, and energy. This quantity appears in every shape and form of its life in the world: in its body, its knowledge, its actions, its feelings, and in all the habits, customs, institutions, nations, wars, in which it activates itself. But it appears truly only in those forms in which, understanding itself, it articulates itself in its ownness as its self by attaining and disclosing its being-with all that truly belongs to it and to which it truly belongs, i.e., by attaining and disclosing the love which it itself genuinely is.

The poem—the right poem, the one that is an epitaph —is such a form. The spirit of the poem first finds its own external shape in the words, images, thoughts, feelings to which it accords their measures; through this external shape it reaches out into the world in search of those other spirits with whom it seeks to be; in its communication with those other spirits, it becomes the ceremony of the marriage sacrament that holds spirits together in communion, the fire dance by which they keep time together, in the rhythm of their love; as the prayer that is spoken in this community it symbolizes the timeless love as it is incarnated in the world, and it does so by the power of the logos that makes it such a symbol, thereby enabling it to participate in the love it points to, to be itself, in its community, an incarnation of that love.

In such a poem, every word is at home. Home is where we start from and where we end. Every word is a beginning and an ending. The here and the now join every other here and now,

> ... a lifetime burning in every moment
> And not the lifetime of one man only
> But of old stones that cannot be deciphered.
> . . . . .
> Love is most nearly itself
> When here and now cease to matter.[81]

Here and now cease to matter only when here and now become of infinite importance, for only then do they participate in the timeless meaning that overcomes their extraneity and joins them in its circle. As Yeats knew of the communion of the old lovers under the shade-hidden lamplight, so Eliot:

> There is a time for the evening under starlight,
> A time for the evening under lamplight
> (The evening with the photograph album).[82]

The moment of looking backwards through the old pictures is a moment that has ceased to matter as moment because it has joined those other moments—in the rose garden, in the English chapel, at the shore of the sea, any one of those moments of which Krishna spoke—in being a point of intersection of the timeless with time, an arrival at the place from which we started, knowing where we are and have been. Every word in the right poem is such a moment: *kairos.* That is why all the words, the phrases, the sentences are able to dance together in complete consort.

The only measuring rod that can gauge the measure of the poem is the rood of the spirits who make it and for whom it is made to be their communal possession. Because in it every word is at home, so with it they are at home with themselves and with one another, being at home with the principle of their own measure, which therein dwells with them.

To be with the other as with one's own is to be in a relation of freedom with that other. To be in the world as in one's home is to be free in the world. To be with oneself as at home with oneself is to be a free ego. The poem—the right one, that is an epitaph—is a symbol of freedom, for it is at home with itself and everything within it is at home with everything else therein. Being such a home, the dwellers therein are free spirits. Because the poem participates in the freedom it symbolizes, we are able to participate in the freedom by knowing and being it in the poem.

In the poem, past and future are conquered and reconciled. The single imagination of the spirit dwells in the first word and the last, remembering the first, envisioning the last, all the while it moves through each intermediary word. Action which otherwise was movement of something moved, driven by demonic, chthonic powers, becomes the circling action of the stillness of the central point. It is right action, in which the doer is at home in his deed.

> ... And right action is freedom
> From past and future also.[83]

Right action, right being, right moving—existing, in which each step is at home, taking its place to support the others, the complete consort stepping the movements of the sacred dance—such being and moving and acting are the prerogatives of the genius of the spirit. For most of us, this aim will never be realized. For most of us

> ... there is only the unattended
> Moment, the moment in and out of time,
> The distraction fit, lost in a shaft of sunlight,
> The wild thyme unseen, or the winter lightning
> Or the waterfall, or music heard so deeply
> That it is not heard at all, but you are the music
> While the music lasts.[84]

The poem is such an unattended moment, too. It is a distraction fit, lost in a shaft of sunlight, a return in imagination to our first world, where the roses have the look of flowers that are looked at, they are there as our guests, accepted and accepting, we moving and they moving in a formal pattern, along the empty alley, into the box circle, to look down into the drained pool.

The poem's pool is filled with water out of sunlight, and in it the lotos rises, quietly, quietly, the surface glitters out of heart of light, and we see them behind us, reflected in the pool.[85]

The lotos, like the rose, blooms for a moment and then is gone. But during that moment Re, the sun-god, appears as a child sitting in it. The lotos is the poem that rises, receiving into its bosom the heart of light returned to its beginning once more. We cannot bear very much reality.

We must go. The cloud passes. The pool is emptied of water, lotos, and light. For the moment, time past and time future pointed to one end, which is always present, and by the power of the logos of the poem, participated therein. In that moment and that participation we have been *there*, in the freedom of the still point of the fire dance of the spirit of love.

8

Being:
The Act of Belonging

The question of the meaning of being stands at the heart of human thought. Thought striving to understand the meaning of being is called "philosophy." Where does this meaning become manifest to philosophical reflection? When we have learned how to look for the meaning of being in the region in which it emerges into view for thought, we shall then perhaps have made a first steady step on the road toward a right understanding of it.

The question is partly one of the meaning of the verb *be*. What we think when we think being must be essentially connected with the ways in which we use this verb. Hence the very first thing that must be done in the inquiry is to investigate the grammar of *be*.

But the question is not only one of linguistic usage. For the grammar of *be* only opens up for thought the general outline, the schema, of the concept of being. It does not give its further determination and specification. The grammar only gives a beginning, which must be followed up by philosophical reflection on the beings that actually are and on the modes of being exemplified by them.

When we enter into this second stage of our inquiry,

two different senses of "meaning" come into play. For as our contemplation advances from inorganic being to living being, and within living being to mental and spiritual being, meaning itself enters into the constitution of the objects we are observing. Inorganic beings do not themselves "mean." They are not intentionalistic beings. But living beings manifest purposiveness, and purpose is a mode of intention. Mentality is essentially intentional. Unconscious mind is already characterized by three basic forms of intention—cognitive, conative, and affective. What is called the "intentionality" of consciousness—namely, the fact that consciousness involves an activity of "meaning," of "being-of-something," as perception is of a perceived object, memory of a remembered event, hope of a hoped-for eventuality—is a clear instance of the essential and constitutive presence of meaning in the contemplated object of our inquiry. Man's being therefore contains within itself its own meaning, and this is the most complex combination of senses and uses of the word "meaning." Even grammar, including the grammar of the verb *be*, falls within the scope of man's being. Hence when we ask about the meaning of being in the case of man we are engaged not only with the grammar of *be* in man's language, i.e., the linguistic meaning of this word, but also with the meaning that belongs to his life, his being, as constitutive of its own inner meaningfulness.

From the question, "What is the meaning of the verb *be?*," we thus eventually arrive at the question, "What is the meaning of human being and, in the end, of all being, insofar as being can be said to have meaning?" The first question is one that belongs to philosophical analysis of language. The second reaches far beyond anything that philosophical analysis of language proposes for itself. It is the question of philosophy itself, not of linguistic analysis alone, and it is, as has been said, philosophy's central question: "the question which was raised of old and is raised now and always, and is always the subject of doubt, viz. what being is."[1]

A question which must first be settled has to do with the etymology of the verb *be.* It is an irregular and defective verb, put together out of the fragments of verbs formed from three roots having the varied senses of to be, remain, dwell, endure, become.* Can recurrence to this etymology be of help in disentangling the meaning of the verb itself?

Leave aside the sense of *es-, to be,* which is after all what has to be explicated. Will it help to understand *be* if we contemplate *remain, dwell, endure, become?* Apparently what is at work here is the familiar process of a meaning being articulated by metaphor. If a man wanted to say that something is, he had to find a word already in use which by its metaphorical power would transfer the mind of the hearer, including his own mind, from the known sense to the new sense. If he wanted to say of a stone that it is, he could say: it dwells. Should his companion reply, "But a

---

*They are:

    es-, a root in many Indo-European languages, Greek, Latin, Germanic, etc., carrying the meaning of *to be, exist.*

    Germanic *wes-,* Sanskrit *vas-,* with a probable Indo-European root *wes-, to remain, to dwell, to continue to be.* Vesta was the goddess of dwellings. Although *wesan,* the Old English form, meant *to be* in the present tense, its eventual derivatives like *was* and *were* became the preterite or imperfect form of the verb.

    an Indo-European root, probably *bheu-,* Sanskrit *bhu-,* Greek *phu-,* Latin *fu-,* Germanic *beo-,* occurring in Old English *beon,* which later became *been,* giving rise to *be.* The meaning centers around *to become.*

    As a result of historical linguistic changes, *be* or *beon,* which earlier was the future tense of the verb *am-was,* came to occupy a more dominant place and to stand for the entire verb.

stone doesn't have a house!," that would result only from his being arrested within the literal meaning. To grasp the real intent of the speaker he would have to see how, in a certain new sense, a stone *does* have something like a house, perhaps the earth with the sky arched above it as an immense vaulted roof. When the hearer grasps this analogy, he begins to get the new sense of the verb: not only does a man dwell, but everything dwells, each in its own way—the tree in the forest, the lion in its lair, the bird in its nest, the stone in its environment. And as the metaphor gains strength the dwelling of things in the new sense becomes something like their dwelling in the world. To be, then, is to dwell, in this new sense of *dwell,* namely, to be a member of the world. What is not does not belong to the world, is outside and away from the world, wholly and fully absent.

I do not offer the foregoing as an actual historical reconstruction of some real aspect of the linguistic creation of the verb *be* in the form, say, of *wesan, wesen,* etc. It is tendered only as an imaginative construction to help us consider the question of the utility of etymology for our problem. And I think that it shows etymology to be suggestive but dangerous. The direction of thinking in such a metaphorical construction is *from* the older and more concrete form *to* the newer form. The metaphor is a leap away from the older to the newer, a change and a transfer. To go back from the newer to the older is to undo the change and therefore to lose hold of the new meaning. To be is *not* literally to remain, dwell, endure, or become. What remains, dwells, endures, or becomes, is. But the being of what is does not conversely resolve merely into remaining, dwelling, enduring, or becoming. Undoubtedly there were features in these more concrete notions that led men to use them to reach the notion of being, the new sense toward which all the older ones strive. Nevertheless our business is with the new sense. The older ones can be used, if at all, only as they were originally meant, namely, to be bridges to the new. If we should adopt the reverse direction, backtracking toward the older senses, then we would be abandoning the possibility of finding what we are searching for.

It is our task to understand being as it has emerged into view for us, as we express it in our language, as we think it in our thought, as we live our own being, and as we relate to the being of that which is. In the end, this is the only understanding of being that we can genuinely have and the only understanding from which we can move into our own historical existence. We belong to our age and our age belongs to us. Our thinking can only be the conscious articulation, in conceptual form, of the meaning of the being of which our own time is the witness. Only insofar as we can truly think the meaning of being as it is disclosed to us in our time and our own being, in its historically conditioned manner of presentation, can there be any talk of a truth in our thinking that can reach beyond our time, backwards and forwards. The question is: What does being mean . . . now?

Be has three main classes of use. It can serve as (1) a substantive verb, (2) a copulative or linking verb, and (3) an auxiliary verb. The first of these uses is apparently the one in which the question of the meaning of being is most directly interested. Here *be* itself serves as the predicate of the sentence, doing the complete job of predicating, not being limited to a partial role. It has its own predicational meaning and does not merely link a subject with a predicate (It is an ancient Mariner) or help another meaningful verb (The Bridegroom's doors are opened wide). Examples of this first use of *be* as a predicate in its own right are: God is; I think, therefore I am; Let things be; To be or not to be; There was a ship, quoth he; There are no such entities as mental states; There is a fly in my soup. Some other uses that the dictionaries and grammars cite as substantive seem to be either on their way toward or back from the copulative use: The meeting will be in Memorial Hall at 8 P.M.; I have not been home for many years; Now I will be on my way once more. Whereas with God or the self, things or Hamlet, it is a question just of being, with the meeting, the absent one, or the traveler it is a question of being where or when, etc. These uses link up with the situational use (There is a fly in my soup; Is there a doctor in the house?) in the sense that they make the being they predicate in some way definite, by placing it in space, time, etc. Apparently, then, the use that should occupy the focus of our attention is the former one, in which *be* is used purely, without such particularization; here being is simply predicated, as such, of God, the self, things, a person, a ship, mental states, etc.

Now the substantive use itself breaks down into a number of differing uses. For example, in "God is" and "I am" there is a close parallelism between the verbs, yet we think of the being of God as atemporal. We may say of Him that He was, is, and always will be; but that is now rather more than anything else a figurative way of expressing His eternity, His being in such a way that He never merely was, never merely is (in the sense of the *now*), never merely will be, but simply and absolutely is in a way that transcends these distinctions. Thus it is not just false but paradoxical and even meaningless to say, "Once upon a time God was, Once upon a time God was not," whereas it is perfectly meaningful to say, "Once upon a time Plato was, Once upon a time Plato was not."* God's being and man's being, in this substantive usage, are thought of as their existence or actuality. If God is, then He exists and is actual; He is not merely possible or potential. Aristotle took as the primary and most complete sense of being *(ousia)* that of *energeia,* actuality, and *entelecheia,* being complete, fully brought out. Possible and potential being have to be expressed by using *be* in a copulative or linking manner or in a substantival manner analogous to the copulative. Whereas "God is actual" can be replaced by "God is," or "I am actual" by "I am," "God is possible, I am possible" cannot be reduced to the purely substantive use of *be.***

In general, the substantive use of *be* will vary in its sense with the kind or category of the subject whose predicate it is. If the subject is an event, then the sense of *be* is to happen or take place. The accident was yesterday, i.e., it happened or took place then. When will the lecture be? Next Monday. That is when it will take place. If the subject is a general concrete thing-noun, like *dragons* or *tigers,* then the sense of the substantive *be* is: occur. "Dragons are," "Dragons exist," i.e., they occur. To deny that they are is to assert that there are no occurrent examples of them; they are not actually exemplified. If the subject

*"God is dead" referred originally to the crucifixion, the death of Christ. Today its meaning is transferred so as to be an ambiguous expression of nihilist rejection of traditional religion, destructive on the one hand, forward-meaning on the other. If it were taken merely literally, like a sentence in a newspaper story about a famous man on the obituary page, it would be pathetically naïve if not linguistically futile.

**The closest we can get to this would be to conceive of possibility as a state or condition of God or my self or something else in relation to actual being, a state or condition of being which is not, but could be, actual. We could thus say: "God is in the condition of possibility," "I am in the condition of possibility," where *is* and *am* carry some of the sense of actual being: "I am—in the state of possibility"—"My actuality is, so far, that of something possible."

names an abstract entity, then we conceive of an abstract sort of actuality or existence that belongs to it in a manner analogous to the way in which factual existence belongs to things of the ordinary spatiotemporal world. So if a philosopher maintains that there is such a thing as causal necessity, a mode of necessary relationship which is exemplified in causal connections among actual events, he is thinking of the being of that necessity itself as in some sense being actual, existing, being present in the structure of reality. This being is not the same as the actuality of a physical object like a stone in the world; yet there is an analogy—if one conceives the world as having a structure, such as that of a structure of law, then one can conceive of some feature as existing in that structure, having its actuality there, occurring in it, taking place there, being present there. These latter expressions are, as it were, metaphorical extensions of the being actual with which we are familiar in the case of environmental things, plants, animals, persons, tools, and the like.

It becomes clear as we peruse illustrations of the foregoing kinds that in its substantively predicational form *be* is used to express various sorts of actuality:

Dragons are: there are actual instances of them.

Causal necessity is: it is actually present in the structure of the world.

God is: He is eternal actuality.

I am: I exist, I am an actual entity.

Once upon a time Plato was: Plato at one time was actual, existent, was an actual entity.

Let things be: let them remain in their own actuality, do not change them from what they actually are; and, in the sense of *Genesis,* let them actually be, let them be actual.

There is a fly in my soup: a fly actually is present in my

soup; the situation or state of affairs a-fly-in-my-soup occurs, is actual, actually exists in fact.

"Actuality" presumably means different things in such
different contexts. It is not the same thing for me to be
actual as it is for God, for dragons, for causal necessity,
etc. Nevertheless there is something that urges language
to use this word in such varied contexts. What is it?

Aristotle's concepts of act and actuality are too limited
to make use of here. He restricted his notion of act to its
relationship to the notion of potency, so that actuality was
the mere correlative of potentiality.* In this limited form
it becomes, as he himself emphasizes, one member of an
opposed pair of correlated concepts, each of which refers
to a different sense of being. So in his catalog of the
senses of be³ he notes that be and that which is mean that
some things "are" potentially and others in complete
reality—we say both of that which sees potentially and of
that which sees actually, that it is "seeing," etc. But presumably that which sees potentially, since it sees potentially, has that power. Hence its power to see is, i.e., exists
as an actual power belonging to it. Visual capacity actually

*"Actuality, then, is the existence of a thing not in the way we express by
'potentially'; we say that potentially, for instance, a statue of Hermes is in the
block of wood and the half-line is in the whole, because it might be separated
out, and we call even the man who is not studying a man of science, if he is
capable of studying; the thing that stands in contrast to each of these exists
actually. Our meaning can be seen in the particular cases by induction, and we
must not seek a definition of everything but be content to grasp the analogy,
that it is as that which is building to that which is capable of building, and the
waking to the sleeping, and that which is seeing to that which has its eyes shut
but has sight, and that which has been shaped out of the matter to the matter,
and that which has been wrought up to the unwrought. Let actuality be defined
by one member of this antithesis, and the potential by the other. But all things
are not said in the *same sense* to exist actually, but only by analogy—as *A* is in
B or to *B*, *C* is in *D* or to *D*; for some are as movement to potency, and the others
as substance to some sort of matter."²

exists in a man who is capable of seeing but not now seeing whereas it does not so exist in a man incurably blind. Thus being belongs both to potential being and to actual being in Aristotle's sense of actuality, potentiality, and being. And even if we were to consider Aristotle's prime matter, matter wholly formless, as being wholly without actuality in his sense, it would nevertheless have actuality in our sense—that is, it would actually exist as just the entity it is, as the ultimate term of the ontological structure of things in the direction of the material as contrasted with the formal component of their being; and in each case—that of this tree, this dog, this man—the primary matter involved in the thing's composition would have this latter sort of actuality.

Our own concept of actuality, of being as it is expressed in the purely substantive use of *be,* in which *be* is a verb of complete predication on its own account and not simply a link between subject and predicate or an auxiliary appendage to another verb—this concept of ours has to be understood in its own terms, as it belongs to us and is effective in the constitution of our own being as the humans who speak this language of being. It is our actual use, itself, of *be* that is determinative for our thought of being.

Let us therefore explore further our uses of *be* as a substantive verb, and let us first turn to the uses intermediate between the fully substantive and the copulative modes. One sense of *be* is: to take place, to happen. The meeting was yesterday; the meeting is now; the meeting is tomorrow; the meeting will be tomorrow; the meeting could have been any day last week; etc. For an event, such as a meeting, to be is to take place, to happen, to come to pass. The expressions are revealing. To take place is to take a place in a context. To happen is to hap, to chance or befall, hence to fall into place in such a context. To come to pass is to come into the context of passage. *Passage, pass,* derive from *pace* in Middle English, *pas* in Old French, *passus* in Latin—a pace or step, originally a spreading or stretching of the legs in walking, from *pandere,* to spread or stretch. When an event comes to pass, it takes its place in the context of the spatiotemporal world, constituting one of the steps, stretches, passages there.

The actuality of an event is its actual happening, its being a passage in the actual world. When we say where and when the event is, we point to the particular place in the spatiotemporal structure of the world which is occupied by that passage. Thus the actual being of an event is its being in and with other events as passages, stretches, of the spatiotemporal structure of the world. It is the event's having its own place in that structure, one of the places available for occupation by events.* In other words the event belongs to the structure; it has its own place there; it is a member of the world, in the way in which events belong to the world. Events that do not happen, purely imaginary events, are not members of the world. The world has no place for them; its company of events excludes them from a place among them. The world never had a place for the meetings of the Pickwick Club. Those meetings took place only in the nonexistent world of Pickwick's England.

But then what of the being, the actuality, of the world?

*I do not mean by this manner of speech to imply that the spatiotemporal structure exists antecedently to its events or that it exists in some mode of abstract separateness from its events, like a Newtonian absolute space and time. It is the structure *of* the events; it makes each event be as it is, but the events also make it be as it is; the events and the structure belong to one another.

Is not a meeting of the Pickwick Club just as actual in the world of Pickwick as a meeting of the poets in our town's Poetry Club? What is the difference between an actual world and an imaginary world? That cannot also be a matter of taking place or not taking place; a world does not take place, since there are no places for it but only in it. Our world *is,* Pickwick's *is not.* The use of *be* depends on the subject of which it is the predicate. We must take *world* here in its most comprehensive sense as referring to the entire universe—not just the human world, my or your world, the world of politics or of history, the earth or the galaxy. What is the actuality of this world? What do we mean when we say simply that it *is?*

A world is, only insofar as it is the world of its events. The actual world is actual because it is the world of actual events. If the event gains its actuality from being a member of the world, the world gains its actuality from being the world whose members are the actual events. We cannot conjure being out of nothing. Being itself has to be in its own way, a way we come to learn only through intimate acquaintance with it. Our language does not attempt to conjure being out of nothing. When it says *universe* it means, first and foremost, "the whole of created or existing things regarded collectively; all things, including the earth, the heavens, and all that is in them, considered as constituting a systematic whole." That definition is from the *Shorter Oxford English Dictionary.* "Created" comes from the tradition and "systematic" perhaps betrays a certain systematic interest of the compilers; but surely, on the whole, the definition speaks with a genuine English accent.

We understand both the being of an event and the being of the universe of all events because we live in the event and, through that event, in the world. The event occupies an immediateness in our living experience, as does our neighborhood in the world. Pickwick's world, Pickwick, its events—these also occupy a place in our experience and world, but their place is different from that of an actual event and their being is different from that of the actual event or the actual world. Pickwick's world is a world we imagine, but which we imagine precisely as not actual. We do not live, suffer, and joy within it. Pickwick lives in it; and we are able to live there with him in sympathy, but not in our primary role as the persons we actually are. We know that our own events are because they come to pass in our world; and we know that our world is because it is the world of just those events.

A decisive point to notice is this: if the being of an event lies in its belonging to the actual world, the being of the world lies in its being the world of the actual events, the world to which they belong. The being of event and of world lies in *their reciprocal belonging to one another.* An event *is*—if and only if it is related to other events in such a way that they are its co-members in the world, so that it belongs to their world as its own world. The world *is*—if and only if it is the collectivity of actual events in such a way that the events belong to it as its members and it belongs to them as their world. If the world were not this collectivity of actual events, it would not be. Not only would it not be the world; it would simply and absolutely not be. The world's being depends on its playing the role of letting actual events belong to it. The events' being depends on their playing the role of member of the world, belonging to the entire company.

In these brief observations I am not trying to spin a theory of the nature of being. I am attempting simply to report on what the language I speak—a language of the unlearned as well as the learned—itself says about the being of an event and the being of the world. If the reader should complain that the above remarks make use of metaphoric or other figurative language, unbefitting a genuine scholar, he should recollect that those remarks are made by the English language. I operate here only as a vehicle through which the language articulates its utterances. Naturally, the mistakes are mine; but I have tried —and tried *only*—to repeat what I have heard by listening to English as it gets itself spoken.

The concept of belonging—along with the several connected families of concepts to which it belongs—is one of the most fundamental concepts of our language.* But we cannot stop with it at present. For we cannot validly say, "To be is to belong," simply in that way. Being is not just belonging. The event *is*, not just because it belongs to the world, but also because the world is *actual*, the actual world. The world *is*, not just because it is the world of the event, but because the event is *actual*, an actual event. The actuality of an event can only be the actuality of an event in the actual world, and the actuality of the world can only be the actuality of the world of actual events, yet there is something in the actuality of both that transcends the

---

*Here is the list of synonyms in Soule's dictionary[4] under the heading "Belong to":

1. Be the property of, be possessed by, be owned by.
2. Be an attribute *or* quality *or* characteristic *or* mark of, characterize, pertain *or* appertain to, inhere in, be the prerogative *or* right of, be the privilege of.
3. Regard, relate to, refer to, have reference to.
4. Be appendant to, constitute a part of, be connected with.
5. Behoove, concern, be incumbent on, be the duty of, devolve on, be the business *or* concern of. The opposites of all these should also be kept in mind.

content of merely belonging to one another. What is it?

The being of event and of world lies in their reciprocal belonging to one another. What is it that thus lies in their belonging? This question is addressed, not to ourselves as thinkers seeking to produce a novel idea, but to our language and its own manner of thinking. What does English say of the being of event and world, which lies in their reciprocal belonging, and *is* their actuality, their actualness? The word the language uses is . . . the word we have been using all along, *actual, actualness, actuality.* What is it to be actual, according to English?

The question does not have to do with the Aristotelian sense, in which the actual is distinguished from and related to the potential. It has in part to do with the sense in which *actual* is correlative to *possible,* for to be, in the primal sense, is not to be merely possible but to be more, namely, actual. What is merely possible *is* not. What is actual *is.* Nevertheless this distinction between actuality and possibility does not represent the language's definition of *actual* but only its usage of *actual* in contrast with *possible.*

The actual is what belongs to, is appropriate to, resembles, or is of the nature of *act, action.* An act is a thing done, a deed. The Latin *agere,* from which *actus, actum* lead to our *act,* means: to drive, to incite, to keep in movement, to be engaged upon, to be concerned, to behave, to do. What is actual acts, operates, does, drives, performs. What does nothing, is nothing. As William James said, imaginary fire does not burn, real fire does. The actuality of fire is displayed in its burning. Actualness is the exercise of power. Actual being is not the actuality of potential being. Actual being is the actuation of the power to do; it is power acting as power, might acting as might, force and energy acting as force and energy. What is, is, and is in the degree and direction that it is, insofar as it is efficacious, exercising the spontaneity that is its very own. An atom is, insofar as it is efficacious as an atom, doing spontaneously what an atom does, being a member of the world in just that way. To be an atom is to act atomically.

When our thinking extends the idea of actual being from the things of the world to things imagined, as when we speak of the abstract entities of mathematics, it carries with it this notion of actuality, developing a metaphorical usage in that sphere. If we say that the number 17 exists, we do so because 17 "behaves" as a number. It is constructible out of other numbers, like 10 and 7; it resists division by any numbers other than 1 and itself, so acting as a prime number; multiplying it by 2 results in another number, 34; etc. We are even led to speak of the world or the universe of discourse of the natural numbers, counting 17 as a member belonging to it in such a way that the being of that world depends as much on 17 as the being of 17 does on that world. The actual being of 17 lies in its belonging to the class of natural numbers as the being of that class lies in its being the class of all of those numbers, owning each of them as one of its members. They belong to one another reciprocally, as event and world belong to one another reciprocally. The character of the belonging differs, for numbers do not act like events, and the world of space and time owns its members in a more concrete way than does the class of natural numbers. But there is a metaphoric closeness of the two senses of being, of the distinctive sort that is characteristic of philosophical concepts.

We may thus say quite generally that as the English language thinks, and we along with it who speak it, being is the efficacity of belonging. I said above that being is not just belonging. On the other hand we must also say, being is exactly belonging: it is the exercise of the force that belongs to the deed, act, doing, effecting of belonging. To be in the world is to take one's place there, to occur there, to exist there; it is to occur as one among the things that belong to the world, taking a place which is one's own and which is a place that belongs to the world as one of its own places. It is to own membership in the world, in virtually every sense of "own."[1] Being is the act of belonging. It runs in two directions. For belonging occurs between at least two beings: it is not a mere quality, but a relation; the co-operation, co-action, of at least two beings is necessary for being to be.

In philosophy we try, among other things, to imagine what an absolute being would be. As absolute it would have to stand by itself alone, depending on no other being, belonging to no other being, having no other being belonging to it, existing in complete isolation simply by its own power to be. But the thought is contradictory. In the very act of isolating itself, standing by itself alone, it would be repelling all other beings from its own being, and thereby aligning itself with them in a group of mutually excluding beings. By its very act of being alone, it would be determining itself to be a member of a group of lone beings.

If we try to think that reality might consist of a single absolute being, no other beings existing, so that the single being no longer had others to repel and could be alone by itself without belonging to any class or group or world, then we fail. For we are there thinking, and by our thinking, repelling the absolute being from ourselves and ourselves from the absolute being. An absolute that does not belong to our world is no absolute; and, belonging to our world, it also is no absolute. An absolute being is not.

Therefore, when philosophers have tried to think an absolute being, they have been compelled to *internalize* belonging within it, so that we who think are within it. The absolute being has to be thought of as producing its own other within itself so that it may belong to that other, the other to it, and the two together with one another.

This thinking gave its structure to absolute idealism in Fichte, Schelling, and Hegel. Absolute idealism was monistic: it thought the single absolute being was the total being. It had to be an idealism, since it had to account for the being of man with his consciousness and self-consciousness as well as the being of the things of nature, and it could do so only by assigning consciousness and self-consciousness to the absolute being. In order to be able to carry out its program of thinking everything as a member of the absolute and thinking the absolute as the owner of all things, it had to develop a method by which the absolute being unfolded within its own being the being of all other beings. This was the dialectical method, by which a being is thought to give rise to its own other and then to appropriate that other as its own. To follow the dialectic in the philosophy of absolute idealism is just to show how, if you were the absolute being, you would generate your own other and then absorb it into your possession. Absolute idealism was, and had to be, an absolute solipsism, as it began in Fichte and ended in Hegel. In order to be, the absolute mind had to be doubled within itself, that is, self-conscious; and in order to be absolute, what it had to be conscious of was, after all, only its own self.

Thus the philosophy which tried hardest and with most success—even if not with final success—to think of being as being by oneself alone, had to cancel the loneliness of the alone in order to make it come alive with being. So we note that Hegel's definition of being—of pure abstract being at first, and of the aspect of pure being that belongs to every more concrete shape of being—is this: being is immediateness, and immediateness is relation to self, *Unmittelbarkeit* which is *Beziehung auf sich selbst.* Interestingly enough, the place in which Hegel gives the clearest and most forthright statement of the meaning of *being* is not either of the logics but the philosophy of religion, at the point at which he is finally concerned with the ontological proof of God's existence, that is, of God's being. Here it is necessary to say exactly what being is, for on it depends the ultimate issue of the being of God.

He has to show that being belongs essentially to God, Whom he conceives of as the absolute concept (notion), the self-determining concept. And he says:

> First of all we ask: what is being, this property, determinateness, reality? Being is nothing more than the unsayable, conceptless; it is not the concrete something that the concept is; it is altogether merely the abstraction of relation to itself. We may say: it is immediateness. Being is the immediate in general, and conversely the immediate is being, is in relation to itself, which means that mediation is negated. This determination, "relation to itself, immediateness," is accordingly for itself in the concept in general and in the absolute concept, in the concept of God, the wholly abstract, wholly poverty-stricken (characteristic) that this concept is relation to itself. Thus this abstract relation to self lies in the concept itself. We have to have this simple insight to begin with.[5]

If being is the act of belonging, then a being that would be absolute could only be one that belongs to itself, for it would have to exercise the power of belonging, act out the act of belonging. This fact lay at the ground of the strength of Hegel's philosophy, and it enabled him to bring into that philosophy everything human and super-human, as well as natural. Belonging-to-self was for Hegel the Heraclitean *gnome* by which his thought guided all things through all. In setting belonging at the center of being he had a hold on the basic truth, a hold that let him bring all the gods of all the religions into the sphere of his Absolute Spirit. So, in the end, he could see the Christian trinity in terms of the realization of self-reference: God the Father knows Himself as Himself in God the Son by a knowledge which is the love of God the Holy Spirit. The Holy Spirit is God distinguishing Himself from Himself as Son and knowing himself therein as the revelation he essentially is, the act of love which is the ultimate act of being. Therefore we understand that and how God is spirit, love, and truth.

If there were an absolute being, then it would have to determine itself to belong to itself; for being is the act of belonging and, in order to be, it would have to act that act.

At the beginning it was said that the substantive use of *be*, in which it serves as a verb of complete predication on its own account, was apparently the one of most direct concern in regard to the problem of the meaning of be-ing. But if we now turn briefly to the use of *be* as copula or linking verb, we see that this use belongs as centrally to the meaning as does the substantive use. For the copulative or linking use is precisely the use that par-ticularizes the different modes of the act of belonging.

"The corridor is narrow." The corridor is a being about which the sentence speaks; it is the sentence's sub-ject. The predicate, narrow, is also a being, namely, an attribute of the subject. The attribute belongs to the subject; the subject possesses the attribute. This possession, whose reflection is belonging, and this belonging, whose reflection is possessing, are the meaning-content of *is* in this sentence. Our language thinks the corridor as owner, possessor of its attribute, and it thinks the attribute as belonging to the subject, owned by it. To be sure, this meaning of *is,* as our language explicates itself, is reached by a metaphorical extension from our thinking about ourselves as owners of our possessions and about the things that belong to us as owned by us, possessions of ours. How else can we get to the thoughts we need to have save by such metaphorical extension from the thoughts we already have? No one is exempt from this indispensable procedure of thinking, however much he may pride himself on his literal-mindedness.

"The man is walking." When a man walks, he acts in a determinate manner in the world. This determinate manner of acting—locomotion, the body in movement from one place to another place in a stretch of time by the alternate striding of its legs—is one particularization of a man's being in the world, hence of his worldly being. Because the world is spatial and temporal and man is a bodily being, it is possible for him to act in this bodily way of walking. Walking is an action of man in his bodily being. This action, attributed to the man, is thought by our language as being *his* action. It is not some other man who is doing the walking; it is he, the man spoken of. The action, as his, has his own self vested in it. The man, if spoken to and in normal condition of health, would (if he deigned to reply, honestly) say: "Yes, it is I who am doing the walking. It is my walking that you are talking about. I am the agent, the walk is my action." This relationship of the walk to the man, denoted by the use of the possessive pronouns *my* and *his,* is a manner of being, namely, action. In English, action is the doing of some act by some agent. The act is the agent's. That is why, when the agent is a man, our thinking tells us that he did it, hence, it is imputable to him as his performance, and he must take the responsibility of being its author. If a man were forced to go through the motions of walking, as when some persons should grab hold of his body and make it advance by alternately pushing and pulling its legs, supporting it upright, etc., we would not say that the man himself was walking; he is not the agent; it is not *his* action but *theirs.*

It is unnecessary to make further comments here on further uses of the linking verb. What Aristotle first and early tried to do—to specify the most universal ways in which predicates could be predicated of subjects, which would be equivalent in English to specifying the most universal ways in which our linking verb *be* could be used, thus arriving at "categories" of being—could be undertaken in regard to English as he tried it with Greek. The old-fashioned logic textbooks are full of this sort of discussion. The theory of predication is the theory of the various possible meanings and uses of predicates, and it explicates the thoughts of language about being a member of a class or a class that possesses members, possessing a quality or belonging as a quality to something, possessing a quantity or belonging as a quantity to something, having a relation to something or belonging to something as its relation to something, performing an action or being an action performed, etc. In every case, since the subject of predication is linked to its predicate as *its* predicate, and the predicate to the subject as *its* subject, the linkage is that of the act of belonging, and that is the reason why the verb *be* is inserted into the position of the link: being is the link that ties beings to beings, the copula that joins them by its unitive power.

In discussing "The man is walking" I took as example of the copulative use an illustration of the use of *be* as auxiliary verb. For this sentence can also be viewed in the latter way: instead of "The man walks," which directly connects verb with noun, we say, "The man is walking," using the *is* with the present participle of *walk* in order to express continuous or progressive action. *Is* thus takes on a phase of time-reference, omitted in the above discussion of the copula. Where beings exist as temporal beings, *be* is used in its tenses. We could say, "The man was walking," "The man will be walking," etc. Where the beings under consideration are not temporal, we do not use the tenses (or: where we do not use the tenses, there we do not think of the beings as temporal). We say, "17 is a prime number," not "17 was a prime number, 17 will be a prime number"; the latter sentences are mathematically meaningless.

The auxiliary use of *be* for tense as well as copula thus does not add something of general interest to the copulative use, but only points in the direction of special meaning-intentions. It is the same with the use of *be* with the past participle of a transitive verb to form the passive voice (I was hired), with the past participle of an intransitive verb to form the perfect tense (He is gone), with the infinitive or present participle to express various meanings such as intention, obligation, etc. (We are coming tomorrow. You are to obey your mother), and with analogous further uses. In each case, a mode of belonging and possessing is brought in and given some particular determination: the undergoing of action, the completion of

action, the intention to act, the assignment and possession of responsibility, etc.

Throughout the use of *be* in English, our language articulates for itself and for us who speak it the meaning of
owning and being owned, belonging and being belonged
to, possessing and being possessed, and, in general, *being
related*—not simply to self, as Hegel's idealistic preoccupation led him to think—but *to other as to own* and its con-
verse, *being related to by other as to its own*. This is the
meaning of *be* as our language speaks it and thinks it in
general.

Once we are able to understand ourselves when we use
the word *be* in accordance with the language we speak, it
becomes possible to turn to philosophical thinking in a
reflective manner, aware of what our project is therein.
Philosophical thinking is thinking about being—and,
therefore also, about not-being. As Aristotle first observed, whereas other cognitive disciplines cut out some
part or aspect of being to study, philosophy turns to being
itself and wishes to understand what it is as such. This
understanding does not consist merely in understanding
the meaning of the verb *be*. Naturally we need to know that
meaning, at least in the sense of being able to use the
words *be* and *being* correctly. But to understand being is to
understand the *content* that the act of belonging comprehends. To say that being is the act of belonging is just
to give, as it were, a nominal or merely verbal definition
of the term *being*. What concretely goes into the act of
belonging? What *is* being in concrete fact?

The question is one of *fact*. It is an "empirical" question. We cannot answer it merely by using the analytico-
logical devices of abstract understanding. No amount of

analysis of words, language, concepts, thoughts will give us the answer. The answer is to be found only in the beings themselves that are. They show the content of being, for they act out the act of belonging. Philosophy is not mere thinking, mere logical analysis, the empty act of the understanding. Philosophy is the study of being, and it can come to know being only by studying the beings that are. Philosophy is thus a positive science, a science of observation. It has to turn to existence to find therein the content of being. It has to look at the physical world and its physical inhabitants, the biological region, the psychological region, and eventually the human region, which reaches up to a spiritual dimension. The act of belonging occurs throughout these regions, for they are all regions of being.

Being is hierarchical. It has levels, a stratified structure, with many devious and complex by-paths in all the strata. The act by which an atom is, so that we can rightly say "There is something atomic; there is something of the nature of an atom," is an act of being just as truly as is the act by which a man is, which enables us to say rightly "There is something human; there is something of the nature of a man." But, on the other hand, the content of the act is in each case different; to be a man is very different from being an atom, different not just in contingent and material details, but different precisely as an act of being, namely, different in point of the nature of the belonging involved. Man belongs and is belonged to in a manner very greatly different from an atom. It is because of the vast difference between the two acts that we place the atom somewhere near the bottom of the hierarchy of being and man close to the top.

As the hierarchy of being ascends, the contents of being become richer. That is, the possibilities of an act of belonging grow more extensive and more intensive, and even further, begin to incorporate the feature of meaning within themselves. Biological entities act in the manner of beings with tropes, drives, and instinctual tendencies, so that their behavior assumes a form that compares with human teleology. It is a question of some philosophical importance how far actual teleology, real purposiveness, belongs to life as such, and where in the hierarchy of being it begins to appear. That problem must obviously be left aside here. Wherever purpose begins, it shows itself surely among animals, especially the higher animals, and it blossoms into full form in man. Similarly, wherever it may be that consciousness first appears, it reaches a great fullness in man.*

Because of the fact that being grows as it rises, and grows particularly in meaning as purpose and consciousness enter, it is possible to affirm that the meaning of being is best and most truly disclosed in the upper reaches rather than the lower strata. The meaning that is constitutive in being, when being grows full of meaning, is better shown there. What it means, in the fullest sense, to belong and be belonged to, is best shown there, and in particular, in the stratum of human being itself.

Consequently I shall here skip over the subjects of biological and psychical being, such as arise in the philosophy of life and of animate being, and turn directly to

*I use the notion of consciousness here in the widest sense it is capable of receiving. Modern psychoanalysis and depth psychology have instructed us about the unconscious and the preconscious. Part of the lesson has been to realize that the unconscious acts on purpose, knowing what it is doing, extremely cunning and skillful in its devices. The victim of a neurosis or a psychosis is not himself conscious of what his unconscious mind is doing with and to him (a form of passiveness in which his humanness is reduced in some degree) but his unconscious mind is not in the same predicament. It is—without the fact being at all paradoxical—"perfectly conscious of what it is doing." It couldn't do what it does as it does it unless it knew what it was doing. My use of *conscious* includes the unconscious' own self-consciousness.

human being as the predominant example of the fullness of being that is shown to us in this world of time and space. This branch of philosophy is sometimes called *philosophical anthropology.*

Understanding the word *be* as we have above, in terms of the act of belonging, what is to be said about the meaning and content of human being?

If being is the act of belonging then the meaning of being is the content of that act, namely, belonging—belonging to and being belonged to. To be is to perform the role of belonging and being belonged to. The meaning of being is the content of that role. Being is acting out one's role of belonging and being belonged to, not belonging and not being belonged to. As the atom is by acting out the role of an atomic member of the physical world, or a blade of grass is by acting out its vegetative role in its environment, so man is by the way in which he acts as belonging to his human world—including the necessary transcending acts as well. What is the essential content of this human role?

That man has a fundamental role to play in being is given in the very fact that man strives to be and have an ego. He strives to be and be able to call himself *I.* Only in periods of great stress, as in mental disease, or in a role of impersonal objectivity, as when writing about himself as one datum among others, does he give way and refer to himself otherwise, as e.g. *he,* and even then he uses a personal pronoun. And if, at an extreme, he were to call himself *it,* it would be his own self that he would be depersonalizing. In doing so he would be at the same time dehumanizing himself. Such depersonalization and dehumanization must be recognized as an extreme possibility of modification of human being. It is so just because it is de-personalization and de-humanization, and therefore contains within itself, as underlying condition, the striving toward the personal as the norm from which deviation occurs. If that norm were not effectively present as a central aim, the deviation would not be possible as such and we could no longer speak of the subject as a human being.

The role of being and having an ego is not given to man as a mere object for contemplation. It is not as though he has presented to himself a concept or plan or project drawn up under the title "I" which then has to be realized in existence. To become, be, and have an ego is not a technical-technological engineering project. It is man's being itself. His role as member of a human world is just to be an ego in that world. That is a first and abstract way of stating the content of the role and therefore the meaning of man's being. Man's belonging is his belonging to his world as an ego. This belonging occurs in his existence as a role to be played. That is, it occurs not in the form of a fact already realized, but in that of a task, an immanent tendency, destiny, opportunity, gift of possibility, on the one side, and a vocation, a calling and a responsibility, on the other.*

However it is not just one role among others (as being

*No single and certainly no simple description of man's being as ego in its relation to time and especially to the future will suffice to state its full reality. Such a description as early Heidegger's, that sees man as "thrown" into the world with the "project" of becoming his ownmost possibility of being, as the neuter entity *Dasein* existing in mood and understanding, has a certain degree of conformity to the facts, but only a certain degree. Man is not simply thrown here. He blossoms here, too, and especially in a domestic environment that cares for him on his own account. His being born is not just a matter of being a neuter *Dasein* cast down from the womb into a world it never made. It is also an emergence from the bodily bosom of the mother into the more open bosom of his family and his home, and of his world itself, insofar as his family and world care for him on his own account as a genuine person whose coming makes a significant difference to his world. Man can be thrown into a quandary but not into a blessed event. Being in the world is not only a predicament; it can be a blessing. The later Heidegger knows this too: the very last line of *Aus der Erfahrung des Denkens* is: "Blessing thinks."

is not just one mode of being among others). The role of father or mother, doctor or patient, newspaper boy or president of a corporation is one among others, which may or may not be assumed by a given person. But the role of being a person is the fundamental role, the role of roles, that is the precondition of the possibility of all other roles, since it is the one that first constitutes the I who can adopt them. And, on the other hand, it is the central role, again, because all the others are needed just to fill it out and make it what it is to be. I am a person, the ego I am, precisely in working out the particular roles that are to concretize the abstract universality of my ego. My being is: to become and be an I, myself, in and through the particular forms of being accessible to an ego.

This primary task is not that of searching for my identity. One searches for his identity when he encounters difficulty in being, in establishing and maintaining himself as an ego, so that in some way his ego comes into question. If my effort to be runs into serious refusals of my world to let me be a member of it, then, unable to attain to the belonging I need in order to become and be my I, I am impélled to cast about in quest of my I, i.e. in quest of the missing belonging. The search for identity is thus a secondary phenomenon which depends for its existence and nature on the primary fact of human being, the task of becoming and being an I, myself, in and through the particular roles of ego-existence. The search for identity is not less important for being secondary; its importance stems exactly from its relation, as secondary, to the primary fact.

Certain religions treat this primary fact as an original sin or a primal unhappiness. Man's being an ego, it is said, is his first sin, the sin involved in his very existence as a man, because it means separation from God, the I as over against the Divine. Or man's being an ego is said to be his entrance into the cycle of being and suffering from which the only escape is into not-being—or the condition of neither being nor not-being—once more. There is profound philosophical truth contained in these myths. Insofar as being an ego entails separation from what is other than the ego, the ego is exposed to the possibilities of negation and suffering; but at the same time separation from the other is a necessary condition for the development of the ego. Thus the ego necessarily, as ego, opens itself up to the possibilities of negation and suffering. This is the "fall"—not a being thrown, but an entering upon the destiny of being an individual human being, a person. When the egg of being is broken, it is hard to put it together again. There is a kind of guilt in breaking out.

Another way of looking at the situation is to note the ambiguity and ambivalence involved in man's being. In order to be my I, I have to differentiate myself from my other; yet in order to be my I, I have to relate myself to my other. Separation and connection are inseparably bound together. I must separate from the other in order to connect with other, and connect with other in order to separate from other. To be an individual I must participate with others; but this participation occurs just for the sake of the individualization, hence, the separation. If I am to be with the other, then I must be other than he; yet I can only be other than he through being with him. These paradoxes, if so they may be called, belong to man's being because it is the being of an ego. An ego is a being whose being lies in establishing its limits by transcending them and transcending them by establishing them. I exist here, as this being, only insofar as I am able to reach across the bounds of my own being so as to participate in the being of an other; but I can participate in his being only insofar as I establish my own being's limits and remain within them. Ego is a principle of distinction. The I is an individual, differentiated from other individuals in its own active being as ego. Whereas a thing—a stone, an atom—simply *is* different from the next thing, an ego, by endeavoring to become and be itself, differentiates itself from what is not itself. Yet ego is also a principle of connection. For, in the very act of differentiating itself from the not-self, it is seeking to unite itself with the not-self.

The fundamental role of human being is this two-in-one act: to unite with other in differentiating from other, to participate in separation, to belong as an ego. Understanding of being, and of the concrete meaning of being, is therefore understanding of the nature of the differentiation and separation by which ego and other are parted and, then, understanding of the nature of the union and participation by which they are brought together. This question of the nature of differentiation and union, of separation and participation, is the central question of philosophy, since it is the question of the constitution of the meaning of being at the place where being is most meaningful. What is the nature of the otherness by which I and my other are other to each other? What is the nature of the union by which the separation in that otherness is overcome? What is the alienation, what the reconciliation, of ego and other?

The philosopher who, more than any other, devoted the full energy of his thinking to this problem was Hegel. We owe more to him than to any other philosopher the groundwork of our understanding of this subject. The whole of his philosophy, as it is represented in the *Phenomenology of Mind* or in the *Encyclopedia of the Philosophical Sciences* is devoted singly to answering this question. It is therefore in order here to consider his view. What follows will be critical of Hegel at the crucial point of his account: it will say that there is an error—even a monstrous error—at the heart of his thinking about the problem. Consequently it is all the more fitting to make an affirmation of respect at the outset.

Hegel is often treated with abuse and contempt. It is easy to find references to him and his failings—in books written by people who have not read or understood him. Many people know that his writings are full of nonsense —for which reason they have never studied them. I wish therefore to say for myself here that the following criticism comes not out of neglect but out of devoted concern. If it is mistaken, the mistake is due to a failure of intelligence, not of effort at responsibility. In the writings of Hegel, after many years of studying and teaching philosophy, I have found more to think about, work with, and build on, than in those of any other philosopher I have read. Schelling runs him a close second. Others will doubtless have had other experiences. Many Catholic philosophers have had this experience with Aquinas. Kant, too, has been to many students a perennially invigorating source of illumination and inspiration, and so it is with other of the greatest thinkers—Plato, Aristotle, Spinoza.

Only in recent times, during which the anti-historical, anti-metaphysical, positivist tendency has achieved a double foothold in the English-speaking world, in the forms of logical empiricism and ordinary-language philosophy, the two chief forms of analytic philosophy, has the study of the great thinkers suffered. The inevitable result is that philosophy itself has suffered and its practitioners grown empty in spirit. Much of what has been produced recently in Britain and the United States in the name of philosophy is vain cleverness, technical ingenuity, word play, along with the studied neglect of questions significant to human existence. It is therefore important to give one's testimony on this matter and to declare that in one page of Hegel—sometimes even in one page of the *Philosophy of Nature,* the weakest, most time-bound, most wrongly thought of all his works—there is often more insight and wisdom regarding the meaning of being than is to be found in the entire corpus of writings of the analytic philosophers. It is so because Hegel understood what it was to seek for philosophical truth but they do not.

The error which I believe is present in Hegelian thought comes from its overplaying of the role of identity in the concept of the overcoming of alienation by reconciliation between ego and other. In his zeal to reach the ultimate in thought and to make it all-inclusively concrete, Hegel interpreted ownness as identity. The unity between form and content, subject and object, ideal and real, finite and infinite, soul and body, was treated by him as an identity. It is important to be clear at the beginning and to keep in mind throughout, that despite all the strenuous effort of his thinking —the most sustained, the most brilliant, the most achieved thinking in the history of philosophy—the one point that Hegel was never able to establish, but at most merely affirmed, was that the *unity* of differents consisted in their *identity.* It is at once the heart and the Achilles' heel of his thinking.

The identity he has in view, which he calls speculative identity, in opposition to the blank, abstract sameness that the understanding thinks of under the name, is a rich and concrete mode of unity, going beyond even the identity of the "indifference of opposites" of Schelling. In simplest terms it is a doubly negative—or as Hegel sometimes says an infinitely negative—relation-to-self. What is truly self-identical distinguishes itself from itself in determining itself as something other than itself, thus negating itself. Yet in this very other it thereupon finds only itself and in it returns to itself, thus performing a second negation. Namely, it negates its own other by returning in that other to itself. The first negation limited it by opposing to it an other (apparently) not itself; the second negation, by identifying the other with itself, removed the limitation and thus reinstated the infinity of the self. Identity is consequently a self-relation that is mediated by a transcending movement out toward an other and a return, in and through that movement, to the immanence of the self. It is a mediated rather than a simple, bare, abstractly immediate relation-to-self.

Hegelian thought consists, wholly and completely from beginning to end, in the concrete working out of this notion of the truth of being as speculative identity. The idea is the concept of identity fulfilled. Nature is identity in its being outside itself. Spirit is self-identity ultimately realized. Truth, freedom, God, the absolute—these are concrete forms of identity. The concept or category of identity itself, in its full sense as identity—namely, the unity of being and not-being, or in reflected form the unity of being-different and not-being-different—is merely the first, purest, most abstract definition of the absolute. (4.78)[6]

God is this: to differentiate himself from himself, to be an object to himself, but to be thoroughly identical with himself in this difference—spirit. (16.191)

Truth is: to relate oneself to the objective as something which is not foreign or alien. (16.257)

Freedom is: relation to something objective as not to something foreign or alien; it is the same determination as truth, except that in freedom the negation of the difference of otherness still receives emphasis, so that it appears in the form of reconciliation. (16.208)

Spirit is essentially this: to come to itself out of its otherness and out of the overcoming of this otherness, by way of the negation of negation; it experiences and goes through its own self-alienation . . . Spirit is eternally this: to die to itself, to make itself finite in naturalness; but it returns to itself by the annulling of its naturalness. (15.435) The evolution of spirit is a going-out, a setting-out-of-self, and at the same time a coming-to-self. This being-with-self of spirit, this its coming-to-self, can be affirmed to be its supreme, absolute goal. (17.51)

The Hegelian *dialectic,* as process and as method, is just the occurrence and procedure of self-diremption and self-recovery in, through, and out of the diremption.

The *Idea* is God's determining of himself to differentiate himself from himself, and the eternal sublating of this difference. (16.230)

The Idea is the realized *concept (notion),* and in the concept—and even more so in the Idea—there is this general content: to be identical with self, to relate self to self, by negation of the sundering or division of self, of which sundering it itself is at the same time the activity of in-stituting. (16.542) There can be only one method in all science, Hegel declares; this is the method of the self-explicating concept, for there is but one such concept, which explicates itself, and the method is just this self-explication. The concept is the activity of positing itself as being identical with being. It is the living, self-mediating process. It consists in this: to overcome its difference from being, to objectivate itself. It is itself the deed of producing itself in being. (16.543)

There is no shape of being, or of not-being, or of their growing forms of unity, which does not find a place some-where in the process of self-diremption and self-recovery. At the very beginning there stands that which alone could be a beginning, namely, pure being itself, which is pure indeterminate immediateness. If we ask what this immedi-ateness consists in, which constitutes being as being, He-gel's answer moves forthrightly into the concept of identity: it is altogether just the abstraction of relation-to-self.[7] That is, it is pure self-relation *before* that which is has moved out beyond itself toward its other, in order to mediate itself there so that it may recover itself in that other. It is the stage of innocence, of pure paradisal con-tainment within self, the stage of being in-itself, *an sich*, merely potential, with nothing out there beyond it that might yet be an other for it. That is why the very first movement of being toward actualization in the dialectic is toward nothing, the only other that being can yet have and find, in which nevertheless it *will* recover itself—in the ceaseless process of becoming, or of transition not only of being into nothing but also of nothing into being.

The point and direction of the Hegelian interpretation of being and of everything that arises out of being is already seen in this poorest and most abstract concept of it, the pure being of the beginning. It is not a mere, blank, static *isness*. Enclosed as it may be within itself, innocent as it may be of what is beyond it and first appears as a mere nothing to it, motionless as it may yet be before it has entered into the unrest of becoming, it still is and contains within itself the impulse to transcend itself toward itself, to thrust outward in search of itself. That is what it is to be *self*-relation even before there is found an other, different from self, in which to recover self. To be self-related, in the sense of being wholly self-enclosed, is yet at the same time and on that very account, to be not so much the actual reaching out toward another as the impulse, the potency, the readiness to do so, a readiness that immediately is and becomes an endeavor. This endeavor is the going-over into nothing with which the movement of the concept starts.

Once the movement starts, the whole constitution of being is set in process. Being is immediateness, relation-to-self. And immediateness recurs, over and over. When being goes over into nothing and nothing in turn goes over again into being, there arises a new immediateness, a more concrete being, which is the truth of pure being and nothing, that is, the recovery of being's identity with itself in the nothing, namely, becoming. Becoming is the identity of being and nothing. Such identity is a relation of being to itself—a relation-to-self, that is, an immediateness. But it is now an immediateness that has been mediated by a diremption or sundering into self and other together with a recovery of self in other. Hence it is a mediated immediateness. If one wished for another word, thought, *logos, gnome* to replace that of idea or spirit it would be: *mediated immediateness*. Immediateness is being;

mediated immediateness is the truth of being. Everywhere the start is made with immediateness, the mere
being of the phenomenon in question; there is a mediation through splitting and opposition; and then there is a
reconciliation, a becoming immediate again, in which
identity-in-difference is attained and the aim of being to
be true is realized at the given stage.

The Hegelian identity is a concept offered to explicate
the truth and freedom of being that are found in genuine
reconciliation. Reconciliation, understood as process as
well as product, is therefore another *logos* and *gnome*,
meaning the same thing as God, truth, freedom, idea,
spirit, though each of these *logoi* has its specialization and
particularized usage. The meaning of the world and its
history lies in the reconciliation of the opposing forces
that being experiences in the living process of its self-
realization in nature and spirit. The whole intent of all
knowing and all doing lies in bringing about a reconciliation between the subjective and the objective. Knowing is
overcoming the alienation of the object of consciousness,
making it into consciousness' own; doing is overcoming
the alienation of the object of will, making it into will's
own. Reconciliation is the aim of philosophy as well as
religion. In religion reconciliation is the negation of the
separation between God and a world that is estranged
from Him. (16.208) Philosophy aims to bring about such
reconciliation through cognition achieved by speculative
thinking. (17.94) As religion is God, who is spirit knowing
himself, so philosophy is spirit knowing itself.

What now is the difficulty with Hegel's theory of identity-in-difference? It is best seen, I think, if we confront the
theory with actual subject-matter which it was intended to

make intelligible. For Hegel's aim was to be responsive to actuality—not to any random, accidental, contingent appearance, but to essential reality, things that truly are, life and mind that are truly free. Hegel's subject-matter was universal: logic, nature, mind. He interpreted all of it in terms of the concept of the recovery of identity in and out of difference or of the mediation and reestablishment of immediateness. Therefore any of the topics in any of his writings would be relevant—from the pure being of the beginning of logic to the absolute thought at the end of the philosophy of mind.

I choose, not arbitrarily, the matter of love. This is not an arbitrary choice because, as Hegel understood, love is one of the names of ultimate being—God is love—and the understanding of it is one of the supreme tests of the truth of a philosophy. No philosophy which does not attempt to understand love and succeed at least in making an approach to its true nature is worth taking the trouble to think about. For Hegel, philosophy could just as well be called the knowing of love as the knowing of God, of truth, of freedom, or of spirit, for love, in its ultimate form, is the Spirit itself, God.[8]

Love shows itself in different forms—of children for parents, parents for children, brother for brother, man for woman, woman for man, friend for friend, individual for his home and his native land, man for God, God for man, and all the many other forms in which the spirit relates itself to its own. In each of these forms Hegel discerned one or other shape of identity-in-difference, mediated immediateness. Here are some of his formulae for love:

(In love) one is not onesidedly in himself, but limits himself willingly in relation to an other, yet knows himself, in this limitation, as his own self.

The first factor in love is that I do not wish to be an independent person for myself, and that, if I were this, I would feel myself to be defective and incomplete. The second factor is that I attain myself in another person, that I am validly there in him, and that he reaches the same condition in me. Love is therefore the most colossal contradiction, which the understanding cannot resolve.

In love an individual has the consciousness of himself in the consciousness of an other; he has divested himself of himself, and in this mutual self-divestment he has gained himself.

In love, in every aspect of its content, these elements are present which we offered as the fundamental concept of Absolute Spirit: reconciled return from its other to itself ... The true essence of love consists in the surrender of consciousness of self, forgetting oneself in another self, and yet having and possessing oneself for the first time in this perishing and forgetting.

The higher union of my self-consciousness in general with the universal, the certainty, security, and feeling of this identity is love, blessedness.

Love is a differentiating of two, who yet are absolutely not different for one another. The feeling and consciousness of this identity is love ... The two are only this consciousness of their being outside one another and of their identity; this intuiting, this feeling, this knowing of unity—this is love ... God is love, i.e. this differentiating and the nullity of this difference, a play of this differentiating which is not taken seriously and which thus is posited as annulled, i.e. the eternal, simple Idea.

(God is) this manifesting, objectivating of self, and being identical with self in this objectivation, eternal love.[9]

Does Hegel have his eyes on the actuality of love? To be sure, he is not thinking of relationships of mere utility, or of pleasure and agreeable feelings, or of lustful passion and its greedy satisfaction. But is he thinking of the genuinely universal nature of love when he thus formulates it as the reconciled return from the self's other to itself in that other?

If it were, then love would not be love; or, rather, all love would then be nothing other at root than self-love. For to love the other not just as itself but only as the reflecting mirror which gives back the image of the self is not really to love the other at all, but only the self. The self is now aggrandized by its absorption of the other into itself and, as it thinks, its absorption into self by the other. It has become (it thinks) a greater self by swallowing the other and letting itself be swallowed by the other, and this is extremely pleasant to it, for the other has been wholly compliant in feeding the self (as well as its own self) in the process. But even such reciprocal, mutually reflecting self-love remains self-love. It is even self-love if the two coalesce so that no difference remains, but now the new *we* loves itself. Self-love is self-love no matter how big the self may become. Hegel's thinking was caught in the toils of self-love. His God is self-love, Narcissus grown infinite.

Such a conception of love does not see the reality of love in its universal truth, but mistakes it for a deviant— though indeed widespread—form of it, a particular that masquerades as the universal. For we must admit that, in some degree, self-love *is* love, not love in its truth and actuality, but love in a deviant and erroneous form, yet nevertheless, in its grotesque body, a still-recognizable form of love.

That Hegel really means to define love as self-love is clear from everything he says about it. The instance of romantic love is of special interest because in it Hegel believes he can discern both its infinity and its finitude or limitation in its being a personal self-love. It may perhaps stand as a signal illustration of his way of philosophizing on the subject.

The infinity of love comes to view, Hegel thinks, when we compare it with what at first seems its opposite, namely, honor, the claims of which often appear to clash with the appeal of the beloved. Though love and honor are opposed, we can, he says, view love also as the *realization* of what already lies in honor. Honor requires that I see myself recognized by another person and that I see the infinity of my person taken up in him. In order to be genuine and total, this recognition cannot merely consist in my personality being respected by others in the abstract or in some isolated and limited instance. Rather, I myself—in my whole subjectivity, with its whole being and contents, as this concrete individual with its past, present, and future—must penetrate the consciousness of the other person. I must constitute his own proper willing and knowing, his striving and possessing. He must live only in me, just as I exist for myself only in him. Both of us become for ourselves in this fulfilled unity; both of us must place our whole soul and world in our identity. Each of us, as a subject with an interior being, having an infinity in himself, opens up and is absorbed into the relationship. The lover apparently, and in a sense actually, loses his consciousness in the beloved; he goes through a show of unselfishness and selflessness; but actually he thereby first rediscovers himself and becomes a self. In this obvious self-forgetfulness—so that the lover to all appearance does not exist for himself and is not concerned for himself—he nevertheless finds the roots of his existence precisely in the other, and enjoys precisely and wholly himself in this other. It is this rounding-out of relation-to-self by the mediation of the other, where the lover is no longer self-related immediately and implicitly but mediately and explicitly through his beloved, that Hegel (in accordance with his accustomed concept of infinity, namely the rounding out of being by the enclosure of other within self) calls: *the infinity of love.*[10]

So for Hegel love becomes infinite by reason of the self's extending itself over the not-self and incorporating it. That indeed is Hegel's basic concept of the ego as infinite relation of mind to itself, absolute negativity, identity in otherness. That is exactly how he describes the ego, the essential feature in consciousness and the form, though not the full content and ultimately developed form, of spirit. Ego, as absolute negativity, is in itself identity-in-otherness. The ego is itself, but yet it also encroaches upon the object as something that is in itself, or implicitly, annulled and raised up. Ego is one side of the relation of consciousness, but also it is the whole relation. Ego is the light which manifests itself but also manifests the object.[11]

This is one way of stating the fundamental principle of idealism, the principle of the ideality of the finite. It is the principle that being is identical with thought; that the truth of existence is its ideality, its being annulled and absorbed by and raised up into mind; that the truth of the objective is ultimately its being *for* a self; that substance is essentially subject. To say that the ego is not only one side of the subject-object relationship but also the whole of it is to set the object down as finite and merely ideal, as merely existent *for* what is not and can never be wholly object, namely, self, subject, mind, spirit. This principle of the ideality of the finite is, according to Hegel, the chief maxim of philosophy and is the reason why every genuine philosophy must be idealism. Infinity can only lie in being-for-self, for only being-for-self can enclose what is not self within self. The fundamental notion of philosophy, Hegel's *gnome,* may thus also be expressed as: the genuine infinite, being-for-self.[12]

If we turn now to the *finitude* of romantic love, the same basic point recurs. The limitation of romantic love—the love of this individual of one sex for that individual of the other, each finding his whole subjectivity in the reciprocal relationship—is just that it is what it is, a merely personal identity reached between two particular, contingently related, selves. It is, says Hegel, the merely *personal* feeling of the singular subject, which shows itself to be filled, not with the eternal interests and objective content of human existence, with family, political aims, fatherland, duties of one's calling, class, freedom, religiosity, but only with its own self, which it wants to receive back again, reflected from another self, the feeling of itself.[13] So, the limitation of romantic love is that it is really a self-love in which the self that loves itself in the other self, and which therefore is the self ultimately loved therein, is only a finite, personal, individual, subjective self, this singular being, existing among all the others and finding one of them, contingently, one pretty girl among thousands, that will serve its self-seeking purpose.

Even in romantic love the self has to be an idealist, according to Hegel; and that one notion is sufficient to display the distortion to which love is subjected by idealism, with its central philosophical doctrine that the truth and infinity of being is being-for-self.

The love that loves itself first and wholly, for which every object of love is only a medium through which it is enabled to love itself, is a false love. It is, on the one hand, a real love in the sense that it is one that exists and continues to exist in the world, just as selfishness is real and continues to exist in the world. It is love because, although the self loves nothing other than itself in an ultimate way, it nevertheless loves itself. It has at least that object of its love. Nor should we try to prove by subtle philosophical distinctions that it does not really love itself. It is true that the self that knows ultimate truth can love —must love—something other than itself as well as itself. You must love your neighbor as yourself. Such a knowing self also loves itself as it does its neighbor. But the self that does not know about the love of neighbor still loves itself, and that is the truth about its condition.

But on the other hand love that only loves itself is not true love. One cannot be truly one's own unless one has the other as one's own just in his otherness. Unless there is someone whom I love just in his otherness, I become empty in myself, shrunken, hardened, cold, lifeless. I become everything but an object of love to myself; I become distasteful, even repulsive, to myself; there is nothing in me that elicits my affection. So, love may try this experiment of making itself its sole object and everything else the vehicle by which it mediates itself with itself, but what in fact happens to it is that it shrinks and withers into a hard, empty core that finally confronts it with its own impossibility.

A God who should only love himself, and love others only as shapes in which he loves himself, would be no true God but a monster. If in thinking, willing, and loving the finite he is in the last analysis thinking, willing, and loving only that in the finite which is essentially himself, then he is not thinking, willing, or loving the finite as just itself, the finite, the not-God. That is why the religious instinct eventually passed by the Hegelian theology as it did the Aristotelian theology. The self-knowing, self-willing, self-loving God is not the God of and for the finite being. If he tries to say to the human individual "I am your God," that individual is compelled to answer—if he himself is genuinely human—"No, you are not my God: it is not me whom you know, will, or love as being your own. You are at most your own God, and in that capacity you are the God of nothing, for you have lost me and everything else finite just in our finitude and therefore just in that which you would need to hold on to in order to be the God of something."

Love has to let what it loves be what it is. It has to love what it loves just as it is. It cannot make the object of love into a means for something else, and in particular it cannot make it into a vehicle simply for the love of self. By attempting to do so it displaces actual love for the object and thereby cuts away the necessary groundwork for its own genuine self-love. By attempting to make its relation to other into a means of self-love it adopts exactly the procedure that, in the end, removes all possibility of self-love.

Another way of saying the same thing is this. If the finite tries to elevate itself to infinity by making the other, which sets limits to it and proves it finite, into a mere self-reflection, thus crossing the border of finitude and straining to become the whole, then it discovers that it has only lost its hold on that other—for the other stubbornly refuses to be dissolved into a mere self-reflection—and, far from having crossed any real border or becoming any real whole, it discovers itself eventually to be the null.

We must therefore thank Hegel for having helped us to

this point, a far distance on the path of thought, and now try to make our way toward the goal that is in sight.

If being is not self-relation, and if truth of being is not self-recovery in the other, then what is it? If the fundamental category of thought is not identity-in-difference, then what is it? If the chief maxim of philosophy is not the ideality of the finite, then what is it? And if genuine philosophy is not idealism, then what is it?

If we look to love, as a developed form of being, for a clue to the answers to these questions, then the first thing that love tells us is that its being consists in a relation to other where, however, the other is one's own.

> My beloved is mine and I am his.
> I am my beloved's and my beloved is mine.[14]

Such is the voice of erotic love. But also the words of the divine love song repeat the mutual ownness.

> And you are my sheep, the sheep of my pasture, and
> I am your God, says the Lord God.[15]

The Johannine Christ takes up the theme.

> I am the good shepherd; I know my own and my own
> know me, as the Father knows me and I know the
> Father.[16]

The loving one does not say, "My beloved is myself in a different garb," but says simply, "My beloved is mine and I am his," "You are mine and I am yours." The loving one does not say, "I know myself in the shape of you," but, "I know you and you know me, each as the other's own."

One cries: O God, thou art my God, I seek thee, my soul thirsts for thee, my flesh faints for thee, as in a dry and weary land where no water is. Because thy steadfast love is better than life, my lips will praise thee.

The other replies: I am the Lord your God, who brought you up out of the land of Egypt. Open your mouth wide, and I will fill it.[17]

Love does not say: I am my own. It says: You are my own. It does not say: You are your own. It says: You are mine. Love is an exchange, not of I-ness but of mine-ness. The narcissistic ego knows as its own in the way of love only itself, the I. It is the object of its love and so it places its mine-ness in that object, namely, in itself. It confuses selfness with mineness; it does not know any other than itself as its own, and therefore is infinitely poor. But the truly loving ego places its mine-ness exactly in the other. It remains itself and does not confuse the other with itself, but it finds the other as its own just in its otherness, as that other whom it calls you and thou, and therefore has become richer. The mystery of love lies in this fact—which can be uttered so simply, so easily—that the other, in its very otherness, should yet be own and mine, and that the self, in its very selfhood, should yet be own to the other, thine. The bond of love is the bond of the ownness of the other—reciprocal when the love is reciprocated, but present one-sidedly even when not reciprocated.

Thus the fundamental category of philosophical thought is not identity-in-difference but ownness-in-otherness. For the truth about love, as about all the other fundamental philosophical matters, like truth, freedom, devotion, actuality, goodness, and holiness, cannot be spoken in the language of identity but only in that of ownness. I find truth when I find reality to be my own, in its otherness. I am free when my action and my destiny, in their otherness, are yet my own. I love when the other is mine and I am the other's.

Being is not self-relation but relation to another. Valid being is not self-recovery in the other but realizing of the ownness of self and other. The fundamental category is ownness-in-otherness. The chief maxim of philosophy is not the ideality of the finite but the ownness of the beings that are other to one another. And genuine philosophy is not idealism but the uncompromising and resolute thinking through of this ownness.

To be own is to belong to the self. What is a man's own belongs to him himself. What is someone else's belongs to that other person himself. What is my own belongs to me myself. What is your own belongs to you yourself.

One might at first suppose that this is a definition of ownness: belongingness to the self. But that would imply that the notions of self and of belonging are themselves independently known. What is a self and what is it to belong to the self? Is the self the unity characteristic of a person's responsive behavior? What is the nature of that unity? Is it not that in his behavior the person distinguishes what is due and what is not due, what is his responsibility and what not, what is his own and what not? What is it for something to belong to the self? Is it anything but to be that self's own—what the self owns and what others owe to it?

To understand what *I* means I have to understand what *my* means, just as to understand what *my* means I have to understand what *I* means. Fundamental philosophical concepts do not seriate themselves like the textbook examples of logical definitions. They form circles and spheres in reciprocal dependence for their mutual illumination. To understand them one has to dwell in the life-experience out of which they are born and receive articulate conceptual shape.

This life-experience is massively varied and complex, for in the end nothing human is alien to it. Everywhere that man turns he has to deal in some way with the question of what is his own and what is not his own. Ownness consequently takes many shapes, lower and higher, less and more developed.

The most obvious experience of ownness is that of the ownership of property. Property is a thing—not necessarily a merely physical thing, but something identifiable as eligible for ownership, so that it can be, say, a copyright as well as a house or a dog—which belongs to a person. A person, in the economic-legal sense, is a being who is eligible to own property, one to whom the rights and duties connected with the holding of property can validly apply. Underlying the idea of property is the ego's capacity to appropriate something, take possession of it, and be willing and able to fight for it if necessary. When the person claims the thing as his property, he claims not so much that he actually has it in his possession (for he still owns what he loans) but that he has a right to the possession of it, which others ought (this is what they owe as own to them) to respect and which the law ought to protect. This claim of his expresses not just a bare conceptual thought but also an act and determination of his will and a feeling of appropriation between the thing and himself.

What is my property is *mine*, and being mine it touches my will and my feeling. It is, as it were, an extension of my self, not literally, but in the shape of what belongs to it. Ideas of desire, of lengthening and stretching, of being suitable and appropriate—all these fall most intimately into the sense of the word *belong*. I desire what belongs to me. I feel its suitability and appropriateness to me in its belonging. It is out there, stretching beyond me, yet close to me, I dependent on it and it dependent on me, the two hanging together. It is because of this intimate life-relationship between property and the individual personal self, the owning ego, that collectivistic culture, which aims at socializing the ego, diminishes the importance of personal property and increases that of social property, while individualistic culture, which aims at loosening the ego from others, does the reverse.

Property is own to its owner by way of his right—originally, the Latin suggests, his private right, *pro priva*—to possess it. This relationship, formal and legal in character, represents just one way in which the owner owns what is his own. The ways in which what is mine can become and be mine are as varied as life itself.

A man's body is his own body, not merely by some private formal legal right, but in a more intimate way. At first, it is his in the sense that he is in and with it in an immediately existential manner, behaving bodily by impulse and instinct, with the pure immediateness of the infant. He has to learn that it is a body and that it belongs to him. His mental relationship has to change from merely feeling himself in his bodily being, indistinguishable from it, to knowing about it, becoming conscious of it. He has to differentiate it from himself in order to be able to take possession of it by identifying it as his own, dealing with it as his own, and mastering it as his own. That is, he has to advance from the mere immediateness of natural life in the body to an intelligent and ultimately spiritual appropriation of the body that lifts it into the sphere of his freedom.

The live body is the embodiment of the self, the center of its powers and activities, the basis of its place, action, and undergoing in the world. It is not merely given to a man; it was always with him, being his always as a charge —a burden, task, opportunity, responsibility, destiny. While it is his, it is in his possession only insofar as he has control over it. What in it he has not mastered behaves toward him as something not altogether his, but other, · with its own power curiously independent of his power and will as a self—as we experience in weakness, incapacity, the suffering of violence, sickness, and finally death—so that in a sense he falls into its possession. When a man's hands can do as he wishes they are his more actually and deeply than when they are inept and clumsy. The random movements of the untrained typist incorporate much that is not his own—which is why we call them random—as compared with the controlled movements of the skilled professional. In the finger and wrist movements of the latter there occurs the realization of the typist's intention, so that they are purposeful—literally full of purpose—rather than random. The degree to which the body is owned by its indwelling self, and the ways in which the self appropriates its own body, are among the essential determinations of the self's freedom. Their importance is proved by the large amount of attention given to them in all religions.

What is true of the body is even truer of the mind. If the body is the embodiment of the self, the mind is the element in which the self actually exists and realizes itself. A man's power to see and hear, to think, feel, and will, to give himself over to this or that cause, to receive and accept offered gifts—all these are parts of his mind, the mind that belongs to him. A man is in and with his mind, as with his body, at first in an immediate and unreflected way. He exists in his intentions, thoughts, and feelings naturally and impulsively. It takes time and experience for him to grow out of this naïveté, to turn upon his self and recognize it in consciousness. The pains and difficulty of psychological therapy testify to the scale of the problem that sometimes has to be faced in order to advance from immediate naturalness of simple being within one's own mind to the free being with one's mind *as* one's own, as recognized and appropriated. The ultimate aim of all individual culture can only be to help man to go through this process, from mere animal-like immediate immersion in selfhood to the free existence that lies in full and responsible self-possession.

The man who is self-possessed thinks thoughts, feels feelings, wills volitions, acts actions that are his, not just in the sense that they happen in and to him, but in the sense that he does them intentionally, choosing and identifying them as his own, as authentic. The self-possessed man is like the skilled craftsman or artist: what he does is done freely and not by chance. His life has become his own, no longer as an event that has happened to him, but now as the pathway of his freedom. To be self-possessed is not only to be possessed by one's self but also to possess one's self. It is the self possessing its own self. Genuine freedom can go no further than this, for which reason again all religions have given primary attention to it.

Everything other than a man's body and his own self is also susceptible to the relationship of ownness to him. Mere physical possession and legal property represent only one mode of the owning of the other. Language suggests to us the wider view. The relationship in which things are own to man and he is own to them is the one we call proper, appropriate—the fitting and befitting relationship. These concepts can become trivialized too easily. For instead of the living relationship between man and other in which the two exist appropriately to one another, we can have in mind an artificial set of conventions, mere external and hollow forms, which serve to define an equally external and hollow propriety. There is, for instance, all the world of difference between genuine human decency and the social unobjectionableness that passes falsely under the name. Philosophy has to guard itself against this kind of degradation of the contents of basic concepts. The concepts of the appropriate and fitting are too important to be lost through abuse.

Man's fitting relationship to things is the one in which, by appropriating them to himself and himself to them, he finally reaches the appropriate, what is appropriate both to him and to them. In such appropriateness of relationships lies the truth of his being, his freedom, the fulfillment of his most fundamental needs, and the only pathway to which he can safely devote himself.

The appropriate is not something that can be defined beforehand, given in a formula which can then be routinely followed. It is an ideal that is subject to constant search. For instance, in knowledge the relationship of appropriation between mind and thing is truth. The thing becomes the mind's own only as the mind comes to know the truth about the thing; and the only way the mind can come to know this truth is to appropriate itself to the thing, to abandon its own predilections in favor of letting the thing itself be what it is and tell what it is. When I have come to know the truth about a thing by yielding my mind to the actuality of the thing, the thing has thereby entered bodily into the domain over which my mind prevails and it has become part of my stock of knowledge. But the truth cannot be defined beforehand, nor is there any artificial method by which one can tell beforehand what the truth is going to turn out to be. It has to be sought. We know beforehand only what we think the appropriation-relationship is; and the nature of this, too, is learned only in the process. What truth is, what the very nature of the appropriation-relationship is between man's mind and reality in so far as man attempts to know reality, is something that man has himself been learning with the ages. The nature of truth is one of the central philosophical problems, largely forgotten by professional philosophers today, but a basic preoccupation of today's living men.

In practice, the appropriation-relation of man to the other occurs by way of the goodness and rightness of his actions. He makes the other his own and makes himself own to the other and himself through actions that are good and right. One way of appropriating nature is to exploit it: to take possession of it for immediate practical purposes, as for instance to mine it for its ores, fish its seas, use the oxygen of its atmosphere for fires. Such appropriation can occur only through right—that is, properly conducted—actions. You cannot take ores from the earth unless you use the right kind of equipment and follow the right procedures. Technology is right action whose purpose is the transformation of natural materials into things aimed at by man.

But there are other ways of relating to nature, too. One of them is represented by man's spiritual attitude toward nature. Technology is part of such a spiritual attitude. The character of the technology itself varies with the spiritual character of man's attitude to nature, and conversely. If man looks out toward nature as the Taoist did, he will see in it not the inhuman vastness of contemporary cosmology, in which man is hardly more than a minute and insignificant accident, but the embodiment of a constantly vital process, circling around from opposite to opposite and balancing the two in an ever living harmony, the coursing of a great vital spirit of which man's spirit is a constituent and smaller example. He cannot, then, so far as he possesses this attitude, set out on the Faustian enterprise of conquering nature to satisfy man's interminable wishes or of coursing through illimitable space with the adventurous hardness of the flying scientist. His culture's action in and upon nature will fit with its intuition of nature, as our culture's action does at present.

The goodness and rightness of actions aimed at other living beings, and above all at other human beings, are again the forms through which man's appropriation of others—his determining of them as own to him and his offering of himself as own to them—comes about. Our general formula for justice, "to each according to his due," expresses one side of this relation: justice consists in rendering to a man what is his own, what is owed to him, what one must own to him. Practical wisdom is knowing what is the fitting thing to do, say, think in the given circumstances; it is the cognitive appropriation of the active relationship between self and other. Courage is the will to face up to responsibility that is ours and carry our charge through in the face of opposition; it is the owning up to responsibility. Temperance is the keeping to due measure and proportion in the things that concern us— appetites, desires, aspirations, and claims; by our temperance we stay within the bounds of what belongs to us, we do not exceed the measures assigned to us by the nature of our being.

Faith is the trust that we exist in a reality that is ultimately our home and in an appropriative relationship to the ultimate. The God of the Old Testament says: "I am the Lord, your God, and you are my people." That is his formula for the appropriation between man and God. The Christian prays, "Our Father which art in Heaven . . . ," thus formulating the fundamental ownness between man and God.

Hope is the trust that we shall reach this appropriative relationship in actuality.

Love, charity, is the actuality of that relationship. The classical expression, cited above from the *Song of Songs*, includes within itself the essential meanings of both *eros* and *agape* and yet descends more profoundly into the nature of love as the unity of which they are only the two sides:

> My beloved is mine, and I am his: he feedeth
> among the lilies.[18]

This mutual ownness of love represents the fullness of actuality of the appropriation-relationship. When we understand it, we understand also that all the other modes of ownness are but shadows of it, perspectival projections of it limning but one of its many facets.

Such are some of the shapes that ownness assumes in the varied structure and process of life. To understand what ownness is and means—this can be attained, not by a curt verbal formula such as ours, namely, "being with what is other as with one's own," but only by participation in the structures and processes of life and by a reflection on them that eventually enables one to articulate them truly in thought.

Philosophy is empirical, not *a priori*. You have to struggle for something and gain it and hold it by force and by right to understand what property is and thus to understand what the "mine" is that relates to property and who the "I" is that owns the property. You have to train and conquer your body, making it into the fit vessel and organ of your self, to understand what it is truly to say, "This is my body." So too it is for one's mind, one's family, one's friends, one's homeland, one's world, one's God.

Hatred teaches us the meaning of "my enemy" and love teaches us the meaning of "my beloved." And in the end, love teaches us the true meaning of hatred but hatred does not teach us the true meaning either of itself or of love. Ownness teaches us its own nature and the nature of its opposite, not-ownness, intractable otherness, alienness, strangeness, hostility. Truth teaches us what is true and not true; but falsehood teaches us only the false, and that falsely.

Just because the ultimate form of ownness is love, all the other forms can be regarded as manifestations of it in circumstances of varied sorts. The ownership by which man owns a plot of land is not the same as that by which he loves and offers himself to be the beloved of someone; yet his relationship to the land is in some manner a love-relationship. He desires it and gives himself over to the holding of it because there is something in it that he loves: its economic value, perhaps, or its scenic outlook, its sentimental value as being the place of his birth or his father's house, or whatever else may attract him in it. It may be that, for some reason unknown to him, the holding of land, more and more of it, is the prime food of the man's self, as though it were a great mother's bosom over which he had constantly to search for nourishment. All these modes of appetite are, to be sure, not love in its ultimate truth; but they are the man's way of understanding, being, and practicing his love—the love he possesses and is possessed by. Similarly, although the ultimate in hatred is the evil person's hatred for the one who deserves only love, a hatred which is essential sin, nevertheless all other forms of alienation and estrangement of the self are, in effect, finite manifestations of hatred in the special circumstances of their occurrence.

Ownness, therefore, is best and most truly understood in terms of love. When one has a veritable understanding of the meaning of "Thou art mine and I am thine" one understands what ownness is. One understands then what a taking is that is a giving and a giving that is a taking. One is then able also to understand what it could be to love a piece of land or a large and glittering automobile—both what is in it and what is missing in it. One is able also to understand what it is to love a wife, a child, a brother, a sister, a mother, a father, a friend, a teacher, a student, God, an enemy.

One understands then the meaning of being as the belonging and being belonged to whose heart is love.

Notes

FOREWORD: THE MEASURE OF MAN

1. W. B. Cannon, *The Wisdom of the Body* (New York, Norton, 1932).

2. William Carlos Williams, *Paterson,* Book Five (New York, New Directions, 1963), p. 278.

3. Robert Duncan, "The Dance," in *The New American Poetry 1945–1960,* edited by Donald M. Allen (New York, Grove, 1960), p. 46.

4. William Carlos Williams, "Spring and All," in *Selected Poems* (New York, New Directions, 1963), p. 35.

5. *Ibid.,* p. 35.

I. WHAT PHILOSOPHY IS AND DOES

1. Martin Heidegger, *An Introduction to Metaphysics,* translated by Ralph Manheim, Anchor Book A 251 (New York, Doubleday, 1961), p. 172.

2. Martin Heidegger, *Aus der Erfahrung des Denkens* (Pfullingen, Neske, 1954), p. 11.

3. Martin Heidegger, "The Origin of the Work of Art," in Albert Hofstadter, and Richard Kuhns, *Philosophies of Art and Beauty* (New York, The Modern Library, Random House, 1964), p. 669.

4. *Hegel's Philosophy of Right,* translated with notes by T. M. Knox (London, Oxford, New York, Oxford University Press, 1952, 1967), pp. 12–13.

5. *Ibid.,* p. 11.

II. THE VOCATION OF CONSCIOUSNESS

1. Edmund Husserl, *Ideas: General Introduction to Pure Phenomenology,* translated by W. R. Boyce Gibson (New York, Macmillan, 1931), pp. 246ff.

IV. THE VOICE OF THE DEAD WIFE

1. Gotthold Ephraim Lessing, *Laokoon, An Essay upon the Limits of Painting and Poetry,* translated by Ellen Froth-

ingham (New York, Noonday, 1957), pp. 8, 11.

2. *Ibid.*, pp. 13–14.

3. *Ibid.*, p. 16.

4. *Ibid.*, pp. 148–157.

5. *Ibid.*, pp. 148–152.

6. *Ibid.*, pp. 153–157.

7. Joseph Addison, *The Spectator*, No. 409, June 19, 1712.

8. Conrad Fiedler, *On Judging Works of Visual Art*, translated by Henri Schaefer-Simmern and Fulmer Mood (Berkeley, Los Angeles, University of California Press, 1949), pp. 5–6.

9. *Ibid.*, p. 48.

10. Henri Matisse, "Notes of a Painter," in Alfred Barr, Jr., *Matisse: His Art and His Public* (New York, Museum of Modern Art, 1951), translated by Margaret Scolari, pp. 119–123.

11. Arnold Schönberg, "New Music, Outmoded Music, Style, and Idea," in his book *Style and Idea* (New York, Philosophical Library, 1950).

12. *The Rodin Book*, in Rainer Maria Rilke, *Selected Works*, vol. 1, "Prose," translated by G. Craig Houston (Norfolk, Connecticut, New Directions, 1960), p. 118.

13. Paul Valéry, *The Art of Poetry*, translated by Denise Folliot (New York, Bollingen Foundation, 1958), "Problems of Poetry."

14. *Ibid.*, pp. 72–73.

15. Gustave Flaubert, letter to George Sand, April 3, 1876, in Steegmuller, F., *The Selected Letters of Gustave Flaubert* (London, H. Hamilton, 1954).

16. Letter to Louise Colet, July 22, 1852, *ibid.*

17. Cited in W. E. Allen, *The Writer on His Art* (New York, 1949), p. 229.

18. Cited by Malcolm Cowley in the introduction to his translation of Gide's *Imaginary Interviews* (New York, Knopf, 1944), xvi–xvii.

19. *Op. cit.*

20. *Ibid.*, "Remarks on Poetry."

21. *Ibid.*, "Concerning the Cimitière Marin."

22. Paul Klee, *Über die moderne Kunst* (Bern-Bümpliz, Benteli, 1945). The translations here are my own. An English translation of the whole appeared under the title *On Modern Art*, translated by Paul Findlay with an introduction by Herbert Read (London, Faber and Faber, 1948).

23. V. Kandinsky, in an article written for *Eri Udstilling* (Copenhagen, 1937) and reprinted under the title "Approach to Art" in his book *Essays über Kunst und Künstler*, edited with commentary by Max Bill (Stuttgart, Gerd Hatje, 1955); the translation is my own.

24. André Gide, *Incidences*, N. R. F. 1924, cited by Henri Peyre in *Le classicisme français* (New York, Editions de la Maison française, 1942), p. 124.

V. THE KIN-CONSCIOUSNESS OF ART

1. Plotinus, *Enneads*, translated by Stephen Mackenna (London, Faber and Faber, 1956), I, vi, 2.

2. Some discussion of these dimensions will be found in the author's *Truth and Art* (New York, Columbia University Press, 1965; paperbound edition, Minerva Press, 1968), Ch. 4, "Language as Articulation of Human Being."

VI. THE POEM IS NOT A SYMBOL

1. Wallace Stevens, "Martial Cadenza," *The Collected Poems of Wallace Stevens* (New York, Knopf, 1955), p. 238.

2. William Butler Yeats, "Sailing to Byzantium," *The Collected Poems of W. B. Yeats,* Definitive edition (New York, Macmillan, 1956).

3. Cf. Curtis B. Bradford, "Yeats's Byzantium Poems: A Study of their Development," in *Yeats, A Collection of Critical Essays,* edited by John Unterecker (Englewood Cliffs, New Jersey, Prentice-Hall, 1963), pp. 94–95.

4. Bradford, *op. cit.,* p. 99.

5. Benjamin Rowland, *The Art and Architecture of India,* 3rd ed. (Baltimore, Maryland, Penguin Books, 1967), pp. 48ff.

6. Bradford, *op. cit.,* p. 115.

7. Yeats, "Meditations in Time of Civil War, My Table," *The Collected Poems.*

8. Bradford, *op. cit.,* p. 104.

9. "Lapis Lazuli," *The Collected Poems,* Definitive edition.

10. "All Souls' Night," *The Collected Poems,* Definitive edition.

11. Bradford, p. 117.

12. Bradford, pp. 117, 118.

13. Bradford, p. 118.

14. Bradford, p. 119.

15. Yeats, "Among School Children," viii, *The Collected Poems.*

16. Bradford, p. 120.

17. Bradford, pp. 119, 120, 123.

18. "One dolphin, one man. Do you know Raphael's statue of the Dolphin carrying one of the Holy Innocents to Heaven?" So Yeats wrote to Sturge Moore in reply to a question about the relation of the dolphin to humanity. Moore was designing a cover for *The Winding Stair.* Cf. Bradford, p. 115.

19. Bradford, pp. 120ff.

20. Yeats, "Politics," *The Collected Poems,* Definitive edition.

21. Wallace Stevens, "Of Modern Poetry," *The Collected Poems of Wallace Stevens.*

22. Wallace Stevens, "Final Soliloquy of the Interior Paramour," *The Collected Poems.*

23. Wallace Stevens, "Extracts from Addresses to the Academy of Fine Ideas," v, *The Collected Poems.*

24. Yeats, "After Long Silence," *The Collected Poems.*

VII. THE POEM IS A SYMBOL

1. John Dewey, *Art as Experience* (New York, Putnam's, 1958), p. 105.

2. Paul Tillich, *Theology of Culture* (New York, Oxford University Press, 1959), pp. 56–57.

3. John Donne, *Holy Sonnets,* "La Corona."

4. T. S. Eliot, *Four Quartets* (New York, Harcourt, Brace & World, 1943), p. 38.

5. "A Note on War Poetry," in the anthology *London Calling,* 1942; quoted in F. O. Mathiessen, *The Achievement of T. S. Eliot* (New York, Oxford University Press, 1959), pp. 196–197.

6. Dr. Robert Freind, headmaster of Westminster School.

7. Sir Walter Raleigh, "Epitaph."

8. *Four Quartets,* pp. 4,5,7.

9. *Ibid.,* p. 7.

10. *Ibid.*, pp. 7–8.
11. *Ibid.*, p. 17.
12. *Ibid.*, p. 17.
13. *Ibid.*, p. 11.
14. *Ibid.*, p. 14.
15. *Ibid.*, p. 17.
16. *Ibid.*, p. 15.
17. *Ibid.*, p. 22.
18. *Ibid.*, p. 23.
19. *Ibid.*, p. 22.
20. *Ibid.*, cf. "Burnt Norton," I, II.
21. *Ibid.*, p. 27.
22. *Ibid.*, p. 27.
23. *Ibid.*, p. 39.
24. *Ibid.*, p. 5.
25. *Ibid.*, p. 5.
26. *Ibid.*, p. 8.
27. *Ibid.*, p. 39.
28. *Ibid.*, p. 32.
29. *Ibid.*, p. 32.
30. *Ibid.*, p. 34.
31. *Ibid.*, cf. "Little Gidding," II.
32. *Ibid.*, pp. 33, 34.
33. *Ibid.*, p. 35.
34. *Ibid.*, p. 16.
35. *Ibid.*, p. 39.
36. *Ibid.*, p. 39.
37. *Ibid.*, p. 39.
38. *Ibid.*, p. 5.
39. *Ibid.*, p. 5.
40. *Ibid.*, p. 4.
41. *Ibid.*, p. 4.
42. *Ibid.*, pp. 4–5.
43. *Ibid.*, p. 4.
44. *Ibid.*, p. 8.
45. *Ibid.*, p. 7.
46. *Ibid.*, p. 6.
47. *Ibid.*, pp. 6–7.
48. *Ibid.*, p. 7.
49. *Ibid.*, p. 15.
50. *Ibid.*, p. 6.
51. *Ibid.*, p. 14.
52. *Ibid.*, p. 14.
53. *Ibid.*, p. 38.
54. *Ibid.*, p. 12.
55. *Ibid.*, p. 12.
56. *Ibid.*, p. 12.
57. *Ibid.*, p. 12.
58. *Ibid.*, p. 5.
59. *Ibid.*, p. 7.
60. *Ibid.*, p. 22.
61. *Ibid.*, pp. 23–24.
62. *Ibid.*, p. 24.
63. *Ibid.*, p. 24.
64. *Ibid.*, p. 5.
65. *Ibid.*, "The Dry Salvages," II and "Burnt Norton," II.
66. *Ibid.*, p. 25.
67. *Ibid.*, p. 32.
68. *Ibid.*, p. 24.
69. *Ibid.*, p. 24.
70. *Ibid.*, p. 24.
71. *Ibid.*, "The Dry Salvages," and "Burnt Norton," III.
72. *Ibid.*, p. 26.
73. *Ibid.*, p. 38.
74. *Ibid.*, p. 37.
75. *Ibid.*, p. 38.
76. 1 *Corinthians* 2.10–11.
77. *Four Quartets*, p. 8.
78. *Ibid.*, p. 39.
79. *Ibid.*, pp. 8, 35.
80. *Ibid.*, p. 13.
81. *Ibid.*, p. 17.
82. *Ibid.*, p. 17.
83. *Ibid.*, p. 28.
84. *Ibid.*, p. 27.
85. *Ibid.*, p. 4.

VIII. BEING: THE ACT OF BELONGING

1. Aristotle, *Metaphysica*, translated by Sir W. D. Ross (London, Oxford University Press, 2nd ed., 1926), 1038b, 2ff.
2. *Ibid.*, Book Theta, 1048a, 30ff.

3. *Ibid.*, Book Delta, Ch. 7, 1017a, 35ff.

4. Richard Soule, *A Dictionary of the English Language*, new edition revised and enlarged by A. D. Sheffield (New York, Tudor, 1946).

5. Hegel, *Vorlesungen über die Philosophie der Religion*, Erster Band, Halbband 1: *Begriff der Religion*, edited by Georg Lasson, (Hamburg, Meiner, 1966, Philosophische Bibliothek Band 59, pp. 221–222). A translation occurs in vol. 3 of *Hegel's Lectures on the Philosophy of Religion*, edited and translated by Rev. E. B. Spiers and J. Burdon Sanderson (New York, Humanities Press, 1962), p. 355. There are many other passages in his varied writings in which Hegel gives essentially the same definition of being. Some of them are noted under the heading of "Sein," pp. 2194–2205 in *Hegel-Lexikon*, Hermann Glockner (Stuttgart, Frommann, 1957).

6. This numerical reference, and those that follow, is to the *Jubiläumsausgabe* of Hegel's works, re-edited from the older collection of Hermann Glockner, under the title of *Sämtliche Werke* (Stuttgart, Frommann Verlag, various dates). The first number refers to the volume, the second to the page, e.g. vol. 4, p. 78. The definitions given in the text, of identity, God, truth, freedom, etc., may be found in the places cited.

7. Cf. *Vorlesungen über die Philosophie der Religion*, edited by Georg Lasson, cited above, Bd. I, pp. 221–222.

8. *Sämtliche Werke*, 16. 227, 314, 318.

9. *Ibid.*, 7. 60; 7. 238; 11. 74; 13. 149; 15. 141; 16. 227; 16. 318.

10. *Ibid.*, 13. 178f.

11. *Ibid.*, 10. 255. Cf. Hegel's *Philosophy of Mind*, translated by William Wallace (Oxford, Clarendon Press, 1894), p. 47.

12. *Sämtliche Werke*, 8. 227ff. Cf. *The Logic of Hegel*, translated by William Wallace (London, Oxford, Humphrey Milford, 2nd ed., 1892, Impression of 1931), pp. 179f.

13. *Sämtliche Werke*, 13. 184.

14. *Song of Solomon*, 2. 16; 5. 3.

15. *Ezekiel*, 34. 31.

16. *John*, 10. 14,15.

17. *Psalms*, 63. 1,3; 81. 10.

18. *Song of Solomon*, 2. 16; cf. 6. 2; 7. 10.

Index

Index of Names

Index of Subjects